ROMANCE MONOGRAPHS, INC.
Number 26

# A CALL TO AUTHENTICITY: THE ESSAYS OF
# EZEQUIEL MARTÍNEZ ESTRADA

ROMANCE MONOGRAPHS, INC.

Number 26

# A CALL TO AUTHENTICITY:
# THE ESSAYS OF
# EZEQUIEL MARTÍNEZ
# ESTRADA

BY

JAMES MAHARG

UNIVERSITY, MISSISSIPPI

ROMANCE MONOGRAPHS, INC.

1 9 7 7

ALL RIGHTS RESERVED

ROMANCE MONOGRAPHS, INC.

P. O. BOX 7553

UNIVERSITY, MISSISSIPPI 38677

IMPRESO EN ESPAÑA
PRINTED IN SPAIN

I.S.B.N. 84-399-7352-7

DEPÓSITO LEGAL: V. 2.515 - 1977

ARTES GRÁFICAS SOLER, S. A. - JÁVEA, 28 - VALENCIA (8) - 1977

**Library of Congress Cataloging in Publication Data**

Maharg, James, 1940-
    A call to authenticity.

    (Romance monographs; no. 26)
    Bibliography: p.

    1. Martínez Estrada, Ezequiel, 1895-1964 — Criticism and interpretation.
I. Title.

PQ7797.M277Z75                    864                    77-7175

# PREFACE

Only Sarmiento, in the history of Argentine literature, can claim to have roused such depths of passion in defence or opposition to a writer, as did his confessed disciple, Ezequiel Martínez Estrada (1895-1964), poet, shortstory-writer, playwright and essayist extraordinary. Jorge Luis Borges once called him a writer of "espléndidas amarguras," Marcel Bataillon the "Unamuno of Argentina," César Fernández Moreno talked of his "ateísmo civil," and Manuel Pedro González of "el escritor más rebelde, iconoclasta y acrático que en la región de la Plata se ha producido en este siglo." Such has been his influence on Argentine culture that to omit him from any serious discussion of the development of Argentinian literature from 1930 onwards would be to overlook a writer who took the spiritual pulse of his country as no one else had done before or has done since.

That Martínez Estrada has not received nearly the same international recognition as other gifted contemporaries such as Eduardo Mallea and Jorge Luis Borges can in part be explained by the rather uneven fate of the essay, as a genre, at the hands of international Hispanic criticism (in contrast to attitudes in the Hispanic countries themselves) rather in the realm of questions of peculiarities of temperament. This same international criticism, which has contributed to the rise of writers such as Borges and Eduardo Mallea, as yet has not given serious attention to the writer who was nominated in 1949 by the Sociedad Argentina de Escritores as its candidate for the Nobel Prize for Literature.

While Martínez Estrada cultivated various literary genres, there is little doubt that it is as an essayist that he is best remembered and read, and if international recognition has been comparatively hesitant, recognition within Argentina, and Latin America generally, has been quite energetic and consistent. Even more than other famous contemporaries, Martínez Estrada has influenced generations of Argentinian intellectuals who have felt themselves constrained to consider him as their principal point of reference to an understanding of contemporary Argentina.

★ ★ ★ ★

The author wishes to thank the Horace H. Rackham Endowment Fund of the University of Michigan, Ann Arbor, with whose partial support the publication of this book was made possible.

# TABLE OF CONTENTS

*To María-Elena Bravo Guerreira*

# INTRODUCTION

*The dimensions of the study*

THE ESSAY WAS THE GENRE that Martínez Estrada cultivated longest and with greatest consistency. Whereas his poems, drama and short-stories are relevant within the totality of his work, neither of these, including his poetry, which he virtually abandoned in 1929, provides the philosophical and emotional span of the essays, twenty-eight of which he published at regular intervals from 1933 until his death in 1964, [1] to say nothing of the some three-hundred and fifty contributions he made to journals from 1917 onwards, more than three hundred of which can accurately be termed short essays. From *Radiografía de la pampa* (1933), it was the essays that enveloped him in continual controversy, and they constitute a corpus of work that has given him his place in Argentine literature, and with which his name is most associated.

Yet there has been a growing tendency to think of Martínez Estrada as the author of one principal essay, *Radiografía de la pampa*, [2] a view not altogether unreasonable in the context of the work's multiple printings over the past forty years. But Martínez Estrada was an essayist of many dimensions, and to consider his first major essay as embodying his essential ideological stance at the end of his life, would be to virtually deny him any real degree of development in his writ-

---

[1] A chronological list of the essays will be found in Appendix II.

[2] Enrique Anderson Imbert and Eugenio Florit, for example, in their *Literatura hispanoamericana: Antología e introducción histórica* (New York: Holt, Rinehart and Winston, Inc., 1960) give one short selection from *Radiografía de la pampa,* and Jean Franco, *The Modern Culture of Latin America* (London: Pall Mall, 1967) draws all her conclusions about Martínez Estrada's views from the book.

ings. Thus we come to one of the principal objectives of this study: the determination and characterization of the evolution in personal philosophy or social stance in the author's essays down the years. Occasionally references will be made to other genres, such as the poetry, in order to establish antecedents to views called into question by critics.

Practically left untouched by critics has been the problem of placing Martínez Estrada in the cultural currents of his age, both foreign as well as native. Clearly his essays did not appear self-engendered, as it were. Argentina, with the rest of Latin America, constituted a type of cultural colony of Europe from Independence onwards, and the prestige of Europe's intellectuals counted heavily among those countries that prided themselves on this cultural dependence. Chapter I then is viewed as an attempt to situate the essayist in the broad perspective of the cultural climate at the turn of the century in Latin America, and to which several outstanding foreign artists and writers contributed, through their writings, and in some cases, by their physical presence.

Another area of comparative neglect has been the matter of the types of criticism his work was subjected to from the beginning and their development throughout his career. Moreover, the important consideration of the relationship of this criticism to an accurate understanding of the essayist's essential personality, with all its idiosyncrasies and conflicts, has, with the recent exception of César Fernández Moreno, received very scant critical attention indeed. Concentrating on the Argentine critics in this manner, the evolution of the essayist's reputation within his own country, as well as the obstacles to it, can be better understood. An examination of the principal types of objections made of Martínez Estrada's work in Argentina, within the framework of certain temperamental attitudes of the essayist, will occupy the main concern of Chapter II. A more general discussion of the reputation of Martínez Estrada in wider Hispanic circles will be found in Appendix I.

Similarly, not one study, as far as this critic has been able to establish, has yet concerned itself with Martínez Estrada's literary view of life. No doubt, as we have suggested elsewhere, the dimensions of the essay as a genre would reveal a conceptual confusion with regard to its susceptibility to effective literary criticism, but given the poetic antecedents alone, in the case of Martínez Estrada, together with his cultivation of other literary modes, a consideration of the evolution of his views on art and aesthetics must assume considerable importance for the critic. Additionally and relatedly, the question as to how the essayist saw the role of the writer in society, and the roles of literature itself in the modern world, must claim the critic's attention. These will be the primary considerations of Chapter III.

Virtually dismissed, when not actually ignored, has been the matter of the relevance of the later period of the author's life in Mexico and Cuba — a period of self-imposed exile — to the whole body of essays, and more importantly, to the personal philosophy of the Martínez Estrada. At the time, many Argentinian intellectuals judged this period, and its motivations, as yet another idiosyncratic quirk of the writer [3] and thus hardly worthy of attention, but critics cannot ignore that Martínez Estrada considered his greatest work came from this phase of his life. [4] Chapter IV, as a result, examines the contributions of the Mexican and above all, the Cuban period to the evolution of the essayist's thought, and general attitudes towards Latin America.

The final chapter represents hitherto untrodden ground in the criticism of the essays of Martínez Estrada. Much more so than other artists such as novelists and poets, the modern essayist is relatively unconstrained by problems of form and structure to express theme and its elaboration, such is the free-ranging nature of the essay. This is not at all to deny form and aesthetic principles to the essay as a genre, but merely to recognize certain of its characteristics. This free-ranging aspect of the essay, well exemplified in those of Martínez Estrada, is not without its critical problems, however. Such are the wider, historical and philosophical implications of the work of the Argentinian that the critic is obliged to consider his work in rather wider perspectives. A purely literary approach, for example, would do little to reveal to what extent Martínez Estrada's historical reinterpretation of Hernández' *Martín Fierro (Muerte y transfiguración de Martín Fierro)* or his lifelong assault on an intellectual cowardice that he saw historically perpetuated throughout Argentinian literature,

---

[3] For a representative synopsis of opinions on this matter, *vide*, "Los escritores frente a una actitud: Martínez Estrada y el país," *Atlántida*, Buenos Aires, 43, 1123 (Sept., 1960), 22-28.

[4] For this expression of the writer's opinion of his work on José Martí, see Roberto Fernández Retamar, "Razón de homenaje," *Casa de las Américas*, 33 (Nov.-Dec., 1965), p. 14.

implied certain methods of approaching history, and even more importantly, to what extent the particular views of Martínez Estrada suggest the presence of distortions in these methods. To a large extent then, this chapter will concern itself, in broad sociological fashion, with the wider implications of the confrontation of the artist with his society.

*The order of study of the essays*

In a letter to Carlos Adam dated 30th April, 1964, that is, some seven months before his death, Martínez Estrada gave rather clear advice as to how his essays should be arranged for bibliographical purposes. [5] The essayist conceived of three categories:

*a)*   Literary essays.

*b)*   Historico-sociological essays.

*c)*   Polemical essays.

Evidently, such an arrangement has particular advantages. Principally it facilitates a comparative thematic study throughout the essays, maintaining at the same time a modicum of structural organization. Moreover, the essayist, in the same letter gave some examples of each category and Adam's final compilation is contained in Appendix II. Given the wide spectrum of themes in the essays of the Argentinian, the above organization is a useful orientation for the critic. One may object that literary and historico-sociological essays may also at the same time be polemical essays, but a closer scrutiny of Martínez Estrada's work would confirm that he came rather close to cultivating the polemical essay almost as a genre.

On the other hand, such a categorization offers an equally obvious disadvantage: Martínez Estrada did not write his essays in that order. Taking the above organization as a key, the actual order of the essays as published would be: b, b, b, a, b, a, b, a, c, c, c, c, a, b, a, b, c, c, c, a, a, b, b, a, a, b; (his *Antología*, 1964, is classified apart). The chronological order, then, can offer a degree of visible thematic

---

[5] Carlos Adam, *Bibliografía y documentos de Ezequiel Martínez Estrada* (La Plata: Univ. Nacional de la Plata, 1968), p. 197. This is the most complete bibliography on Martínez Estrada to date and is quite invaluable for source materials, as well as a generous selection of the essayist's correspondence and some selected critical comments by various figures.

development that the above scheme would not, and to considerable extent, a chronological order will be followed in the main body of the study. Fundamentally an overview of the following chapters (which individually subscribe to and participate in this overview) will reveal that the principal concern of the study will be the unfolding drama of the personality of Ezequiel Martínez Estrada as revealed in a chronological analysis that participates fully in the thematic considerations also outlined above. This, in other words, is a middle position between the author's own scheme (which would give little sense of thematic evolution) and the purely chronological order (which would overlook the undeniable susceptibility of the essays to broader classifications).

Since the study has the dual aim of relating thematic concerns and the elucidation of fundamental traits of personality, and the necessary interaction of both, particular essays have not been considered with the aim of providing a thematic catalogue of their content; moreover, the concerns of some chapters have afforded more importance to lesser-known works that are relevant to the characterization of the essayist, than that normally given to essays containing a richer thematic vein. Where pertinent, other source materials such as periodical articles and correspondence have been introduced to corroborate or contrast positions outlined in the essays themselves. Similarly, occasional essays, such as *El nuevo mundo, la isla de Utopía y la isla de Cuba* (1963), bear little thematic or temperamental relevance to points discussed, and thus have received little attention. True to this same orientation, literary essays have been studied not from the point of view of establishing a successful evocation of the writer in question (for example, *Nietzsche,* 1947, or *Realidad y fantasía en Balzac,* 1964) but rather have been approached from the question of what they reveal of the essayist's temperamental postures and thematic preoccupations.

## Brief outline of the life and works of Ezequiel Martínez Estrada

Documentary sources reveal very little about the childhood and early manhood of the essayist, and frequently the critic is obliged to "read between the lines" to reconstruct phases and attitudes in his past. Born on the 14th of September, 1895, in San José de la Esquina, province of Santa Fe, Ezequiel Eduardo Martínez Estrada was the eldest of three male children born to Ezequiel Martínez and Manuela

Estrada, both of Spanish stock. The early years of his life were particularly somber, if a letter he wrote in later life to Victoria Ocampo is taken as a faithful reconstruction. In it he stated, "Debo confesar que no recuerdo ninguna época que haya vivido la ingenuidad de la niñez," further observing that "Repasando mi vida, sólo veo que he sido yo el culpable de una valoración pesimista, y que prolongar la existencia más allá de la pubertad es un funesto error que se paga con la misma supervivencia." [6] In 1900 the family moved to Buenos Aires, and Martínez Estrada was enrolled in a rather prestigious school, the Colegio Avellaneda. The differences in social station between himself and his schoolmates soon became evident, and he attempted to compensate for it by becoming an outstanding student. Despite this success, his parents could not afford to underwrite his higher education, and in 1915 Martínez Estrada entered the postal service at the General Post Office in Buenos Aires, "en la categoría 19a, cargo provisional, y en la sección clasificación," and he was to remain a postal employee until his retirement in 1946.

Most bibliographies of the writer consider 1918, the date of his first collection of poems (*Oro y piedra*), as his first publication, but a series of three articles published in *Nosotros*, Buenos Aires, in 1917 and 1918 offer clear antecedents to the pessimism expressed above. [7] Imbued with an early distrust of the ordering and organization of life, the author also was affected by a deep sense of *desengaño* concerning the ultimate possession of happiness and truth in this life, and eventually came to realize that the real human value of these preoccupations resided in the striving itself and not in their doubtful possession. [8] Such sceptical attitudes are evident at various points in the

---

[6] See "Carta a Victoria Ocampo," *Sur*, 295 (July-Aug., 1965), 3-7.

[7] The bibliography published by *Casa de las Américas*, 33 (Nov.-Dec., 1965) in its special number dedicated to "Homenaje a Ezequiel Martínez Estrada," gives no mention of these early articles. The very first publications of the author (all from 1917) however, are almost all occasional poems published either in *Fray Mocho* or *Caras y Caretas*, both Buenos Aires periodicals; they number some nine contributions in all, and precede the *Nosotros* articles.

[8] Martin S. Stabb was virtually the first to point to the significance of these articles with regard to the development of certain temperamental tendencies in the author's work. See "Ezequiel Martínez Estrada: The Formative Writings," *Hispania*, XXXIX (March, 1966), 54-60. Practically the same sentiments were echoed much later in life, in *Meditaciones sarmientinas* (Santiago de Chile: Editorial Universitaria, 1968), pp. 170-171. Nonetheless,

work of the author, and many of them, especially that of the impact of mechanized culture or *cultura kitsch* (as he frequently referred to it) on human values, was to become almost an obsession right until the end of his life.

The second collection of poems, *Nefelibal* (1922) was to be awarded the Third National Prize for Literature and was naturally a significant encouragement to his poetic career. The previous year Martínez Estrada married Agustina Marriconi, who was to be his constant companion in Cuba and Mexico as well as in Argentina; the marriage, however, produced no children. *Motivos del cielo,* the third poetic collection, came out in 1924, in which year Martínez Estrada saw a brief experience as a Professor of Literature in the Colegio Nacional of the Universidad Nacional de la Plata in temporary replacement of Rafael Alberto Arrieta (author of a fundamental history of Argentinian literature), although the writer was to remain associated with the Escuelas Superiores of the University until 1946. 1927 witnessed the awarding to the author of the First Municipal Prize for Literature by the city of Buenos Aires for the fourth collection of poetry, *Argentina,* and Martínez Estrada reached the height of his poetic career two years later with his *Humoresca* and *Titeres de pies ligeros* (a drama), both of which won the First National Prize for Literature.

In 1927 both the writer and his wife made a first trip to Europe, visiting France, Spain, Portugal and Italy, and was to be the first of many trips outside of Argentina. In 1929 he met for the first time that other great voyager, the North American Waldo Frank, a man who enjoyed friendship with many leading Latin American intellectuals. Two years later the Asociación Wagneriana of Buenos Aires gave a production of *Titeres de pies ligeros.*

The publication of *Radiografía de la pampa* in 1933 — it was given rather tardy recognition in 1937 with the Second National Prize for

---

despite Stabb's reference to the (undoubted) presence of anti-rationalist sentiments in these articles which was to appear almost as a leitmotif throughout the author's work, it is pertinent to remember here his great personal struggles to overcome such tendencies. In the same letter to Victoria Ocampo referred to above, he also noted (p. 5):

> Soy una madriguera de complejos, una red subterránea en que el subconsciente posee sus mapas precisos. Nunca quise aprovechar de ese tesoro soterrado, dejando libre el juego de la fantasía, sino que me esforcé por que la razón lúcida rigiera mi pensamiento.

Literature — clearly marked a change of direction in his literary career and to a large extent, also, in the intensity of his personal philosophy. The exact motives for this definitive change towards the essay as his chief means of expression, and consequently away from poetry, will no doubt continue to be a problem for the biographers of Martínez Estrada. The fundamental question will continue to be whether the decision to virtually abandon poetry [9] came as a result of the writer's association with Horacio Quiroga or a disenchantment with the social state of Argentina as defined in the military *coup d'état* of 1930, or whether, in fact, it was a combination of these and other events. The author did not offer an unequivocal explanation. On the one hand he suggested that it was as a result of the "paso de un régimen político y económico de la nueva historia fascista del mundo," [10] while on another occasion he affirmed that Quiroga, "extinguió en mí la lámpara mortecina de la poesía." [11] Whatever the exact reason was, *Radiografía de la pampa* — which reached six editions by 1968 — was to be the work with which the author was most associated, thus identifying Martínez Estrada first and foremost as an essayist.

During this period — from 1917 onwards — the writer published regularly in a host of periodicals that included *La Nación* (his first publication in the famous newspaper was in March, 1924), *Babel* (Buenos Aires), *Fray Mocho* (Buenos Aires), *Síntesis* (Buenos Aires), *Trapalanda* (Buenos Aires), *Propósitos* (Buenos Aires) and frequently in *La vida literaria* (Buenos Aires), the editorship of which magazine he was to share with Luis Emilio Soto, Francisco Romero and others, in later years. Given the "laureles de oro" that his poetry had earned him, it was to be expected that many publications would seek his collaboration.

Martínez Estrada's next major publication, *La cabeza de Goliat* (1940) an extensive essay on the abominations of Buenos Aires, marked two curious hiates in his literary production, characterized by no major essay publications, and in the first, by very little activity in

---

[9] The author made a brief return to poetry again in 1959, with the collection *Coplas de ciego*.

[10] See "Prólogo inútil," in Ezequiel Martínez Estrada, *Antología* (Mexico: Fondo de Cultura Económica, 1964), pp. 7-19 and especially p. 13.

[11] Ezequiel Martínez Estrada, *El hermano Quiroga*, 2nd ed. (Montevideo: Arca, 1966), p. 70.

periodicals: 1933-1940 and 1940-1946. [12] 1941, however, did see the appearance of two dramas, *Lo que no vemos morir* and *Sombras* (the first of which was produced in the Teatro del Pueblo the same year) and three years later Martínez Estrada published his first short story, *La inundación,* a genre to which he was not to give serious attention again, for various reasons, among them those of his health, until 1956.

Professionally, however, the years 1940-1946 were not inactive. Martínez Estrada, having been one of the founding members of the Sociedad Argentina de Escritores and was President during 1933-1934, became President again for the period 1942-1946, and in 1941 he presided over the Tercer Congreso de Escritores de Tucumán. During July to September, 1942, the writer visited the United States as a guest of the Department of State, in company with other Argentinian intellectuals. The following year he visited Bolivia, invited by the Exposición del Libro in La Paz, and in August of the same year (1943) gave some lectures in Montevideo. In 1946 he occupied the post of Editor on the editorial board of *Sur* and almost at the same time retired from his post as a postal employee, having been so for thirty-one years. [13]

*Sarmiento,* one of the important essays of the historico-sociological classification suggested by the author (as we have noted above) appeared in 1946, as did *Panorama de las literaturas,* a rather textbookish work characterized by rather arbitrary judgements at times, and hardly among the essayist's most creative works. *Sarmiento* accentuated the extent to which the famous educator and President of the Republic had influenced Martínez Estrada's thinking, as did *Los invariantes históricos en el Facundo,* published the following year, a little known but important work which provided a useful synthesis of the essayist's views on Argentina. 1947 also saw the appearance of *Nietzsche,* and pointed to the intellectual debt that, at least at one stage in his life, the essayist owed to the German philosopher.

---

[12] Another is that of the years 1951-1956, although it is quite obvious in this case that it was due to the long illness caused by a skin condition that affected him extensively during exactly this time.

[13] For these aspects of Martínez Estrada, as well as for much of the material in this section, I have relied heavily upon Adam, *Bibliografía y documentos de Ezequiel Martínez Estrada,* 245-247.

The years 1948 and 1949 brought the author more honours. Returning from a visit to Brazil in 1947 (a visit to his wife's family) he went on to Cuba the following year to become a Caballero de la Orden Nacional de Mérito Carlos Manuel de Céspedes. Later in 1948 the essayist also received the Gran Premio de Honor de la Sociedad Argentina de Escritores and the same society, in 1949, proposed him as their candidate for the Nobel Prize; a second visit to Cuba, also in 1949, gave the writer the added distinction of being named a member of the Cuban Academy of History. This year also Martínez Estrada and his wife set up a permanent home in Bahía Blanca. An important work of 1951, *El mundo maravilloso de Guillermo Enrique Hudson*, basic for an appreciation of the author's views on "authenticity" in Argentine literature, preceded almost five years of silence as the essayist was confined to bed almost throughout the whole period because of an excruciating skin disease, eventually diagnosed as *neurodermitis melánica*.[14] Unable to read or write, Martínez Estrada went from hospital to hospital during these years until the disease was finally brought under control in 1955.

Consequently, after such a long period bereft of literary and other activity, 1956 and 1957 saw a sudden spurt of publications. With *Tres cuentos sin amor, Sábado de gloria* and *Marta Riquelme* (all of 1956) Martínez Estrada returned to the genre he had not worked since *La inundación,* in 1944.[15] Also published the same year were two of his polemical essays, *Cuadrante del pampero* and the bitterly anti-Peronist work, *¿Qué es esto?* 1956 also witnessed the brief return of the essayist to the Colegio Nacional de la Plata, but due to a rather obscure controversy with student groups, he renounced the post in September, after a stay of little more than six months. In 1957, however, Martínez Estrada was named "profesor extraordinario" at the Universidad Nacional del Sur, in Bahía Blanca; the same year saw the essayist and his wife on an extended visit to Europe that included Russia, Roumania (where the governments had invited him), and France and Italy.

---

[14] This is the author's own description of the disease, as revealed in a letter to Enrique Anderson Imbert, of 1st August, 1952. See Adam, p. 168.

[15] Carlos Adam cites Juan Carlos Ghiano as having been told by Martínez Estrada that these short-stories were in fact written much earlier. See Adam, p. 25.

Two important essays, from the point of view of the author's personal philosophy, *Exhortaciones* and *Las 40*, very polemical in nature, were published in 1957. Even more illuminating with reference to certain developments in the essayist's personal philosophy was the rather moving *El hermano Quiroga*. A return to other genres, the drama and short story, also took place in 1957 with *Tres dramas* (a republication of *Lo que no vemos morir* and *Sombras*, both of 1941, and the new *Cazadores*) and *La tos y otros entretenimientos*, a collection of thirteen short stories; during 1957, also, Martínez Estrada presided over the Liga Argentina por los Derechos del Hombre.

Apart from the publication of his 51 *Coplas de ciego* in 1959, Martínez Estrada published only essays from then until his death, and as we shall shortly consider, all the posthumous works are also essays. At this juncture, therefore, it is pertinent to consider the intervals at which the author published in the various genres. The tableau is as follows:

*Poetry*

1918, 1922, 1924, 1927, 1929, 1947 (re-issue), 1959

*Short story*

1944, 1956, 1957, 1965 (re-issue)

*Drama*

1929, 1941, 1957 (Partial re-issue)

*Essay*

1933, 1940, 1946, 1947, 1948, 1951, 1956, 1957, 1958, 1960, 1962, 1963, 1964, 1965, 1966, 1967, 1968, 1969.

The concentration of the essay is thus readily aparent, even more so if we consider the *Nosotros* articles, that we have discussed earlier, as essays. The question as to how Martínez Estrada saw himself will be discussed in the main body of this study, although it may be said at this point that he never for a moment relinquished for himself the title of "artist." [16]

---

[16] In the prologue to his *Antología* of 1964, the essayist insists upon his work being judged, above all, as "la producción de un artista y un pensador." See *Antología*, p. 19.

*Heraldos de la verdad,* of 1958, illustrated the writer's debt to Montaigne, Nietzsche and Balzac, the latter receiving a much larger treatment in *Realidad y fantasía en Balzac* published just before his death in 1964. These works together with the posthumous *Para una revisión de las letras argentinas* (1967) and *En torno a Kafka y otros ensayos,* of the same year, provide rather useful material for the consideration of the author's views on literature, and are dealt with in Chapter III. Yet another important essay was the 1960 *Análisis funcional de la cultura,* which earned for Martínez Estrada his last literary prize, that awarded by the Cuban *Casa de las Américas.*

On a personal level, the years 1959-1962 were very important for Martínez Estrada. Increasingly disappointed and frustrated by the continual neglect of his diagnosis of Argentina's social and spiritual ills, which constituted the *raison d'être* of so many of his essays, he decided to go to México in a type of self-imposed exile in 1959. In reality he was invited by the Fondo de Cultura Económica, and in the same year he also visited Chile and Austria, and directed a Seminar in the Escuela de Ciencias Políticas of the Universidad de México. Explaining his reasons for leaving Argentina in a now-famous speech given at the annual dinner of the staff and friends of the Mexican journal *Cuadernos Americanos* (and discussed in detail in Chapter II), he went on to state in terms strongly reminiscent of his polemical essays, that now in Mexico,

> Me siento rejuvenecido, sin rencor y con ánimo, no diré con fuerzas, para cumplir la etapa final de mi destino, y si no me consideran ustedes, amigos y camaradas, estigmatizado por haber visto el rostro terrible de la verdad, dénme las manos y ayúdenme a escalar el último tramo de mi Calvario. [17]

Yet the pathos of these words soon dissipated itself when the author answered a call from the *Casa de las Américas* to work in Cuba, and it was then (1960-62) that he found himself with strength to undertake a fundamental study of José Martí, published in two parts, posthumously, as *Martí: el héroe y su acción revolucionaria* (1966) and the much longer *Martí revolucionario* (1967). There can be little

---

[17] Ezequiel Martínez Estrada, "Los escritores frente a una actitud," *Atlántida,* Buenos Aires, 1123 (Sept., 1960), p. 23. The *Cuadernos Americanos* dinner speech was reproduced here.

doubt that given the above expression of self-pity (even if, in the author's terms, well-motivated) the work in Cuba came at the right moment psychologically for Martínez Estrada; it gave him the reassurance of the efficacy of his work precisely when he needed it, and it was the beginning of a renewed enthusiasm. Other publications at this time were the short pamphlet, *Familia de Martí* (1962), the impressive and voluminous *Diferencias y semejanzas entre los países de la América Latina* (1962), which posterity may well designate as one of the author's most accomplished works, and, in contrast, the crudely partisan *El verdadero cuento del Tío Sam*, of 1963.

The tone of this latter work (not completely without precedent, as can be seen in polemical essays such as *Exhortaciones* or *Cuadrante del pampero*) in reality pointed to an increasing radicalization of the essayist, and at the same time, an increasing "Americanization," which grew out of his experiences in Mexico and Cuba. It should be remembered that the years 1960-1962 were particularly difficult ones in Cuban history; the Missile Crisis, the Bay of Pigs incident, the ending of the Sugar Quota normally accepted by the United States, no doubt helped engender the feeling in Cuba that full-scale invasion was imminent, and to a hardened iconoclast like Martínez Estrada there was no question as to where his sympathies lay. Accordingly, one notices in the more polemical essays of the period (above all in *En Cuba y al servicio de la revolución cubana*, 1963) more and more efforts by the essayist to defend the Cuban régime from its international detractors. Thus in an energetic reply to a declaration of Argentine intellectuals (including Borges, Mallea and Bioy Casares) against the increasing Marxist orientation of the Cuban government, Martínez Estrada charged:

> En fin esa declaración con la que desengañan a los aficiona-
> dos a la literatura de imaginación que creyeron que pertene-
> cían ustedes a la intelectualidad argentina — a la alta, por
> supuesto —, deja la convicción de que ignoran ustedes cómo
> se vive, se trabaja, se estudia y se construye sobre las ruinas
> de un régimen ominoso un nuevo mundo de paz y de con-
> fraternidad en Cuba. Yo estoy aquí y lo veo. [18]

---

[18] Ezequiel Martínez Estrada, *En Cuba y al servicio de la revolución cubana* (La Habana: Ediciones Unión/Ensayo, 1963), p. 99.

And in the same source there are many strong attacks on the United States, as well as an evocation of his compatriot Che Guevara. [19] From the same period, but published posthumously was *La poesía afrocubana de Nicolás Guillén* (1966), a work that is discernibly affected by the author's abundance of enthusiasm in favour of the new Cuban order; unfortunately it was also marred by some very arbitrary remarks about modern Spanish poetry that did not always appear pertinent to his discussions. *En torno a Kafka* (1967), *Meditaciones sarmientinas* (1968), *Leopoldo Lugones: retrato sin retocar* (1968) and *Leer y escribir* (1969) — all compiled by Enrique Espinoza, who has undertaken the task of re-issuing diverse material of Martínez Estrada on a thematic basis — constituted useful reminders of antecedents to positions in his major essays, and as such have aided critics in search of the essential personality of the essayist. Particularly memorable are the exchanges between the author and a group of Russian students (during the former's visit to the University of Moscow in 1957) on the subject of socialist realism and the whole question of the portrayal of "reality" in literature, in *En torno a Kafka*. Similarly *Meditaciones sarmientinas* brought into timely focus his concept of Argentine literary history, while *Leer y escribir* offered light on the early years of his literary career, in particular "Reflexiones acerca del error," which dealt with his views on the acquisition of human truth. The *Antología* which appeared in 1964 offered little new in the way of texts, but the prologue, by the essayist himself, proved quite valuable for the appreciation of certain historical motivations in the author, and was illustrative too of the demagogic style typical of his more polemical essays:

> Después de ese libro [*Radiografía de la pampa*] he escrito unas decenas de otros, orientados en la misma dirección del esclarecimiento honrado de nuestra realidad ... Todas aquellas obras mías que se refieren al mismo tema de *Radiografía de la pampa*, como *La cabeza de Goliat, Muerte y transfiguración de Martín Fierro, Sarmiento, Invariantes históricos en el Facundo* y algunas otras, me adjudican el papel de maniático disconforme, el cual tengo que aceptar resignadamente, porque en nuestro vocabulario no existe todavía palabra para designar al estudioso imparcial de los estratos de la vida

---

[19] *Ibid.*, pp. 79-84.

social de un país por sobre el que los ciudadanos transitan mirando a lo lejos. [20]

Yet the highlight of these last years of his life for Martínez Estrada was unquestionably his quite moving encounter with the whole personality of José Martí, and one of his major preoccupations during this time was precisely the possibility that he might die before he saw his work on Martí in print. [21] This final pleasure, indeed, consolation, was to be denied him. He returned to Buenos Aires in November of 1962, and exactly one year later, resident again in Bahía Blanca, he wrote to Carlos Adam:

> Un año de residencia en este *bel paese* de riqueza y cultura prominentes, me han arrancado las pocas ganas que tenía para vivir. Viejos, enfermos y solos... "esperando el coche." [22]

The following year, almost to the day, on the 4th of November, 1964, Ezequiel Martínez Estrada died at his home in Bahía Blanca, "old, ill and alone." The following day *La Nación* offered a realistic yet moving evocation of one of the country's greatest intellectuals:

> ... su espíritu, cansado de andar por el mundo de lo ideal, se autoconsumía al no encontrar lo que buscaba. La vida histórica y humana argentina, la cultura de las minorías y la visión de nuestros estadistas lo arrinconaban contra el muro de las imposibilidades con que tropiezan todos los idealistas que analizan la historia como si fuera el resultado de la obra perfecta, de unos hombres también perfectos. Martínez Estrada era un fanático de la verdad. [23]

---

[20] *Antología*, p. 14.
[21] The impact of the personality of Martí on Martínez Estrada is discussed in detail in Chapter IV.
[22] *Bibliografía y documentos de Ezequiel Martínez Estrada*, p. 196.
[23] "Ezequiel Martínez Estrada falleció en Bahía Blanca," *La Nación*, 5th November, 1964.

## CHAPTER I

## CULTURAL ANTECEDENTS TO THE
## HISTORICO-SOCIOLOGICAL ESSAYS

WHILE THE PRECISE ORIGINS of nationalism [1] admit of no exact historical delimitation, Bertrand Russell rightly asserts that our modern versions owe a fundamental debt to the Romantics who assumed a nation "to be race, descended from common ancestors, and sharing some sort of 'blood-consciousness.' " [2] Naturally, the whole concept has revealed a range of subtleties in its development from the 18th century that the original Romantic conception appears markedly dated in its relevance to 20th century Latin America.

Nonetheless, each of these "categories," in turn, received generous attention by essayists throughout Latin America in the striving towards a concrete conceptualization and eventual institution of ideas such as Nation, State, Fatherland, which hitherto had remained the prerogative of the respective *madre patria*. The clear ascendancy of French culture, in retrospect, did not achieve such a position in Latin America purely as a result of its undeniably very strong intellectual prestige; increasingly, the repudiation of the mother country inevitably implied a cultural "severing" too, and France increasingly filled the cultural needs of the continent. Thus the concept of "race and common ancestors" at least on a cultural level, until almost the beginning of the 20th century, did not find many cultivators. Equally, the idea of a common "blood-consciousness" throughout the continent did not develop to any appreciable degree, except in repudiation of

---

[1] The term is used here in the sense of "cultural nationalism."
[2] Bertrand Russell, *History of Western Philosophy* (London: Allen and Unwin, 1969), p. 658.

the colonial heritage, when writers such as Francisco Bilbao (1832-1865) denounced the Spanish heritage as the source of Chile's and the continent's ills, in very acerbic fashion.

Yet, in indirect ways, other forces were at work which were to eventually see an approximation of Gallic and Hispanic values in the affirmation of a mutual subscription to a common Mediterranean experience, to a type of *patrimonio común*. The increasingly expansionist policies of the United States, her burgeoning economy, and continental investments, together with the impact of the Spanish-American War of 1898, more than ever raised fears of the *coloso del norte*. But the economic and political threats were indicative of more deep-seated fears with regard to the cultural effects of such North American power. Psychologically, the last years of the century seemed to be ripe for a reassurance that Spanish America was not condemned to forever be the "poor relation" of the American family. The proverb that *la edad suple al hombre*, found its realization in the figure of José Enrique Rodó (1871-1917) whose essays, principally *Ariel* (1900) and *Motivos de Proteo* (1909), almost alone engendered the long awaited spiritual reawakening. Directed at the youth of Latin America, Rodó's work was conceived as an attempt to re-imbue Latin America with a sense of mission, of a heroic view of life, that must not be threatened by the "sacro imperio del utilitarismo," [3] represented by the United States.

Not unexpectedly, *arielismo* gave rise to many oversimplifications with regard to the "pristine purity of the Latin spirit" and "gross utilitarianism" of North America. Manuel Ugarte (1878-1951) in his *El porvenir de la América latina* (1911) together with Columbian Carlos Arturo Torres (1867-1911) and Venezuelan Rufino Blanco Fombona (1874-1944) adumbrated this view of the spiritual "superiority" of Latin America. [4] Nonetheless, the newly found confidence of those who supported Rodó's basic postulations (and those who could resist them were very few indeed) did have some markedly positive results. First of all, Rodó's work reemphasized the role that a moral concept of life (ideals and ideas) had to play in the continued development of society, which necessarily gave impulse to new ideas

---

[3] José Enrique Rodó, *Ariel*, 3rd ed. (México: Espasa-Calpe, 1963), p. 73.
[4] Jean Franco, *The Modern Culture of Latin America* (London: Pall Mall, 1967), pp. 51-52.

on educational reform. [5] Secondly, the emphasis on a continental, Latin-American spiritual awareness, had the effect of liberating many intellectuals from the suffocating confines of a narrow nationalism. It was the advent of a supranational ideal, and one probably would have to go back to Bolívar to find such continental adhesion to the work of one writer. Yet in another, more basic sense, *arielismo* came as a liberating and unifying force. Fundamentally, Rodó reminded Latin-American intellectuals of their full membership in the neo-Latin family; the hitherto intellectual mentors of Latin America, the French, could at last be approached on a level approaching if not of equality of achievement, at least on that of a common mission, of a mutual spirituality.

Thus, for many Latin-American intellectuals, the sense of belonging to a marginally intellectual community increasingly dissipated itself in the wide appeal of the new *arielista* self-assertion. Yet at the same time voices of dissent became more and more audible, encouraged no doubt by the more exaggerated claims of a Manuel Ugarte or of a Blanco Fambona. But deeper, more fundamental reasons were not hard to arrive at. The exultation of neo-Classical values, the reminder to Latin Americans of their Mediterranean heritage, and of traditions to be cultivated in face of a very real utilitarian "threat," would have a great deal of plausibility for countries like Argentina and Uruguay. [6] But could these ideals constitute a genuine *American* idearium? Could the American interpreter of Taine and Renan offer viable solutions to the spiritual problems of those countries of predominantly Indian cultures? Did not Rodó's fear of "la tiranía irresponsable del número" and of his clear promotion of the creation of an intellectual élite [7] to rule the destiny of nations appear as a tacit justification of merely another form of *caudillismo*, of oligarchic rule?

---

[5] José Vasconcelos (1882-1959), Mexican Minister of Education, 1921-24, was a great believer in the cultural unity of America, and attempted to implement his ideas in concrete educational programmes.

[6] It is pertinent here to pause on the apparent anomaly that Argentina, the country with the greatest "white" population in Latin America, has produced essayists in numbers whose theories on America have given considerable importance to the indigenous cultures. Martínez Estrada himself, together with H. A. Murena have stressed the influence of the land in shaping aesthetic attitudes. See *La tesis andina* (1920) of Bolivian Jaime Mendoza (1874-1939), an Indian novelist, for a rather similar concept.

[7] José Enrique Rodó, *op. cit.*, pp. 84, 85.

## Questions of race

In the last analysis, Rodó's doctrines could not hope to fundamentally inspire those who saw the indigenous cultures as central to any consideration of an American, truly American reality. Certainly there were those who, from predominantly "Indian" countries, would find particular consolation in the postulates of Rodó. Bolivian Alcides Arguedas (1879-1946) espoused an unashamedly racist view of the non-European, holding that the Indian was incapable of advancing beyond the point of an agricultural worker or soldier. [8] The ills of Bolivia, he advanced, could in great measure be attributed to racial miscegenation; his *Pueblo enfermo* (1901) and *Raza de bronce* (1919) both bear witness to a conception of the Indian cultures as having caused the degeneration of European culture in his country. [9] More in harmony with the implicit opposition in Rodó's work of Latin and Anglo-Saxon cultures were the writings of Peruvian Francisco García Calderón (1883-1953) who wrote almost entirely in French. *Les democraties latines de L'Amerique* (1912) and *Le Péru contemporain* (1907) espouse a view that the material and educational progress of countries such as Argentina, Uruguay and Chile was the result of their largely white populations, the author stating further in a later work that it was the inevitable consequence of "la depuración de las razas, de la abundancia de inmigraciones viriles, del desarrollo de la vida industrial." [10]

Not unexpectedly, given the powerful antecedent of Domingo Sarmiento (1811-1888) and his maniacal deprecation of indigenous contributions to his country's development, it was Argentina that produced probably the continent's most coherent and consistent defender of the racist interpretation. Published in 1903, *Nuestra América*, by Carlos Octavio Bunge (1875-1918), undoubtedly influenced Arguedas and García Calderón, since it was practically the first social study of its kind. In his completely negative attitude towards the racial composition of Argentina and Spanish American society he was very much

---

[8] Martin S. Stabb, *In Quest of Identity* (Chapel Hill: University of North Carolina Press, 1967), p. 23.

[9] *Ibid.*, p. 23.

[10] Francisco García Calderón, *La creación de un continente* (Paris: Paul Ollendorff, 1913), pp. 256-257.

a forerunner of the racial theories of the Andean essayists. Hence for Bunge:

> Cada raza física es una raza psíquica. Cada raza posee un carácter típico ... los españoles nos dan arrogancia, indolencia, indiferencia, uniformidad teológica, decoro; los indios, fatalismo y ferocidad; los negros, servilismo, maleabilidad, y, cuando entroncan con los blancos, cierta sobreexcitación de la facultad de aspirar que podría bien llamarse *hiperestesia de la ambición.* [11]

As could be anticipated, Bunge called for increased Europeanization of Argentina and clearly too, he stands in direct succession to writers like Sarmiento and Alberdi and to the corresponding slogans, "civilización y barbarie," and "gobernar es poblar." At the same time, Bunge's more recent spiritual mentors were Positivists; his affinity, for example, with Frenchman Gustave le Bon, a prestigious social scientist or "social organicist" at the turn of the century, who considered the racial character of a nation to be immutable, [12] was obviously reflected in his own introduction to *Nuestra América.* Outlining his view of the question he states:

   i. Each people possesses its own social psychology.

   ii. The collective psychology of any society, even if susceptible to evolutionary transformations, is relatively "cut and dried" ("neto") and stable.

   iii. The typical qualities that constitute the social psychology of a people are only peculiar to it, to the extent of their intensity and form. [13]

Hence, while his "methodology" perforce would lead to rather pessimistic conclusions about America at large, the relatively large "white" population of Argentina could allow him to advocate immigration as the chief instrument for achieving the elusive political stability and material progress of his country.

---

[11] Carlos Octavio Bunge, *Nuestra América* (Buenos Aires: Casa Vaccaro, 1918), pp. 118-119.

[12] Martin S. Stabb, *op. cit.,* p. 14.

[13] José Luis Romero, *El desarrollo de las ideas en la sociedad argentina del siglo XX* (México: Fondo de Cultura Económica, 1965), p. 53.

Although Bunge was not an anti-Hispanist in the sense of a Francisco Bilbao, who contributed to fanning the flames of the "leyenda negra," there were rather vociferous contemporaries such as Agustín Álvarez and Juan Agustín García. Álvarez, in his *Manual de patología política* and pamphlet *El continente enfermo* (both 1899) expressed the fear that immigrants would be absorbed into the "medio ambiente de tradición española" and that the country would not receive the benefit of their new ideas. [14] Mexico, probably the one Latin American country (with the exception of Brazil) [15] where Positivism struck particularly deep roots, saw a sustained interest in questions of indigenism and racism in the last decades of the XIXth century and up until the Revolution. There were those, like Francisco Bulnes (1847-1924), in his *El porvenir de las naciones latino-americanas* (1899), who outlined "environmentalist" analyses of Indian "inferiority" based upon dietary considerations (protein content of cereals and their importance to brain formation, placing the wheat eaters — the whites — in a "superior" position over the maize and rice eaters — Indian and "yellow" races respectively). Yet there was very little genuine racism, as one critic has pointed out, of the biological type, evident in contemporary Mexican social thought, unlike other parts of the continent:

> If one were to compare the race-thinking of the Mexicans with the literature of what may be called the "classic" school of nineteenth-century European racism — the works of Arthur de Gobineau, Houston Stewart Chamberlain and Gustave le Bon — it would be perfectly clear that Mexican thought remained relatively uncontaminated by these doctrines. It may be noted in passing that the virus of "classical racism" had by contrast made considerable headway in the late nine-

---

[14] José Luis Romero, *op. cit.*, p. 54.

[15] While there is as yet, as far as can be traced, no basic study of the intricate and complicated relationship between Positivism and the development of indigenous and racist theories, it would be a distortion to see in Positivism, from the examples we have used in this chapter, an ideological base used to justify the continued neglect of the indigenous masses. In Brazil, for example, Positivism was largely instrumental in forcing the issue of abolition of slavery in 1888; Miguel Lemos, one of the "guiding lights" of Brazilian Positivism, was a leading abolitionist. See the chapter, "The Advent of Positivism" in João Cruz Costa, *A History of Ideas in Brazil* (Berkeley: University of California Press, 1964), pp. 82-175.

teenth and early twentieth century in other parts of Spanish America. [16]

Moreover, Justo Sierra (1848-1912), surely the outstanding Positivist of the Díaz régime, attacked the "biological" racism of Gustave le Bon:

> Mucho se ha dicho en pro y en contra de las familias mezcladas o mestizas. Ha tiempo que los sabios extranjeros nos han acostumbrado a declaraciones dogmáticas respecto de los antecedentes y consecuentes de nuestro estado político y social, y esas sentencias son por tal modo desconsoladoras, que si ellas fueran conclusiones realmente científicas, desesperaríamos de nosotros mismos... protestamos contra sus inducciones, que no son científicas porque dimanan de observaciones deficientes de los hechos;...
>
> Uno de los etnologistas que cometen este pecado lógico, el doctor Gustavo Le Bon... ha formulado así su opinión sobre la familia mestiza en un flamante estudio intitulado *La influencia de la raza en la historia. (Revue scientifique.* Abril, 1888) [17]

Hence, Mexico was spared the more extreme aberrations, at least at an influential level (Sierra was also a leading educator) of racist doctrine. Clearly the polemics of race and environment grew out of that offshoot of Positivism — social Darwinism —, Sarmiento and the Brazilian Euclides da Cunha (1866-1909) probably being the best known examples of this. Both *Facundo* and *Os Sertões* rely heavily on a method of "geographical determinism," and da Cunha was at times hard pressed to reconcile contemporary racial theories and empirical evidence to the contrary. [18] Martínez Estrada too, as we shall

---

[16] Martin S. Stabb, "Indigenism and Racism in Mexican Thought: 1857-1911," *Journal of Inter-American Studies*, I, 4 (Oct., 1959), 420-421.

[17] *Obras completas del maestro Justo Sierra*, revisada y ordenada por Agustín Yañez (México: Universidad Autónoma, 1948), V, 213. Quoted in Martin S. Stabb, "Indigenism and Racism in Mexican Thought: 1857-1911," p. 406.

[18] "Their [the sertanejos] heroic courage aroused not only da Cunha's sympathy and admiration but also his curiosity. He found an explanation for their courage and their ferocious desire for independence in the constant struggle they waged against the natural environment. But how could this be reconciled with the fact that the *sertanejos*, or inhabitants of the *sertão*, were racially mixed descendants of Portuguese and Indian and therefore presumably

see later, employed a type of "geographical determinism," but with some major differences and very pessimistic results.

## The rise of America

In retrospect, the first decade of the twentieth century would appear to be an era of enormous intellectual activity. Various tendencies seemed to be converging upon one single point: an increasing awareness of, and an attempt to define, an American reality. As we have seen, the publication of Rodó's *Ariel* in 1900 laid the foundations for a whole reassessment of what it meant to be American, and what particular destiny fate held in hand for the continent. Thus there was an upsurge of interest in questions of indigenism and racism, particularly with regard to the Indian and his importance to the entire question of *americanismo*. Yet it is equally obvious that there was a persistence of some nineteenth century attitudes. Positivism still continued to be the primary "doctrine" with regard to the administration of the state and its ancillary institutions, particularly that of education, and it was not until 1910 that Mexico, where the *científicos* were more entrenched than anywhere else, bore witness to the eventual collapse of the "religion of Humanity." Similarly, literary tastes continued to reflect the prevailing Modernism of the preceding decades; *Cantos de vida y esperanza* by Darío appeared in 1905, and the greatest example of Modernist narrative prose, *La gloria de Don Ramiro* by the Argentinian Enrique Larreta, in 1908.

The year 1911 [19] marks the beginning of the end for both the political and aesthetic *status quo*. The Mexican Revolution was a year old and Mexican Enrique González Martínez published his famous sonnet "Tuércele el cuello al cisne" as an overt attack on the hollow imitators of Darío. And increasingly, Spanish America was beginning to experience the stirrings of a reaction to the "Futurist manifiesto" of Italian Marinetti published in 1909, seen in movements such as the *estridentistas* in Mexico (in 1922) and the *Martín Fierro* group in Argentina in 1923.

---

degenerate? Da Cunha could only conclude that the struggle with the environment had offset their racial defects." Jean Franco, *The Modern Culture of Latin America*, p. 45.

[19] It is of course possible to trace the revolt against Modernism to an earlier date, such as to the publication of Santos Chocano's *Alma América* in 1906, replete with themes of national, historical and political interest.

However, the changing directions of intellectual activity were also in response to the profound disillusionment caused by the European turmoil of 1914-1918. Suddenly that font of everything truly cultural and creative — Europe — had shown itself capable of a degree of barbarity that many intellectuals in Latin America had hitherto thought to be their own fate. Suddenly European immigration, that well-worn panacea to the continent's ills (and particularly those of Argentina), began to lose some of its previously irresistible lustre. From the feeling of involvement, of much greater participation in a neo-Latin, "Mediterranean" world-view, which the work of Rodó [20] had set in motion, gave way to a feeling, not of equality or superiority [21] with regard to Europe, but rather that America's contributions to the world cultural community could be conceived in terms that did not necessarily stress Europe as the principal point of reference.

More than ever in those years following the War, there was an evolving climate of newly-found confidence in America and her destiny, even if, somewhat paradoxically, it was a small group of European intellectuals that contributed signally to that confidence. While Ezequiel Martínez Estrada did not share the optimism of the times, there can be little doubt that he, in many ways, as we hope to illustrate, was deeply affected by some of these thinkers.

## A decadent Europe

Chronologically, [22] the works of Oswald Spengler (1880-1936) and in particular his *Decline of the West*, which appeared from 1917

---

[20] The literary-philosophical essay *Los motivos de Proteo* (1909) on the theme of Spanish America's spiritual vocation, was a development of the appeal made in *Ariel* nine years previously.

[21] Jean Franco, however, does interpret Spengler's work as implying a superiority on the part of the American indigenous cultures. See Jean Franco, *op. cit.*, p. 104-105.

[22] It is indeed difficult to fix with certainty a chronological list of influences from foreign sources. The most obvious difficulty is not that of tracing the impact of a certain work from its date of publication, but rather from the date of its translation. Hence those writers writing in a Romance language (e.g. French) will be read more quickly and more widely than those writing in German. Thus, of the writers under discussion one could make a case for treating Ortega y Gasset first, since important works such as *Meditaciones del Quijote*, *España invertebrada*, and *El tema de nuestro tiempo*, published in 1914, 1921, and 1923, respectively, in all probability had an impact previous to *The Decline of the West*, which first began to appear in 1917 in

onwards (in German) were the first to catch the imagination of many intellectuals with reference to the theme of European decadence. Spengler held that Western civilization (European) was in its last agony, and that it was not necessarily the greatest of many civilizations that had declined and disappeared. One of his fundamental ideas that readily seemed to apply to Latin America was that parliamentary democracy was doomed to fall and would be superceded by a type of "caesarism." Naturally, the long tradition of *caudillismo* in Latin America was an obvious example of this, thus implying that the continent was more "advanced" than other cultures, including Europe. The inversion in values is evident: what was previously considered a reason for political underdevelopment is now a hallmark of a society at a more advanced stage of development. The effect of this particular concept in many Latin-American intellectual circles can be appreciated by the content of a lecture [23] given in Santiago de Chile, at the University, in 1927, by R. Carlos Keller:

> Cómo, se dirá, ¿no somos nosotros, los iberoamericanos los que nos consideramos inferiores a los europeos y que tratamos de progresar según aquel modelo? Y ahora viene un

---

German. However, since the essays of Ortega we shall discuss are from 1929, he is treated second. Another important foreign influence that should be mentioned is that of the North American Waldo Frank (1889-1967) whose personality and work (*Our America*, 1919) caused him to enjoy a rather special relationship with many Latin American intellectuals of the time. In one of his many contributions to Spanish-American literary journals he saw the breakup of the modern state as beginning with the replacement of Christian brotherhood by nationalism, which was finally to cause the decadence of Europe:

> Podeis medir el estado de la descomposición cultural de Europa, por contraste con el Conjunto en que habitó Dante. Allí todo tenía su sito [*sic*], su movimiento con ritmo designado en el Todo. De Dios al sacerdote, del Emperador al siervo, del cielo al infierno, de la estrella al átomo, de lo bueno a lo malo, todo era integral. Era un mundo, además, en el que Dante vivió junto con su cocinero. Ese conjunto está muerto. Pero organismo muerto no significa inanición. Mirad a cualquier cadáver haciendo progreso en su descomposición, ved como eso también es vivir. Europa hormiguea en su muerte. (Waldo Frank, "El Redescubrimiento de América; los últimos días de Europa," *Amauta* (Lima), núm. 11, año 2 (enero, 1928), p. 2.

[23] R. Carlos Keller, *Spengler y la situación político-cultural de la América Ibérica*. Conferencia dada en el Salón de Honor de la Universidad de Chile, el 25 de mayo de 1927 (Santiago de Chile; Imprenta Universitaria, 1927), p. 8.

autor alemán a comprobarnos que hemos avanzado mucho
más que aquéllos?

The tone of Keller's speech indicates that many intellectuals suffered from a sense of inferiority faced with Europe and that he is
clearly intent on redressing the balance:

> ... si preparamos bien el barbecho, basándonos en los prin-
> cipios de la sociología moderna, cuyo más caracterizado re-
> presentante es Spengler, adaptando los métodos europeos, no
> los resultados, inculcando a nuestra juventud el espíritu de
> crear, no de imitar, y fomentando cuidadosamente toda ma-
> nifestación de vida propia y original que descubramos, creo
> yo que hemos hecho todo lo que está de nuestra parte, para
> que el soplo milagroso de la evolución cultural se comunique
> a nuestra juventud y le imprima su espíritu maravilloso. [24]

## The telluric reality

Yet Spengler's spectacular success in Latin America was not merely
as a bolster for continental neurosis. Instinctively his audience realized
that this European was attuned to their American reality. Stressing
an intuitive concept that was later to be developed by Count Hermann
Keyserling, Spengler referred to the particular relationship that existed
between American man and the land. Typical of this sensitivity is the
following:

> Primeval man is a *ranging* animal, keen and anxious in its
> senses, ever alert to drive off some element of Hostile Nature.
> A deep transformation sets in first with agriculture. He who
> digs and ploughs is seeking not to plunder, but to alter
> Nature. To plant implies, not to take something, but to pro-
> duce something. *But with this man himself becomes plant*
> — namely, as peasant. He roots in the earth that he tends.
> The soul of man discovers a soul in the countryside. A new
> earth-boundness of being, a new feeling, pronounces itself.
> Hostile Nature becomes a friend; earth becomes *Mother
> Earth*. Between sowing and begetting, harvest and death, the
> child and the grain, a profound affinity is set up. [25]

---

[24] *Ibid.*, p. 282.
[25] Edwin Franden Dakin, *Today and Destiny: Vital extracts from Decline
of the West* (New York: A. A. Knopf, 1940), p. 205.

This statement of affinity with Nature — *lo telúrico* — was one that found an immediate echo in Latin America, and enhanced the notion that at last there were Europeans who really understood the peculiar American reality not in the manner of a Chateaubriand or of a cult of exoticism for its own sake, but rather in the sense of a fully viable culture. At the same time, most intellectuals were willing to overlook a rather conservative vein in Spengler, which if properly examined, would raise rather similar objections ultimately, as those against Rodó: the promotion of patrician attitudes, of an "enlightened" minority rule. The following, for example would not be unworthy of the Uruguayan:

> The traditions of an old monarchy, of an old aristocracy, of an old polite family, in so much as they are still healthy enough to keep clear of professional and professorial politics; in so far as they possess honour, abnegation, discipline, the genuine sense of a great mission, sense of duty and sacrifice — can become a centre that holds together the being-stream of an entire people, and enables it to outlast this time and make its landfall in the future. [26]

Nonetheless, the German's influence was profound. In addition to his main contributions to a deep sense of cultural *aggiornamento* in Latin America, probably his greatest single offering was the idea that, just as individuals, nations possess souls, [27] a concept that was destined to preoccupy a whole generation of Latin American intellectuals, including Martínez Estrada, which, combining with a configuration of historical, political and ethnic considerations, helped to foment a crisis of identity in many countries:

> Nations are *the true city-building peoples*. In the strongholds they arose, with the cities they ripen to the full height of their world-consciousness, and in the world-cities they dissolve. Every town-formation that has character has also *national* character. The village, which is wholly a thing of race, does not yet possess it; the megopolis possesses it no longer. Of this essential, national character, which so colours

---

[26] *Ibid.,* p. 282.

[27] It will be obvious that Spengler did not conceive of "soul" in a theological manner, but rather after the fashion of the Hegelian *Volksgeist*. A further example of his conservative attitudes may be seen from his views on the impossibility of communication between the "souls" of two cultures. See the chapter, "What is Race?" in Dakin, *op. cit.,* pp. 159-177.

the nation's public life that its slightest manifestation iden-
tifies it, we cannot exaggerate — we can hardly imagine —
the force, the self-sufficingness, and the *loneliness* ... Between the souls of Cultures the screen is impenetrable. [28]

## Ortegean meditations

Also of immense influence at this time, was the work of Ortega
y Gasset (1883-1955) and the role of popularization of German
philosophy undertaken by his periodical *Revista de Occidente* from
1923 onwards, although important works, like *España invertebrada,*
were published earlier. Yet Ortega's contributions were not always
accepted without criticism, and as one critic has shrewdly pointed
out, Ortega was particularly adept at handing out left-handed compli-
ments to Spanish America, [29] and Argentinians, more than most, felt
a sense of outrage from time to time, at some of the Spanish philosopher's comments. A clear example of this tendency of simultaneous
praise/criticism can be seen in a famous essay on Argentina, "El
hombre a la defensiva" together with "La Pampa ... promesas" both
published in 1929. On the one hand Ortega stated,

> Lo que sí creo es que esa alta idea de sí propio anidada en
> este pueblo [argentino] es la causa mayor de su progreso, y
> no la fertilidad de su tierra ni ningún otro factor económico. [30]

Then, shortly afterwards he pointed out that,

> El argentino actual es un hombre a la defensiva ... En la
> relación normal el argentino no se abandona; por el con-
> trario, cuando el prójimo se acerca hermetiza más su alma y
> se dispone a la defensiva ... Que el atacado se defienda es
> lo más congruente, pero vivir en estado de sitio cuando nadie
> nos asedia es una propensión superlativamente extraña. [31]

In similar vein he goes on to say,

> No hay modo de eludir la única expresión rigorosa: el argen-
> tino se gusta a sí mismo ... Al argentino le gusta la imagen

---

[28] *Ibid.,* p. 167.

[29] Martin S. Stabb, *In Quest of Identity,* p. 70.

[30] José Ortega y Gasset, *El Espectador* (Madrid: Espasa Calpe, 1966),
Colección Austral, 7 & 8 (2 tomos en 1), p. 104. Both these articles, under
the heading of "Intimidades" were first published in September, 1929.

[31] *Ibid.,* pp. 110-111.

> que de sí mismo tiene ... Es sobremanera Narciso. Es Nar-
> ciso y la fuente de Narciso. Lo lleva todo consigo: la reali-
> dad, la imagen y el espejo. [32]

yet still feels constrained to add,

> Quien sabe eludir los *trompe l'œil* psicológicos y ha visto,
> como por una rendija, la magnífica intimidad que el hombre
> argentino llega a paralizar dentro de sí por reducirse a la
> fruición de su imagen, se impacientará pensando en todo lo
> que podría ser ya este pueblo ... Se impacientará de que en
> el *pueblo con más vigorosos resortes históricos que existe
> hoy*, haya faltado una minoría enérgica que suscite una nue-
> va moral en la sociedad ... [33]

It is interesting at this point to recognize the extent to which the
three principal figures we have been discussing up to this juncture
— Rodó, Spengler and Ortega — all subscribed to a belief in the
efforts of an *élite*, of an enlightened minority, to effectively lead a
given country towards its moral/historical destiny. The differences of
kind between "intellectual *élite*" (Rodó), "old aristocracy" (Spengler)
and "energetic minority" (Ortega) are really non-existent; it is in
fact a question of degree. One may speculate on the basis for the
appeal of these three men in terms of whether these attitudes enhanced
the acceptance of their main ideological appeal or that they were
accepted in spite of them. [34]

As one young essayist has noted, the principal objection that may
be levelled at Ortega's American meditations is that they conceive of
the continent only in terms of Argentina and the United States; [35]
and Ortega himself made an unequivocal affirmation of debt, intellectual and *vital*, to his experience of Argentina. [36] Yet the Spanish
thinker was not always received with uniform acclaim, and he pro-

---

[32] *Ibid.*, pp. 122, 124.

[33] *Ibid.*, p. 426.

[34] See Jean Franco's discussion of this and related themes in her chapter
"The Select Minority: Arielism and Criollismo, 1900-1918," in *The Modern
Culture of Latin America*, pp. 40-68.

[35] Juan Francisco Marsal, "Las meditaciones argentinas de Ortega," *Ciudad*, 4-5, Buenos Aires (1956), p. 10.

[36] "Por qué he escrito 'El hombre a la defensiva,' " *Obras completas*, 4th
ed. (Madrid: Revista de Occidente, 1957), IV, 70. This was first published
in *La Nación*, Buenos Aires, 13th April, 1930.

pounded two concepts in particular that were controversial. The first was the curious concept of the State (according to Ortega) that he found in existence among Argentinians. Basically, his objection was that the then operative conception of the State constituted a continuation of European models that had long been abandoned in Europe. Thus he wrote,

> Para mí es cosa clara que entre la realidad social argentina y su idea del Estado hay un curioso desequilibrio y como anacronismo. Esta va muy por delante de aquélla, y pareja incoincidencia acusan en conjunto muchas cosas buenas y malas, plausibles y peligrosas. [37]

This, as can be clearly inferred, was tantamount to saying that the imitators had imitated badly, and that a basic source of the country's ills was the very heart of its social institutions. At the same level of criticism Ortega proceeded to the lack of discipline, the lack of sense of mission on the part of educated minorities in the country:

> ...el argentino es un hombre admirablemente dotado, que no se entrega a nada, que no ha sumergido irrevocablemente su existencia en el servicio a alguna cosa distinta de él... El europeo se entrega a la vida, al destino, y, por tanto, hace del destino su vida misma, lo toma y acepta. A esto llamo sentir la vida como misión... Pero el argentino tiende a resbalar sobre toda ocupación o destino concreto... [38]

The second fundamental idea that also raised a great deal of controversy was the particular relation that he judged existent between Argentinian man and the land. We must hasten to add, however, that this was not at all the "telluric" forces as outlined by Spengler and later to be developed by Count Hermann Keyserling, [39] as we will soon consider. Ortega, in other words rejected "el determinismo del medio" as Juan Francisco Marsal put it. [40] He saw nature not as something apart from man, without him, but rather part of him; hence nature under this relationship becomes "humanized," and man dwells

[37] *Obras completas*, II, 643.
[38] *El espectador*, p. 97.
[39] See Ortega's article, "Sobre los Estados Unidos," *Obras completas*, IV, 387. This was first published in *Luz* (Madrid), July 30, 1932.
[40] Juan Francisco Marsal, p. 11.

on it. Moreover, *paisaje,* as used by the philosopher in this context is really referring to a spiritual nature, *paisaje del alma.* Thus the all-embracing, all-pervasive dimensions of the Pampa reflect themselves in Argentine man, and, by extension, in Argentine society. Hence, the absence of clear-cut dimensions, of concrete contours, in the Pampa is reflected in the form-less character of the Argentinian's concept of himself and of society; thus he does not "feel life as a mission" as Ortega pointed out. Because of this very lack of form, of concreteness, the Pampa — and the Pampa within every Argentinian — is in a constant state of becoming; it is the continuous promise of things to come. The image of the eternal circle appears to present itself: the Argentinian does not feel life as a mission, among other things, because he is always in wait of a national/spiritual realization, progress that never quite manages to manifest itself:

> En rigor, el alma criolla está llena de promesas heridas, su-
> fre radicalmente de un divino descontento — ya lo dije en
> 1916 — siente dolor en miembros que le faltan y que, sin
> embargo, no ha tenido nunca. Frente a la Tierra Prometida
> es la Pampa la tierra promisora. Si yo pudiese asomarme al
> alma de cualquier viejo criollo creo que sorprendería su se-
> creta impresión de que se le ha ido la vida toda en vano por
> el arco de la esperanza, es decir, *de que se le ha ido sin*
> *haber pasado* ... Por eso, cuando al llegar a la vejez mira
> atrás, no encuentra su vida, que no ha pasado por él, a la
> que no ha atendido y halla sólo la huella dolorida y román-
> tica de una existencia que no existió. Encuentra, pues, en
> rigor, el vacío, el hueco de su propia vida. [41]

Yet not all was pure analysis in Ortega's Argentine meditations. If the Argentinians' morale was, as he diagnosed, very low, and if one could accuse Ortega precisely of contributing to such a condition, the philosopher was equally energetic in his encouragement:

> ... el hombre argentino está desmoralizado y lo está en un
> momento grave de su historia nacional, cuando — después
> de dos generaciones en que ha vivido fuera — tiene que vol-
> ver a vivir de su propia sustancia en todos los órdenes: eco-
> nómico, político, intelectual. Tal es mi convicción madurada
> calladamente durante muchos años y que no es fácil hagan

---

[41] *El espectador,* p. 97.

vacilar lo más mínimo las diatribas, insolencias y chistes de esos jóvenes intelectuales argentinos que emplean en gesticulaciones narcisistas su tiempo, en vez de arrimar el hombro, como yo, sin posturas, sin "maneras", a la tarea de hacer una nación que, por fortuna no merecida de ellos, puede ser una formidable nación. [42]

Thus we see that Ortega, basically, shared Spengler's view of Argentina/America as embodying a great "becoming"; Spengler's faith in the "essential national character" and Ortega's reliance upon, and stressing of, "los resortes históricos" are not at all radically different from each other. Nevertheless, while both also share a rather conservative view of national/cultural survival and development (the subscription to the concept of a "saving" minority) Ortega, as we have noted, rejected the "telluric" interpretation of American man. By 1932 the Spanish philosopher's opinions with regard to Argentina had become more crystallized and there is an unmistakable tone of impatience to his reflections, occasioned, no doubt, by increased attacks directed at him by some of the younger critics. Rejecting the idea of *telurismo* as expounded by surely its greatest interpreter, Count Hermann Keyserling, we can notice that the somewhat cautious lan-

---

[42] *Obras completas*, IV, 72. One matter discussed by Ortega in "El hombre a la defensiva" that did nothing to increase his prestige in Argentina was that of the *guaranguería* of Argentinians. In fact it occasioned a sense of outrage in intellectual circles, and many writers rushed into print to refute his views, among them Martínez Estrada. His reactions were moderate compared to others, but he accused Ortega of a basic ignorance about the country. See "El guaranguismo de Ortega y Gasset," *Leer y escribir* (Mexico: Joaquín Mortiz, 1969), 91-96. Young Argentine intellectuals, however, were not the only source of criticism of Ortega's views on America; others were not slow to voice their impatience with the condescension that they saw in the Spaniard's attitudes. Consider the clear irony of the following:

América, España mayor, le hace olvidar divisiones, le incita y consuela. En Buenos Aires ha hallado dos veces el camino de Damasco, en esa ciudad tentacular donde la riqueza sirve de basamento, como en Florencia, a graciosas torres que albergan a Ariel entre dos vuelos. Regresa a su patria, grávido de dones, rico en fe y de caridad.

...El gran místico español enseñaba que la unidad debe poner su silla sobre todo. El guiador de nuestro tiempo invoca el amor que desciende desde los cielos más altos a la tierra para que todo en el universo viva en conexión.

(F. García Calderón, "Ortega y Gasset y nuestro tiempo," *El Repertorio Americano*, San José, Costa Rica, XX [1930], 147).

guage of the "left-hand compliment" has given way to a much more
affirmative position:

> Ser joven es no ser todavía. Y esto, con otras palabras, es lo
> que intento decir respecto a América. América no es todavía.
>
> Por eso, en medio de grandes aciertos, considero un error
> que Keyserling se coloque ante América del Norte o América
> del Sur e intente decirnos lo que son, como si tratase de
> pueblos viejos, cuyo espíritu es ya macizo y vive desde el
> centro radical de sí mismo. Este error le lleva a tomar como
> rasgos característicos modos transitorios y mostrencos de la
> vida colonial. ¿Es tan seguro, por ejemplo, que el americano
> del Sur esté constitutivamente unido a la tierra mientras el
> del Norte no tiene relación profunda con ella? ¿Hubiera
> dicho lo mismo Keyserling si su viaje hubiese acontecido en
> 1860? No; todavía no se puede definir el ser americano por
> la sencilla razón de que aún no es, aún no ha puesto irre-
> vocablemente su existencia a un naipe, es decir, a un modo
> de ser hombre determinado. Aún no ha empezado su his-
> toria. Vive la prehistoria de sí mismo. Y en la prehistoria
> no hay protagonistas, no hay destino particular, domina la
> pura circunstancia. América no ha sido hasta ahora el nom-
> bre de un pueblo o de varios pueblos, sino que es el nombre
> de una situación, de un estadio; la situación y el estadio
> coloniales. [43]

### The prophet of lo telúrico

Keyserling's long, rambling and rather uneven work, *Meditaciones
suramericanas* (published in Spanish in 1931) lent itself to the type
of objection made by Ortega. In reality, he was in many ways close
to the Spaniard's conception of America. It is pertinent, for example,
to compare the above citation with the following:

> The South America of today is as yet too unfinished and
> immature, too dependent on foreign ideas which it has taken
> over, as to be profound. But irresistibly it is evolving in the
> direction of Indianism. And thus I doubt not that in the days
> to come it will create a culture of great depth, in the sense
> of nearness to earth. Even that part of South America which
> is of European blood is not Christian in its depths. It is
> determined by primordial life, not by Spirit. It is essentially

---

[43] *Ibid.*, p. 378.

blind. Again and again, it seeks to be guided by ideals; it cultivates narcissistic tendencies ... But its world of ideas and ideals is too indistinct and too weak to take the lead ... South America's true life is the very opposite of a play: it is nought but darkness of the netherworld. [44]

Apart from a wish to give fundamental importance to prehistory in his conceptions, Keyserling's stance here is remarkably close to the outline of Ortega's American meditations that we have given above. Martínez Estrada, on the other hand (and as we shall soon proceed to illustrate), is much more in tune, intellectually and above all, intuitively, with the German. Various criticisms have been levelled at Keyserling's works, [45] but most commentators credit him as the principal perpretrator of the concept of *lo telúrico* — that special relationship between man and the land — that he considered so essential to the understanding of Latin American man:

> Blood and that for which it stands belong entirely to earth ... Thus, meditation of the problem of Blood of itself merges into meditation of the connexion between man and the soil on which he dwells ... Every live creature adapts itself to its surroundings, or is shaped by them. Owing to the extreme variability and peculiar sensibility of man, this is true of him in the highest degree. In the long run, there always emerges as the ultimate unit a synthesis of Blood and Earth which is so firm and so tenacious ... once a connexion between Blood and earth has been created, it represents an insoluble unity. [46]

This, of course, is a clear instance of the "determinismo del medio" that Ortega could not accept. While as we have pointed out, Keyserling and the Spaniard often reached similar conclusions (Ortega as we have seen spoke of the "grandes aciertos" of the German), Ortega is ultimately convinced that Argentina's spiritual crisis is in the moral/

---

[44] Count Hermann Keyserling, *South American Meditations: On Hell and Heaven in the Soul of Man* (New York: Harper Bros., 1932), p. 155.

[45] Some critics have disapproved of Keyserling's reliance at times on Spanish-American literary models — principally *La vorágine* (1924) by the Colombian José Eustasio Rivera, and freely admitted by Keyserling — as a basis for his conception of South American man as "primordial." Jean Franco, for example, sees his formulation of *lo telúrico* as "probably more harmful than helpful." (*The Modern Culture of Latin America*, p. 106).

[46] *South American Meditations*, pp. 96-97.

historical realm, and "history" for him means, *grosso modo*, colonial history. Keyserling, on the other hand, seeks an explanation for various manifestations of South American character traits (unlike Ortega he was not *comprometido* or committed to the analysis and search for solutions of any national malaise) in terms of pre-hispanic, primordial "manifestations" that he experienced in his travels and readings in South America. Like Ortega, he had his detractors, among those who felt alienated by his "primitive" descriptions, like the following:

> In the frenzied reptilian sexuality of the South American also lies *one* of the roots of the deep sadness pervading the continent. *Post coitum animal triste.* The mood of the exhausted male frog or of the female bursting with the abundance of its eggs is dominant there. Just as man feels swallowed up in the primeval forest of the Amazonas, even so does he feel engulfed in the morass of the netherworld within himself . . . [47]

This type of language, bordering at times on the escatological, most probably limited the diffusion of his work in certain circles. Nonetheless, *Meditaciones suramericanas* influenced a great deal of Argentinian intellectuals, Ezequiel Martínez Estrada among them. [48]

---

[47] *Ibid.,* p. 31.

[48] It should be stated here that the whole matter of the influence of Keyserling upon Martínez Estrada is in need of further research. Basically, it is a question of whether there existed between the two a temperamental affinity, the thesis I support, or a direct influence of *South American Meditations* on *Radiografía de la pampa,* the position adopted by Peter G. Earle in his *A Prophet in the Wilderness: The Works of Ezequiel Martínez Estrada,* p. 80. The subject of influences is always a thorny one, but in this case there is evidence which cannot be overlooked. In an interview concerning the genesis of *Radiografía* conducted in 1958, and in reply to the specific question of influences on that work, Martínez Estrada stated that these were, in order, Sarmiento, Groussac, Spengler, Freud and Simmel, but made no mention of Keyserling (*Leer y escribir,* Mexico: Joaquín Mortiz, 1969, pp. 133-136). Moreover, in his essay of two years previously, *¿Qué es esto?* (2nd. ed. Buenos Aires: Lautaro, 1956, p. 265) he stated:

> Una de las impresiones más exactas y vívidas de Keyserling, cuando nos visitara, fue la de que entre nosotros existía un estado de ánimo potencial y difuso que calificó de miedo. Encontró la frase 'no te metás' era expresiva de ese estado de ánimo. Uno de los capítulos de *Meditaciones suramericanas* es 'Miedo'; y sin conocer ese libro, antes que llegara a Buenos Aires, yo titulé con esa palabra una parte de mi *Radiografía de la pampa.*

Clearly Martínez Estrada is struck by the coincidence, which was to appear as the fifth of six chapters in his 1933 work. Even such a clear statement

The discussion of cultural themes and tendencies, within the framework of the formulation of concepts of cultural nationalism and national self-definition, that we have carried to this point, has been, as we shall see, an attempt to situate the early sociological works (dealing with a specific Argentine context) of Martínez Estrada in a historical/cultural dimension to which they clearly conform, on the one hand, and from which they also differ, in radical manner. In this way, the originality of the essayist may be better appreciated.

## Some Argentinian antecedents

Apart from these foreign influences (although Ortega could hardly be termed "foreign") recently commented upon, Martínez Estrada's investigation of Argentine historical/cultural reality drew upon some specifically Argentinian antecedents. Ricardo Rojas (1882-1957) published an essay in 1909 called *La restauración nacionalista,* in which he called for a return to the Indo-Hispanic values and a turning away from the strong policy of immigration so strongly advocated by Sarmiento and Alberdi in the previous century. Basically, he did not favour a rejection of European culture but rather its assimilation — not imposition — into Argentine culture. [49] Rojas too, was to some extent a "telluricist" in that he considered the root of the American character and *argentinidad* in particular (the latter phrase itself being coined in 1916 by Rojas' work of the same name) as a transformation of

---

would not be definitive however (the chapter "Miedo" could have been written out of published order) if it could be established that there was serious re-writing of the manuscript *on that account* before its publication. There is no evidence of this. Additionally, the chronological consideration cannot be conclusive about a possible direct influence. It is known that Martínez Estrada used a 1932 French translation of *Südamerikanische Meditationen* (Earle, p. 237), and the first reviews of *Radiografía de la pampa* in Argentina appeared in August of 1933. It now appears rather improbable that between the actual arrival of the French version in Argentina and the handing into press of *Radiografía de la pampa* there was time for a direct influence upon, and a serious re-writing of, the latter. On the other hand Martínez Estrada knew Keyserling from at least 1931 (See "Hermann y Josefina," *Leer y escribir,* 97-100). Could he have been privy to some edition of Keyserling's work prior to 1932? The above statement from *¿Qué es esto?* discounts this. In short, there is insufficient evidence to support the thesis of a direct influence of Keyserling on Martínez Estrada at this point; on the other hand there is ample to suggest my position of a temperamental coincidence.

[49] Jean Franco, p. 90.

the conquering European by a (mystical) contact with the land. [50] Another essayist of seminal importance in this literature of "search for essence" was Carlos Alberto Erro (b. 1899), particularly in his *Medida del criollismo* of 1929 and *Tiempo lacerado* of 1936. Yet rather than state precisely what the Argentinian *ethos* is, he analyses the historical/moral situation of the country in order to suggest attitudes that national leaders might realize in political action; this of course, entailed the need for analysis and self-knowledge and an affirmation of *argentinidad*. And shortly after this Eduardo Mallea (b. 1903) published his famous dichotomy of the Argentine soul as between "la Argentina visible" and "la Argentina invisible" in *Historia de una pasión argentina* (1937).

### The Bible of Pessimism

*Radiografía de la pampa,* "la biblia del pesimismo" as Zum Felde has called it, [51] was published in 1933 and constituted Martínez Estrada's first major excursion into the genre of the essay. While there are those who see a continuation of earlier themes, particularly those of his poetry, in this first attempt, [52] it was, in very basic fashion, a clear cut, a definite break, in the type of essay that had as its central theme that of the definition of the national "way of being." The particular reasons for its originality we shall deal with elsewhere; an originality that relied as much upon freshness of method as upon the particular temperament of the author.

Yet, there can be little doubt that *Radiografía de la pampa* was also thematically related to an earlier, equally fundamental work — Sarmiento's *Facundo*. The earlier interpretation of Argentinian life presented the now famous division between "civilization" and "barbarism" as characteristic of the country; Martínez Estrada, on the other hand, sharply differs in that he repudiates such a simplistic vision:

---

[50] I have relied heavily for these considerations of Rojas and Erro on Stabb's chapter "Argentina's Quest for Identity" in *In Quest of Identity,* pp. 146-181.

[51] Alberto Zum Felde, *Índice crítico de la literatura hispanoamericana,* Tomo I: *El ensayo y la crítica* (México: Editorial Guarania, 1954), p. 474.

[52] Martin S. Stabb, "Ezequiel Martínez Estrada: the Formative Writings," pp. 54-60. A rather similar thesis is expounded by Eugenio Pucciarelli, in "La imagen de la Argentina en la obra de Martínez Estrada," *Sur,* 295 (July-Aug. 1965).

Lo que Sarmiento no vio es que civilización y barbarie eran una misma cosa, como fuerzas centrífugas y centrípetas de un sistema en equilibrio. No vio que la ciudad era como el campo y que dentro de los cuerpos nuevos reencarnaban las almas de los muertos. [53]

The origins of such barbarity in Argentina are traced by Martínez Estrada, as by Sarmiento, to the Colonial past. Basically he sees Spain as totally unequipped spiritually and culturally to have undertaken the Conquest:

Es que no somos un pueblo nuevo, ni un paisaje nuevo, ni un ensayo último. Eramos antigüedad y fuimos poblados por una nación de tipo antiguo, que era ya arcaica en la Europa de 1500. Espiritualmente heredamos una cultura que permanecía estacionaria, y que carecía de poder íntimo para evolucionar con intrepidez en el movimiento general de la época, hacia formas civiles complejas. Véase lo que significa España en las postrimerías del siglo xv, comparada con los pueblos germanos, galos, itálicos, sajones; era un pueblo esclerosado, pétreo, rupestre. Era un pueblo "americano." [54]

Thus from the beginning, according to this interpretation, the whole enterprise was destined to failure, in the sense of the future development of the colonies. Concomitant with this view of the conquerors in their cultural background, was the impact of their arrival in America. Very soon the disillusionment at not finding an El Dorado in the River Plate region occasioned the development of an all-pervasive spiritual disillusionment that seems to strengthen the author's earlier affirmation that "Cada día de navegación, las caravelas desandaron cien años." [55] The Spaniard, then, physically engendered this cultural poverty and spiritual "malaise" in the sexual association with the Indian woman, causing as a result, the whole shame of the colonial past to be concentrated in the *mestizo*:

... también dejaban [los españoles] una sustancia inmortal y avergonzada, que en cada cópula perpetuaría la humillación de la hembra... Entre el matrimonio y el concubinato abríase un abismo; la ley de Dios no era la ley de América.

---

[53] Ezequiel Martínez Estrada, *Radiografía de la pampa*, 6th ed. (Buenos Aires: Losada, 1968), p. 341.

[54] *Ibid.*, p. 76.

[55] *Ibid.*, p. 75.

> La unión azarosa de los sexos engendra en los espíritus la
> inseguridad y la transmite; el acto realizado de manera in-
> completa produce una de las formas de la angustia neurótica:
> el apuro, el disgusto, el asesinato de la propia vida. [56]

Clearly the author is entering the realm of the genesis of a "national
psychology" built upon a historical neurosis which, by extension,
America was to inherit and develop. From this we can appreciate the
central importance of the now famous concept of the "hijo humillado."
Its importance to the author's central thesis — outlined above — becomes obvious:

> Nunca se comprendería bien la psicología del gaucho, ni el
> alma de las multitudes anárquicas argentinas, si no se piensa
> en la psicología del hijo humillado, en lo que un complejo
> de inferioridad irritado por la ignorancia puede llegar a pro-
> ducir en un medio propicio a la violencia y al capricho. [57]

Not unexpectedly, independence from Spain is interpreted as partial
liberation from a state of ignorance exacerbated by the complex of
humiliation. Partial it has to be, according to the author's reasoning,
because since it is still a key well into the nineteenth century for
understanding Argentine social reality, the act (or "the act and the
thesis" as he puts it) of Independence could not hope to be a complete break from the presence of the Mother Country. Naturally, this
conception of the beginnings of Ibero-America, leads on to even deeper
fatalism. Typical of his method, Martínez Estrada "lifts" the simple
statement of fact to an apocalyptic level:

> Entre el cristiano y el indio no hubo amistad posible; tenían
> diversos intereses, una distinta concepción cósmica de las
> cosas. Sus relaciones eran fingidas y el indio llevaba la peor
> parte.
>
> Mezcla de sangre indígena y europea, el mestizo dio un tipo
> étnico inferior a la madre y al padre. [58]

Slightly later he called this wholesale fornication "la siembra de los
hijos de nadie." [59] Nor could there have been any hope of a tempering

---

[56] *Ibid.*, p. 28.
[57] *Ibid.*, p. 35.
[58] *Ibid.*, pp. 31, 33.
[59] *Ibid.*, p. 34.

force in the shape of the Church; like many other institutions, as the author notes in a later chapter on "seudoestructuras," it was a negative force. Earlier too, the relationship between invasion and conversion was ironically evoked:

> Los misioneros eran un complemento de la invasión armada, no con el propósito de legitimar ante el Papa y el Rey los despojos y la esclavitud, sino con el ánimo de fijar un reinado pacífico y seguro al Dogma. Fue una empresa eclesiástica y no religiosa, la evangelización de la América española. [60]

Gradually, it becomes evident that the enumeration and treatment of themes revolve around a central thesis: the absolute lack of authenticity in Argentine life born of the conviction that this part of America at least (Keyserling would have said "all") never belonged to "history," concurring to a great extent with what Ortega postulated on the same theme. [61] Thus — and this is the fulcrum of his thesis — America (and hence Argentina) owes its present state of inauthenticity to a series of deterministic forces; Martínez Estrada's resulting pessimism and fatalism is therefore well motivated. In other words, he is a determinist to a considerable degree. This, with some interesting variations, is evident in one of the book's major themes: the interaction of man and his environment. Here the affinity with Keyserling is evident:

> En términos generales [América] era un área botánica y geológica, detenida antes de que se abriesen los horizontes de la Edad de Hierro. Lo que ya había desaparecido en otras regiones, lo que en otros parajes se había transformado y puesto al servicio de la inteligencia, aquí conservaba su telúrica virginidad y su carácter mecánico de ensayo siempre repetido.

> Toda América era la tierra del Terciario y formaba una unidad con sus vertebrados inmensos, ambulantes moles de huesos y tejidos. [62]

The Argentine Pampa, in Martínez Estrada's conception of nature, transcends the botanical/geographical dimension it undoubtedly con-

---

[60] *Ibid.*, p. 179.
[61] See above, p. 39.
[62] Ezequiel Martínez Estrada, *Radiografía de la pampa*, pp. 73, 74.

stitutes. More than anything else it is spiritual reality, an all-pervasive force that makes its imprint upon the Argentinian, whether he lives in rural areas or in the "barrios-fronteras" of the "gran Aldea" of Buenos Aires. Naturally, as in the foregoing, the author does not offer empirical data to support this; in these discussions of the importance of nature in the interpretation of the *alma argentina*, he gives a free rein to the intuitive approach:

> El baquiano no necesita haber pasado muchas veces por un mismo lugar; puede no haberlo visto nunca. Pero por cierta experiencia de las hierbas, de los colores de la tierra, de las remotas cumbres; asociando presagios y sugestiones infini-tesimales, liga el pedazo de campo o de selva que tiene ante la vista, a un todo inmenso ... Está dotado de esos órganos sutiles de los insectos y las aves, para registrar en su sistema nervioso vibraciones delicadísimas ... Más bien que en el conocimiento de las cosas externas, hállase en el secreto del *modus operandi* de la naturaleza ... [63]

In his conception of nature, Martínez Estrada displays a strong af-finity to the "telluric" ideas of Keyserling. Governed by a strongly intuitive method, both men conceive of the physical environment as the ultimate reality in America/Argentina. For the Argentinian, the Pampa is an invincible, vital force that leaves its mark upon all life that dwells on it. This force of the Tertiary (Martínez Estrada) of the Third Day of Creation (Keyserling) never allows man to forget that any victories (in the shape of attempts to populate, exploit, the earth) are always partial ones, never final. Martínez Estrada sums it up in his now famous words: "... la tierra es la verdad definitiva, la primera y la última: es la muerte." [64]

Again and again the author turns to pre-history and the Conquest to find the key to the subsequent development of the continent. Quite apart from his judgement that the Spaniards were not spiritually or culturally equipped to bequeath anything of permanent value to the colonies, there is the accompanying belief that something went fun-damentally wrong from their very arrival in America. While the native Indian had arrived at a certain "compromise" in his attitudes towards the land, the conqueror refused to do so, spiritually disillusioned at

---

[63] *Ibid.*, p. 139.
[64] *Ibid.*, p. 16.

his failure to find the fabled riches of the continent in Argentina. This really was the start of the *pecado original* concept that Martínez Estrada alludes to on various occasions, but which was to find probably its most coherent exposition in his disciple, H. A. Murena. [65] Thus,

> ... lo que estaba al alcance de quienquiera, sembrar, construir, resignarse y aguardar, resultaba deprimente y fuera de la tabla de valores de conquista y dominio. Trabajar, ceder un poco a las exigencias de la naturaleza era ser vencido, barbarizarse. Así nació una escala de valores falsos y los hombres y las cosas marcharon por caminos distintos. [66]

Such have been the attitudes examined up to this point, that, characterized by an irremediable pessimism that reflects a strongly deterministic attitude, it is not surprising that the author does not offer a metaphorical "baptism" to the idea of "original sin." In practically the only words of encouragement in the whole work (the last lines of the book) he exhorts:

> ... vuelve a nosotros la realidad profunda. Tenemos que aceptarla con valor, para que deje de perturbarnos; traerla a la conciencia, para que se esfume y podamos vivir unidos en la salud. [67]

## The Eternal Pampa

The fifteen years that separate *Radiografía de la pampa* and *Muerte y transfiguración de Martín Fierro* [68] bear witness to a prolongation of thematic preoccupations of the former, together with a discernible relaxation in the acrimonious tone so typical of that work. Widely appreciated as the most exhaustive treatment of Hernández' famous poem produced to date, *Muerte y transfiguración* ... is even more properly understood if it is approached in the manner of the exemplifying in a fundamental work of Argentine literature of the vision of Argentina presented in *Radiografía de la pampa*. In the hands

---

[65] H. A. Murena, *El pecado original de América,* 2nd ed. (Buenos Aires: Editorial Sudamericana, 1965).

[66] Ezequiel Martínez Estrada, *Radiografía de la pampa,* p. 10.

[67] *Ibid.,* p. 342.

[68] Ezequiel Martínez Estrada, *Muerte y transfiguración de Martín Fierro: Ensayo de interpretación de la vida argentina,* 2 tomos (México: Fondo de Cultura Económica, 1948).

of Martínez Estrada the 1948 work offers a perspective of national history that practically reverses Sarmiento's identification of *ciudad/ campo* with *civilización/barbarie*. This does not come as a surprise, since as we have pointed out, [69] one of Martínez Estrada's basic postulations in *Radiografía de la pampa* was precisely the primacy the land had in any considerations of Argentine reality. Thus in this "radiografía de Martín Fierro" we again encounter the constant of the Conquest as the principal source of Argentina's mal-adjustment:

> En su aspecto literario, quiero decir humano y de conciencia, la Conquista no tuvo aquí, como lo tuvo en México y algo menos en el Perú, el ímpetu religioso que prolongaba, desde Pelayo hasta los Reyes Católicos, la misión de España dentro de la Cristiandad. Como por arte de magia, aquí la empresa quedó reducida a una parodia tragicómica: lanzas en los indios, sables en los cristianos, cabalgaduras en ambos bandos, y nada más, es lo que resta en la memoria de aquellas glorias pasadas. De aquellas bestiales cruzadas nos libramos, pero alguna compensación tiene siempre todo ideal fallido. [70]

The fine irony of the final sentence does not escape the reader, nor does the tone, whose hint of optimism, however slight, indicates a clear change from the uniform pessimism of *Radiografía de la pampa*. In another reference to this same theme in the second volume of *Muerte y transfiguración* ... we again see the absence of a willingness to express the object/phenomenon in apocalyptic terms; this has now given way to matter-of-fact statement:

> *Martín Fierro* ... una protesta ... contra un estado social heredado de la Colonia, que siempre hemos conservado latente y resignadamente como una enfermedad hereditaria. [71]

Interpreting the theme of the poem to be that of injustice, [72] of personal and social injustice as the author does, it is immediately evident that it falls into an evolving pattern that we have seen traced in the previous work. From that work of monumental (and indelible)

---

[69] See above, p. 46.
[70] *Muerte y transfiguración de Martín Fierro*, I, 357.
[71] *Ibid.*, II, p. 137.
[72] *Ibid.*, I, p. 380.

injustice that was the Conquest, as a result of which "los hombres y las cosas marcharon por caminos distintos," [73] the distance, in a spiritual and political sense, between town and country increasingly widened to produce a degree of barbarism in the institution of the social order never existent in the country (*campo*). Hence the interpretation that,

> Para Hernández, las ciudades — y en primer término la ciudad de las ciudades, Buenos Aires — encierran casi todos los males políticos: El sermón de las discordias, el manejo arbitrario de las rentas, los gobiernos unitarios y despóticos, el olvido y desprecio del campesino. [74]

This pessimism, albeit somewhat lightened, as we have noted, is still very much in evidence in the author's treatment of, or rather, evocation of, the Pampa. His "telluricism" or geographical determinism, to which it bears a close relationship, is still the principal method of evocation:

> Hay que tomar en cuenta que el mundo del *Martín Fierro* es ese mundo informe, el del caos primitivo, el de las regiones del planeta aún no civilizadas, el de los climas que rechazan la vida, el de las temperaturas malsanas, el de las zonas epidémicas: el mundo inhabitable. Todos sus representantes están al servicio de potestades incógnitas, como en *La muralla china* de Kafka.... Podéis cambiar uno a uno a todos los habitantes de ese mundo y poner otros: harán lo mismo, y esa es la nota trágica más intensa del Poema, ésa la concepción realmente asombrosa de Hernández cuando ningún autor había penetrado tan hondo en la urdimbre secreta de la sociedad, de la familia, porque pone al descubierto los toscos hilos de su trama. [75]

Here, however, one must underline the two important inferences of Martínez Estrada. According to this interpretation, Hernández not only possessed a natural "telluric" intuition of the Pampa and its reality, but also had the gift of the "primitive vision" conceived by Freud and later interpreted by Jung as the hallmark of the truly creative genius, artistically speaking. Hernández, artistically, is therefore a "primitive" himself in so far as he has intuitively been able

---

[73] *Ibid.*, I, p. 10.
[74] *Ibid.*, I, p. 303.
[75] *Ibid.*, II, p. 380.

to arrive at, in the author's opinion, a successful recreation of the netherworld reality of the real gauchesque:

> Es terrible un mundo así; un mundo siniestro — que Keyserling denominó... el del Tercer Día de la Creación — donde el individuo flota sin arraigo y sin amparo, acometido por los mismos encargos de velar por su estabilidad y seguridad... [76]

> Lo gauchesco es una posición total de la psique: un estilo, un contenido, un uso del lenguaje, una cualidad étnica, un cariz geográfico y temporal, un mundo.

> ...lo gauchesco es lo que Ortega y Gasset vio en la postura defensiva del argentino; lo que Keyserling intuyó como un sedimento geológico de un mundo de vivir y de ser del hombre de épocas muy antiguas. [77]

The ending of *Martín Fierro,* because of a lack of clear-cut, final resolution, has caused some critics to see this as a defect, if not a fundamental one, nonetheless a defect. For Martínez Estrada, on the other hand, it constitutes probably the crowning example of his "telluric determinism." Just as in real life, so in literature reflecting that reality, the *medio ambiente* inexhorably exerts its final victory over man:

> Este Final, abierto como la pampa, desemboca en lo impreciso, que es el elemento de que todo el Poema se nutrió. Nada concreto había en él.... Lo informe, lo enigmático, roía los perfiles, devoraba cuerpos y almas, y ahora termina ingurgitándolo todo. Es simplemente el predominio de lo inmenso y latente sobre lo concreto y efímero; la inmersión del evento en el reino de lo perdurable, sin formas pero, susceptible de adoptar unas o otras formas. El Final configura el "mundo" en que las historias se proyectaron por un azar cuya razón de ser no pertenecía a los personajes. Ese "mundo" no estaba condicionado por las personas y sus hechos, sino por lo que los rodeaba. Eran sombras, eran sueños, y al desvanecerse ellos algo recobra su papel de verdadero Protagonista. Algo que vagamente alcanzaban a intuir y que, por darle un nombre, a veces nombraban "destino." [78]

---

[76] *Ibid.,* II, p. 380.
[77] *Ibid.,* II, p. 465.
[78] *Ibid.,* II, p. 116.

From this one may extract a pattern of what is really an evolving existentialist position. Against such determinism, the concept of the "absurd" of life, of existence itself, is very close to formulation. Martínez Estrada does not in fact formulate it, as such, but there is an obvious "sartrian" impression to the following:

> Así contempla Martín Fierro con estupor que todo se rompe y se disipa como un sueño, y que la ley que gobernaba antes su relación con el mundo, que es la misma, es la que hace de su existencia un conflicto incomprensible. Es el mundo en que vive el que se ha transfigurado, desplazándolo a él como un ente absurdo. [79]

> El transcurrir del Poema es como si se tirara de un hilo que deshace un tejido que ya contiene un cuadro. Los personajes y las cosas que están en él sienten que se desarman, que se desvanecen, que son absorbidos como por una inmensa y lenta serpiente, sin comprender cuál sea la causa ni que todo ocurre así porque están en un tejido que se deshace. Sienten que desde afuera alguien tira del hilo que los constituye y llaman a esa mano destino. [80]

It can also be appreciated that despite a greater general discipline, a more rigorous analysis, Martín Estrada has still relied upon the strongly intuitive method used in such virtuoso fashion in *Radiografía de la pampa*. The real development, however, has been the gaining of a greater precision, a greater coherence of statement, imposed, no doubt, by the more restricted dimensions of the poem itself, as opposed to the free-ranging character of the 1933 work. Moreover, as

---

[79] *Ibid.*, II, p. 502.

[80] *Ibid.*, II, 503. It is also convenient to note at this point that this technique of evocation by Martínez Estrada was not universally accepted. More than one critic considered it to be a distortion of historical fact. In his book, *Civilización y barbarie en la historia de la cultura argentina* (Buenos Aires: Theoría, 1965), Fermín Chávez states that:

> En esas invenciones ha caído M. E. [*sic*] a lo largo de su extensa y malograda *Muerte y transfiguración de Martín Fierro*. Su falta es grande, pero su culpa es menor... Su pecado es la parte que le corresponde del pecado de toda una generación propensa a *mistificar* los temas argentinos. Y mistificar, según la sabia definición de Leonardo Castellani, no es otra cosa que remedar la filosofía, sin poseer el instrumento conceptual del filósofo. Remedar la filosofía mediante un lenguaje críptico y nebuloso que impresiona a los incautos. (pp. 95-96).

has been outlined above, there has also been the formulation, in virtually explicit form, of an existentialist vision of man and his relationship to his environment. A discernible lightening of the stark pessimism of *Radiografía de la pampa* is also evident in *Muerte y transfiguración* ..., although it would be inexact to speak in terms of basic changes.

## The monstrous metropolis

The other fundamental work in the essays belonging to the historico-sociological cycle is *La cabeza de Goliat,* and in fact precedes *Muerte y transfiguración de Martín Fierro* chronologically. [81] As had been treated in *Radiografía de la pampa,* the author's view of Buenos Aires in Argentine history was, broadly speaking, that it was an artificial creation, something *contra natura* and the biggest danger to the existence, as a nation, of Argentina itself. This theme was to be constant throughout his work, and in 1955 we see no relaxation in the *manía.* In a letter of that year to General Don Pedro Eugenio Aramburu, then President of the Republic, Martínez Estrada wrote:

> Para abreviar mi exposición, no es historia lo que quiero exponer ante V. E. ni confirmarle que seguimos siendo un país ciertamente muy culto, a pesar de todo. V. E. conoce la historia patria mejor que yo y, sobre toda otra ventaja, la está haciendo, en tanto yo la veo hacer. Lo que quiero es exponerle de nuevo este viejo problema crucial de la unión del norte y el sur, del abrazo de la hermana rica y la hermana pobre. Pues todos sabemos bien que en 1880 el nudo no se desató sino que se lo cortó, y con la espada para mayor insensatez. Ahora V. E. debe desatar el nudo sin cortarlo.... Esa sería su mayor gloria ...

> La situación debe observarse imparcialmente y hasta donde sea posible desde puntos de vista esencialmente utilitarios. "Si tu ojo es causa de pecado arráncatelo," dijo Jesús. Cuando una ciudad se convierte en boca que succiona la sangre

---

[81] *La cabeza de Goliat: Microscopía de Buenos Aires,* was first published in 1940. Since the material studied in this chapter has as its first principle the attempt at the approximation of the world-view of the author through the tracing of development in his work, the greater thematic similarity between *Radiografía de la pampa* and *Muerte y transfiguración de Martín Fierro* has been judged to outweigh chronological objections that naturally arise in this case.

de toda la nación, no sólo hay que pensar en desmantelarla sino en hacerla volar con dinamita. Tenemos por las razones expuestas, que desmantelar a Buenos Aires, y otro día le diré a V. E. cómo, si me lo permite. Desmantelar quiere significar asimismo que hay que recomponer el gigante decapitado, poniéndole la cabeza en su sitio, para que girándola abarque todo el horizonte, el pasado y el futuro, el norte y el sur. [82]

"El gigante decapitado," then, is the principal focus of *La cabeza de Goliat*. Yet this attitude is really indicative of a strong dislike of cities as such, and an extreme example of the city is Buenos Aires. Implicit too, in the above, is a moral approach which, as we shall see later, is part of the religious/moral vision of the author. Equally implied is the notion that the city is inevitably a corrupting influence upon those who have known rural life. Thus, for Martínez Estrada, Chicago's Al Capone, New York's John Dillinger and Buenos Aires' Scarfó come to be engendered *naturally* by the city. [83] A good example of the author's position is the following:

> Es que la ciudad coloca al individuo en un aislamiento que le corta todo ligamen con la naturaleza o con Dios, quiero decir con el misterio de lo visible y lo invisible. El hombre necesita sentir que el mundo es incomprensible y necesita explicárselo a su modo, para poder vivir y morir satisfecho: como necesita ver para caminar... La ciudad crea la metafísica, que es la angustia del entendimiento, y la angustia que es la metafísica de los que no saben razonar. [84]

Martínez Estrada's conception of "Goliath's head" is almost bucolic in the primitiveness of its vision. The abandonment of rural life (later developed in *Muerte y transfiguración*...) assumes the proportions of a type of "Paradise Lost" in which man has lost the only possibility of self-realization that he had, and the city — clearly Buenos Aires, but logically extendable to any large city — increases the deep sense of alienation from that previous "pastoral" state; hence one can

---

[82] From "Al Sr. Presidente de la República, Gral. Pedro Eugenio Aramburu," in Carlos Adams, *Bibliografía y documentos de Ezequiel Martínez Estrada* (Universidad Nacional de La Plata, Serie "Textos, documentos y bibliografías," III, 1968), pp. 178-179.

[83] Ezequiel Martínez Estrada, *La cabeza de Goliat: Microscopía de Buenos Aires,* 2nd ed. (Buenos Aires: Emecé, 1947), p. 157.

[84] *Ibid.,* p. 207.

appreciate the inversion we have noted in Sarmiento's traditional dichotomy [85] in the hands of our author. The real civilizing force was not the city but the rural areas since it did not possess in anywhere nearly the same measure, the corruption and falseness of urban values.

Yet, curiously enough, Martínez Estrada is not totally opposed to the city of Buenos Aires. One critic goes as far as to see a certain affection towards the city in the tone of certain descriptions of streets and corners. [86] This is evident, too, in a very probable autobiographical note on *carteros* (Martínez Estrada was a postal clerk for many years) where there are descriptions of their situation, accompanied by a very fine sarcasm that borders closely upon that rarest of rarities in Martínez Estrada: humour. [87] Evident, too, is the notion that the city is not entirely responsible for the spiritual destruction that it engenders, that in many ways it is helplessly bound up in its own past. [88]

While *La cabeza de Goliat* does not offer the same ideological span and depth of *Radiografía de la pampa* or *Muerte y transfiguración de Martín Fierro,* it is nonetheless an example of the institutionalization of that great spiritual error, in the past, when irrevocably men and reality went their separate ways.

---

[85] See above, p. 43.
[86] Martin S. Stabb, *In Quest of Identity,* p. 178.
[87] *La cabeza de Goliat,* pp. 164-166.
[88] *Ibid.,* p. 94.

## CHAPTER II

CRITICAL REACTION TO THE HISTORICO-SOCIOLOGICAL
AND POLEMICAL ESSAYS

THE FUNDAMENTAL PESSIMISM of the intuitivist approach, well exemplified in the essays of Martínez Estrada we have considered to
this point, if not peculiar to certain individuals, is at least indicative
of a particular type of temperament, the main tenets of which we
shall consider in another chapter. Such pessimism, and that of *Radiografía de la pampa* above all, is inevitably indicative of a spiritual
isolation so pervasive that occasional attempts at relieving it almost
pass unnoticed. Thus we have noted that the final lines of the above
work constitute an exhortation, an appeal for the facing up to the
essential rootlessness of Argentine life, which in itself is the *sine qua
non* of the search for authenticity. And this, clearly, is a measure
of optimism, albeit slight.

But equally clearly the basic assertions of Martínez Estrada in
these three fundamental essays concerned chiefly with an Argentine
— and by extension — American reality, were in direct opposition
to, say, the idealistic positivism of José Enrique Rodó, who, as we
have noted, envisaged a regenerative, spiritual role for the continent,
based upon its undeniable relationship to the Greco-Roman tradition.
The Argentinian vehemently denies the existence of such a tradition
in America, or rather that even if it were to exist it would have no
relevance to the realities of the continent. Naturally, once one accepts
the concept of geographical determinism, the geological substrata
theory, as to the evolution of an American spirit, then the idea that
neo-Classical values in such a context can at best be considered a
cultural "graft" on to an essentially primitive subsoil, is not at all

unconvincing. Yet one need not be a confirmed Classicist in order to find such an interpretation of America unacceptable, although, as we have suggested, the pessimism of such theories implies, conversely, the rejection, *a priori*, of the postulates of Rodó. This opposition between pessimism/primordialness, and optimism/neo-Classicism, is well represented in the work of a more recent critic, and sums up a whole body of criticism of the "primordial vision." Keyserling, of course, is the frequent target of those who would reject such a vision:

> Con todo, la pregunta por el ser de América siempre irá acompañada de la desazón; aquélla no posee la segura respuesta de historia que tiene la pregunta europea. A la pregunta por el ser de Europa responde, claramente, su cultura. Pero esta poca densidad histórica de nuestra América ha llevado a la conciencia de nuestra pobreza, ha forzado a la actitud subjetivista a responder negando la historia, diciendo que América no es historia; acaso mera primordialidad. Este fue un error en el que incurrió Keyserling al enjuiciar nuestro continente.... Keyserling interpretó a los sudamericanos con categorías naturales, biológicas, exclusivamente; éste fue el error que frustró el núcleo principal de sus *Meditaciones.*... Todas sus intuiciones eran remitidas a grandes estructuras cosmológicas. A Keyserling... se le escapó, justamente el ser humano. Al pensar en América, su mente sólo intuía una simbiosis de plantas, animales y fuerzas ciegas.... Cuando se nos dice que de las ocho obras maestras de barroco en el mundo, cuatro se hallan en estas tierras, se nos ocurre pensar hasta qué extremo la reciente afirmación de América como vida primordial, como el continente sin historia, no es otra cosa que una ligereza conceptual, un desconocimiento del pasado o la expresión de una voluntad de olvido. [1]

The selections made above are indicative to what extent the intuitions of Keyserling had found fertile ground in America. Moreover, a closer examination of the tone of the above, the implied rejection of questions of "el ser de América," the dismissal of Keyserling and those who would continue his basic affirmations [2] as representative of "una

---

[1] Víctor Massuh, *América como inteligencia y pasión* (México: Fondo de Cultura Económica, 1955), pp. 99-103.

[2] It is fairly obvious that the target of Massuh's attacks is not only Keyserling himself, but also people like Martínez Estrada, one of the first to propagate the idea of America's "original sin," but logically too, his disciple

ligereza conceptual" reveal too, a certain uneasiness faced with such meditations, and a clear readiness to deny any validity to them whatsoever. The critic in question, Víctor Massuh, also overlooks the fact, as we have pointed out,[3] that Ortega y Gasset also subscribed to the idea that "América no es historia," preferring to underline its immense "recursos históricos," which is not the same thing. From these negations, Massuh proceeds to a type of moral reassurance (which is probably too, as we have suggested, reflective of a need for a personal reassurance) for the continent:

> Como cualquier otro pueblo de la tierra, los hispanoamericanos podemos crear cultura, afirmar valores. No nos domina ninguna frustración metafísica, ninguna culpa original, ninguna inhibición histórica. Con ser la naturaleza un personaje importante en nuestro drama histórico, ella no cae sobre nosotros como una fatalidad. Nuestra vida histórica no sólo lleva la rúbrica de su acatamiento: abunda en momentos de rebeldía, de plena autoposesión. Y si nos asalta la desazón ante ciertas formas primarias o malignas de nuestra cultura, no hemos de remitirnos a patéticas e improbables raíces ontológicas.[4]

Then Massuh offers a concrete alternative to such pessimistic conceptions of America, personified, as he frequently points out, by men of culture such as Pedro Henríquez Ureña and Alfonso Reyes, two of the best known Classicists among Latin American essayists:

> Aspiramos al cumplimiento de un ideal del hombre que no lo defina como agonía, como tensión de contrarios. La existencia no es un cuarto cerrado y a oscuras donde nuestro ser se despedaza en vano. Necesitamos realizar una imagen que lo defina como integración, como totalidad armónica, sobre todo como el portador de la serenidad y la alegría. Un ideal que proyecte nuevas claridades sobre la frente del atormentado *yo* contemporáneo; esto es, sobre los frutos de los precursores, nuestros padres agonistas, Kierkegaard, Nietzsche y Unamuno.[5]

H. A. Murena who contributed frequently to the periodical *Sur* for some years before the publication of his *Pecado original de América* in 1959. Since Argentina is not the particular focus of Massuh's work, all geographical determinists would feel the point of his criticism.

[3] See above, p. 39.
[4] Massuh, *América como inteligencia y pasión*, p. 107.
[5] *Ibid.*, p. 9.

From this we may conclude that Massuh espouses a position that is practically diametrically opposed to that of Martínez Estrada. From the telluric ramifications of the latter's concept of the primacy of the geological, and its fundamental formatory implications for the emergence of American man, to what is virtually a neo-*arielista* position as expounded by Massuh, the distance is indeed great.

## The Europeans of America

The corollary of this critical posture is that of those who see the origins of the Argentine crisis of identity as in the *absence* of a telluric relationship between man and earth in Argentina, suggesting that it is precisely in the absence of a strongly American tradition that the source of the national character is to be found. José Edmundo Clemente is representative of such views:

> Buenos Aires es platea hacia Europa, pero el interior del país también es Europa. Si no lo es, será barbarie. Depende de la Gran Ciudad. Los argentinos carecemos de tradición indígena ancestral para auscultar en las entrañas de la tierra el futuro latente; futuro que siempre está contenido en el pasado. Por ello nuestro pasado sigue todavía en el porvenir. Somos europeos por sangre, y por idioma. Profundamente. Los vecinos de América pocas veces lo comprenden. Al carecer de una cultura telúrica para sustituir la cultura heredada, nuestro permanente dilema será entonces el gritado por Sarmiento: civilización europea o barbarie. De ahí que el Facundo sea el libro que los argentinos leemos como si nos leyéramos las líneas de la mano. [6]

At the same time it should be noticed that there is no obvious regret at the non-indigenous tradition in Argentina, on the part of Clemente; on the contrary there is a plainly discernible pride at the European tradition there, all of which constitutes a neo-Sarmientian position with its attendant oversimplifications.

A frequent criticism leveled at Martínez Estrada is that his views on Argentina, when they are not rejected for their actual content, reflect only a partial view of reality, and that basic premises apart, at best lead to merely a partially-true vision of matters. A constant

---

[6] José Edmundo Clemente, *El ensayo* (Buenos Aires: Ministerio de Educación y Justicia, 1961), p. 21.

companion of this affirmation is that Martínez Estrada suggests no ways out of the pessimism in which he is so deeply immersed. Thus, Dardo Cúneo states,

> La verdad de la batalla de Martínez Estrada — su verdad —, lo que perdurará de su obra es, precisamente, esa resolución enérgica y audaz de discutir los mitos. La crítica cierta que puede formulársele a Martínez Estrada es que cuando convoca los materiales de la realidad argentina valoriza los inferiores como si en ellos se encontrara radicada toda la realidad.... Martínez Estrada, que despliega gran calidad de negador no asume fuerzas para crear o hallar posibles afirmaciones nuevas. Negando cree haber cumplido. Más allá de la negación para él no hay nada. Ahí, concluye su tránsito. Zona de esperanza, de recobración, no es zona suya. Pareciera que la negación devora al negador. Exactamente: el negador se consume en ella. [7]

Cúneo's affirmations here are additionally interesting in that they also constitute an example of the universal distrust of extreme positions, particularly a deeply pessimistic position. Society does not easily tolerate an unalleviated pessimism, and this, as we shall consider later, is central to the eventual ostracism of Martínez Estrada from Argentine society. At this point, however, it is pertinent to observe that while it is perfectly valid to advance that the personal idiosyncrasies of temperament, be they virtues or aberrations, in no way affect the power, accuracy or ultimate truth of what is affirmed by an individual author; such an attitude naïvely overlooks the peculiar social and historical moment in which Martínez Estrada lived, and above all the unyielding character of the man himself. Again as we shall see later, it is in remembering these realities that one can explain to a considerable extent why the rather oversimplified dichotomy made by his famous contemporary, Eduardo Mallea in *Historia de una pasión argentina* (that of the two Argentinas, the "visible" and the "invisible") has not suffered the same fate as, say, *Radiografía de la pampa,* and the general acceptance of Mallea in literary/social circles, compared with the isolation of Martínez Estrada from the same society.

---

[7] Dardo Cúneo, *Aventura y letra de América* (Buenos Aires: Ediciones Pleamar, 1964), pp. 135-139.

*The pessimistic pontification*

Cúneo, in another work, points to other objections in Martínez Estrada, which were fundamental to the Argentinian literary generation of 1945, and whose position with respect to the previous generation of 1925 we shall discuss elsewhere: the alleged "alienation" of Martínez Estrada from what he was attacking, a sort of detached pontificating that pointed to no solution whatsoever. Cúneo proceeds to draw a parallel with Miguel de Unamuno:

> Unamuno es España porque él riñe desde dentro de ella. M. E. [sic] no consigue ser la Argentina porque no la siente desde su interior: la vigila desde afuera. . . . *Radiografía de la pampa* no deja ver la punta de ningún camino. Es un libro del momento en que la crisis se mira a sí misma hacia dentro y hacia detrás. Con este libro la crisis no revierte sus conflictos hacia afuera y mucho menos hacia delante. . . . Hay, evidentemente, dos maneras de hablar de nuestros defectos e insuficiencias. Una, lo es con ansioso amor, en el que se comprometen todos los votos de la fe y de la acción para rehacer y completar lo que sabemos defectuoso e insuficiente. Así se comportó Unamuno con su España: la riñó con rezongos que tenían voces esperanzadas de plegarias. La otra manera es extender tras la observación un acta de inapelables culpas y sus correspondientes condenas, acumulando todas las posibles minucias que nos digan que nuestras imposibilidades de hoy son definitivas, eternas. En el primer caso la observación termina por ser incitación para empeñar fuerza. En el segundo, un pretexto para dejarse morir. Aunque no se haya propuesto esta consecuencia, el análisis de M. E. [sic] importa una lección despiadada, desertora. [8]

Although it has not been stated explicitly up to this point, it readily becomes obvious that the concept of a national collective identity, "el modo de ser argentino," "el alma argentina" underlies the whole work of Martínez Estrada together with the critics we have discussed up to this point. Yet while the idea is almost universally accepted, of only on the level of a starting-point to discussion, there are some notable exceptions. Of the same generation as Martínez Estrada, Jorge Luis Borges was never quite convinced by Oswald

---

[8] Dardo Cúneo, *El desencuentro argentino* (Buenos Aires: Ediciones Pleamar, 1965), pp. 156-157.

Spengler and other formulators of the idea of the "national soul" such as Keyserling and André Siegfried. With gentle irony he stated:

> Algunos alemanes intensos (entre los que se hubiera desta-
> cado el inglés De Quincy, a ser contemporáneo nuestro) han
> inventado un género literario: la interpretación patética de
> la historia y aún de la geografía.... Lo circunstancial no
> interesa a los nuevos intérpretes de la historia, ni tampoco
> los destinos individuales, lo mutuo. Juego de actos y de pa-
> siones. Su tema no es la sucesión, es la eternidad de cada
> hombre o de cada tipo de hombre... Mucho de la manera
> patética de Spengler... hay en la obra de Martínez Estra-
> da, pero siempre asistido y agraciado de honesta observa-
> ción.... Es autor de espléndidas amarguras. Diré más: de
> la amargura más ardiente y difícil, la que se lleva bien con la
> pasión y hasta con el cariño. [9]

Much later in life it would appear that Borges has come rather closer to the national-collectivity idea, but even here he is far from admitting that there are any immutable characteristics in such a concept, and there can be little doubt that the immutability aspect of the concept is central to its acceptance:

> La asidua reverencia que nuestras escuelas dedican a la his-
> toria argentina ha servido para borrarla o, mejor dicho, para
> simplificarla y endurecerla curiosamente... Nuestra historia
> es un frígido museo. No la sentimos o la sentimos de ma-
> nera elegíaca. Una de las razones es el hecho de que ahora
> somos otros. Aquel tiempo arriesgado y azaroso ya no es el
> nuestro; algo, silenciosamente, se ha roto. [10]

## Marxist objections

Adopting an even more sceptical attitude in a recent study on Argentine intellectuals and their attitudes towards society, Adelmo Montenegro views the willingness of certain writers to have recourse to philosophical and metaphysical explanation to the whole question of the *ser nacional* as not only a basically conservative tendency but

---

[9] Jorge Luis Borges, "*Radiografía de la Pampa,* por Ezequiel Martínez Estrada," *Crítica* (Buenos Aires), I, 6 (Sept. 1933), 5.

[10] Jorge Luis Borges, "Nota sobre los argentinos" in *Argentina: análisis y autoanálisis,* ed. H. Ernest Lewald (Buenos Aires: Editorial Sudamericana, 1969), p. 78.

evidence too of an ignorance of very feasible sociological/economic explanations of the phenomenon:

> Los argentinos, y en general los americanos, hemos hecho de la nacionalidad un presupuesto teórico y práctico, una categoría del pensar y del actuar, y nunca, salvo las excepciones que no conozco, hemos pasado más allá de la línea de un escepticismo metódico, fruto, probablemente, del desencanto que se apodera de nosotros, al comprobar las periódicas frustraciones en los niveles políticos y económicos de la vida nacional.... Los caracteres nacionales, son pues, un mito detrás del cual se disimula un pensamiento conservador que se niega a aceptar la categoría del cambio, como la revelación sociológica o histórica de la verdadera naturaleza de los pueblos. [11]

Certainly, as Montenegro affirms, to subscribe to the idea of a national *ethos* as something finished and immutable (as does Martínez Estrada) would clearly appear a basically conservative way of conceiving national history. [12] Yet, equally, such a view may be representive of a fatalistic view of history, a philosophy of history as a constant repetition and not as a straight continuum. And such fatalism can be consonant with many radical attitudes. This distinction, as we shall consider later, is central in the philosophical stance of Martínez Estrada.

It will become increasingly apparent that Montenegro's posture is not very distant from what may be called a classical Marxist position.

---

[11] Adelmo Montenegro, "Las ideas acerca del hombre argentino," in *Los intelectuales argentinos y su sociedad,* ed. Norberto Rodríguez Bustamante (Buenos Aires: Ediciones Libera, 1967), pp. 114-115.

[12] Conservatism with regard to attitudes towards alleged cultural constants can also be seen in a view of André Siegfried, one of the earlier formulators of the concept of the national *ethos.* He, with many others saw the advent of the technological age as ultimately constituting a threat to civilization:

> Today all continents, all countries and all peoples clamour after the machine. But it is one thing to use a machine once it is made and quite another thing to invent it or replace it, and it is this circumstance that forms the basis, still solid despite everything, on which Western superiority rests... It is at this point that we can see the possibility of a crisis on the horizon of our civilization; its technique derives essentially from its culture, and in denying its culture, or leaning too far towards the technical side, it would risk compromising the very sources of its vitality. (*Nations Have Souls,* trans. Edward Fitzgerald [New York: Putnam, 1952], p. 192.)

The orthodox Marxist would also reject such a view of history as inherently conservative and diametrically opposed to the dialectic of history conceived as the continuous revelation of man as determined by material/economic factors leading towards the eventual classless society. In similar terms, too, the Marxist view of crisis in society is presented in terms of class/economic conflict. Dismissing Spengler and Keyserling as "herederos ... del romanticismo espiritualista," [13] Juan Carlos Portantiero goes on to criticize the excesses of the Argentinian intuitivists:

> El pensamiento de los intuicionistas — Martínez Estrada, Mallea, Scalabrini Ortiz, — era una desesperada tentativa de reencontrar vínculos entre los intelectuales y el pueblo-nación. Es claro que esa intención se abarata en el mundo de las mistificaciones que envolvía los puntos de partida del razonamiento, pero de todas formas significaba la aceptación fundamental de que una crisis muy honda conmovía al país ... Esa desesperación significaba una primera toma de conciencia con la desagradable realidad, una nota de discordancia con el coro del optimismo liberal. Es claro que tenía sus vicios ... pero era un punto de partida ... contra la torre de marfil. [14]

The important point here is that for Martínez Estrada (and Scalabrini Ortiz in *El hombre que está solo y espera,* of 1931, and Mallea in *Historia de una pasión argentina* of 1937) the "mistificaciones" were fundamental, as it is practically certain that Portantiero here is alluding to concepts such as "sentimiento de culpa" and "fatalismo telúrico" of Martínez Estrada, the almost mystical amalgam of criollo and immigrant of Scalabrini Ortiz, and the aristocratic stoical qualities of the old criollo as seen in Mallea's work, the dichotomy of "Argentina visible" and "Argentina invisible" itself containing the impression of mystification. Again as we shall consider later, the concepts formulated by Martínez Estrada, were none the less valid or true for proceeding from an intuitivist premise, as Portantiero himself concedes in the last two lines of the above quoted statement.

---

[13] Juan Carlos Portantiero, *Realismo y realidad en la narrativa argentina* (Buenos Aires: Ediciones Procyón, 1961), p. 74.
[14] *Ibid.,* pp. 76, 85.

*Sebreli's anathemas*

Another Marxist, Juan José Sebreli, has provided the single most comprehensive criticism of Martínez Estrada's work, in terms revealed by the title of his study: *Martínez Estrada: una rebelión inútil,* published in 1960. [15] It should be stressed, however, that neither Portantiero nor Sebreli, both Marxists, are concerned with the systematic application of a Marxist aesthetic to the work of Martínez Estrada; the latter's contributions to the world of art and culture is of little concern to Sebreli. Both he and Portantiero are interested in measuring the effect of Martínez Estrada's work on the Argentinian socioeconomic reality at a given historical moment. And it is here that there is an attempt at the application of the Marxist concept of history to the Argentine *milieu.*

Sebreli, predictably, has little patience with the historical fatalism of Martínez Estrada, since, in his view, it has helped to obscure the real reasons, social and economic, of the Argentine spiritual crisis:

> Si la Naturaleza es un ciclo cerrado y sin porvenir, la historia humana, en cambio, es una serie conexa de desarrollos, de desenvolvimientos, de procesos que se encuentran interconectados y que actúan recíprocamente unos sobre otros. El hombre histórico es creador, niega el pasado a la vez que lo conserva y se proyecta hacia el porvenir: no siempre ha sido lo que es y no será nunca más lo que ha sido. En el tiempo histórico, el hombre no vuelve nunca al punto de partida y sólo se encuentra con su pasado en un nivel superior. El movimiento es ilusorio, sostiene Martínez Estrada, cuando lo ilusorio es en verdad, la inmovilidad, la rigidez.... Martínez Estrada ... negó al progreso, pero la objetividad del progreso es cruel y a su vez lo niega a Martínez Estrada. [16]

Equally predictable is Sebreli's rejection of "fatalismo telúrico," not as a concept, but rather the importance given to it by Martínez Estrada:

> La influencia de la tierra sobre el hombre, sólo existe en la medida en que el hombre influye a su vez sobre la tierra. El

---

[15] Juan José Sebreli, *Martínez Estrada: una rebelión inútil* (Buenos Aires: Editorial Palestra, 1960).

[16] *Ibid.,* pp. 46-47.

hombre puede ejercer sobre el paisaje, que lo condiciona
pero no lo determina, una influencia decisiva y aun modifi-
carlo substancialmente.... El paisaje puede guiarnos hacia
un determinado estilo de vida pero no arrastrarnos inexora-
blemente.... Ninguna realidad histórica admite ser reducida
a una realidad exclusivamente geográfica o biológica, aunque
toda ella esté impregnada de significaciones geográficas o bio-
lógicas. [17]

rejecting, in turn, any metaphysical basis for the country's ills:

El terrible problema de la tierra americana, presentado por
Martínez Estrada en términos teológicos de pecado, culpa y
fatalidad, no es sino un problema de orden principalmente
económico y social. La enfermedad de nuestra pampa que
su radiólogo no ha sabido mostrar es el latifundismo y el
monocultivo. [18]

The corner-stone of Sebreli's however, that of the "uselessness" of
Martínez Estrada's "rebellion," is that, in Martínez Estrada's own
terms of "fatalismo," "inexorabilidad," "pecado original," his impact
upon Argentine society cannot but be destined to failure. Thus, if,
according to Martínez Estrada, Argentine man, or American man, is
imprisoned within a pre-ordained set of cultural, social and "telluric"
circumstances that effectively govern his cultural and spiritual growth,
then, as Sebreli logically concludes, he cannot be held responsible for
the subsequent aberrations that arise from these circumstances. Thus,
he states, Martínez Estrada, inadvertently or not, has played into
the hands of those sectors of society that he would most attack:

Si la oligarquía lo aplaude y lo corona con "laureles de oro",
es porque *Radiografía de la pampa* le está dando las más
elevadas excusas para tranquilizar su conciencia. En efecto,
¿cómo sentirse responsable de un mundo donde reina la
fatalidad? ¿Cómo reprocharse por el atraso en que se encuentra el país cuando ese atraso es insuperable?... Con
Martínez Estrada, todas las injusticias, todos los atropellos
entran en el orden natural. Las estructuras económicas, políticas, y sociales retrógradas de nuestro país no son la consecuencia de una clase social retrógrada, están determinadas
por la fatalidad étnica y geográfica. [19]

---

[17] *Ibid.*, pp. 32-33.
[18] *Ibid.*, p. 32.
[19] *Ibid.*, pp. 30-31.

This in fact constitutes the nucleus of Sebreli's case against Martínez Estrada. Yet he also touches upon a theme in the work of Martínez Estrada that few critics have treated: the existence of a type of death-wish implicit in many of his works:

> Las acusaciones de Martínez Estrada a la obra de Sarmiento, pueden ser verdaderas, pero son abstractas, no parten de ninguna situación histórica concreta. Es la suya, la perspectiva del intelectual aislado, "au dessus de la mêle [*sic*]".... Para Martínez Estrada la eficacia política debe identificarse, en todo momento, con la verdad y la moralidad, y cuando esto no ocurre prefiere convencerse de que, al fin, en condiciones objetivas desfavorables, el sacrificio y la renuncia pueden ser la mejor manera de servir a la humanidad, o sea un afrontamiento con la muerte ... [20]

Sebreli thus strongly suggests that Martínez Estrada was totally ill-equipped for the work of renewal needed in Argentine society — as interpreted by Sebreli. Ill-equipped temperamentally, most of all. Finally, Sebreli is in agreement with the view of Dardo Cúneo that there is an unmistakable sense of detachment in Martínez Estrada's attitudes, admitting, at the same time, that it was governed by an attempt to reach the greatest amount of objectivity in his search for truth. [21] Also Sebreli sees certain traits in Martínez Estrada's works that bear witness to virtually masochistic sentiments in the face of the problem of the attaining of the ideal: ·

> Como el neurótico se aferra a su enfermedad, Martínez Estrada se aferra a su escepticismo y no quiere la construcción de un mundo mejor ya que tendría que aceptarlo y resignarse a ser como todos.... Martínez Estrada no quiere ser vencedor, sino conservarse en su calidad de luchador pues no cree tener más valor que por esa lucha.... La rebelión contra el estado de cosas intolerables es necesaria para todo hombre auténtico — nos dice Martínez Estrada — pero a la vez imposible, porque nada se puede cambiar: estamos condenados pues a una tarea absolutamente gratuita y vana: la rebelión inútil. [22]

---

[20] *Ibid.*, p. 87.
[21] *Ibid.*, p. 87.
[22] *Ibid.*, p. 92.

The Marxist critic here is clearly accusing Martínez Estrada of bad faith, particularly in the first few lines, where we also find inferred that the particular psychic make-up of the author is really in the proportions of a medical condition, over which he has no control. Implicit, too, is the suggestion that Martínez Estrada is suffering from certain illusions of grandeur, an implied reluctance to "ser como todos." Quite apart from any other objections against Sebreli's views, however, one may justifiably accuse him of having strayed from his Marxist method in order to indulge in an attempt at the description of the gradual development of a neurosis in Martínez Estrada.

Yet it is also pertinent to note that Sebreli is not only concerned with a refutation of Martínez Estrada's contributions to Argentine literature, but fundamentally with the work of Martínez Estrada as representative of a whole type of literature that — in Sebreli's terms — has successfully lulled the Argentine intellectual community into a preoccupation with a reality of highly dubious rational foundation, and away from what the critic affirms should be the real concern of that community: that Argentina's problems are essentially economic and political in nature, and effectively dominated by a landed oligarchy absolutely dedicated to the conservation of its power. [23] Thus Sebreli accuses,

> El fatalismo telúrico de Martínez Estrada y de sus derivados — el "pecado original de América" de Murena, el "demonio americano" de Solero, el "demonismo vegetal" de Kusch, el "desarraigo argentino" de Mafud, la "personalidad argentina" de Canto — son, a pesar de la variedad de ideo-

---

[23] It would constitute a substantial exaggeration, however, to restrict the "economic" arguments against Martínez Estrada's view of Argentine reality to a uniquely Marxist framework. The nationalist Left in Argentina often viewed his work with misgivings rather similar to those of Sebreli, but without the dialectic overtones. For a coherent example of such criticism, see Arturo Jauretche, *Los profetas del odio* (Buenos Aires: Ediciones Trafac, 1957), especially p. 39. Moreover, a much earlier objection to the fatalism of *Radiografía de la pampa* on economic/political grounds is that of Bernardo Canal Feijóo, a non-Marxist and generally unaligned politically:

> El 80 % de nuestros errores actuales son el fruto mecánico de la etapa histórica universal en que le tocó entrar a la existencia internacional a nuestro país... [*Radiografía de la pampa*] toma por signos constitucionales, de una especie de fatum orgánico, lo que sólo son, sin lugar a dudas, meros errores de política social y económica. ("Radiografías fatídicas," *Sur*, VII, 37 [Oct., 1937]).

logías que van de la extrema derecha a la seudo izquierda, la expresión inconsciente del pesimismo irracionalista de una clase que se niega a reconocer las causas concretas de su decadencia y prefiere pensar que es el mundo entero, o por lo menos el país entero el que cae.... El mito de la Pampa irá perdiendo vigencia, otros mitos, otros ritos, otras tareas, otras esperanzas, ocuparán su lugar en la literatura argentina.[24]

Sebreli's critical method, then, has been to situate a very personal attack on Martínez Estrada — the particular, temperamental aberrations of the man — in the wider context of its representativeness of the historical/intuitivist genre as cultivated in Argentina.

Posterity no doubt will show that the most durable dimension of Sebreli's objections will prove to be his attempt at an explanation of Martínez Estrada's peculiarities of thought through an analysis of his temperamental peculiarities. In effect, a very fundamental element visible in practically the whole of Martínez Estrada's work — and understandably accentuated in the later period of his life — is the unshakable conviction that he was essentially alone in the world, and destined to fulfill, no matter the personal sacrifices involved, a personal and social mission with regard to Argentina. Thus Martínez Estrada himself rejected the role that Sebreli has assigned him: that of the originator of a certain "school" of thought in Argentina. The essayist felt a sense of solidarity with a very limited group of people and would almost certainly have espoused Rubén Darío's celebrated remark, "No imitar a nadie, y sobre todo a mí." We might add at this stage that such sentiments should not be confused with an "ivory tower" attitude on the part of the essayist. We shall soon discuss what may be termed "withdrawal symptoms" of the later stages of Martínez Estrada's production, but it is an exaggeration to talk, as Sebreli has done, of the essayist being "above the strife."[25]

*Some kindred spirits*

Before proceeding to a consideration of some of the salient features of Martínez Estrada's personality, as manifestated in his works, it is relevant to note that the body of foreign influences we have noted in the previous chapter were obviously not restricted to Martínez

---

[24] *Ibid.*, pp. 34-35.
[25] See above, p. 74.

Estrada. The essayist in question fed upon a variety of influences impinging upon the Argentine literary generation of 1925 and affecting a whole cultural atmosphere. Without compromising the originality and uniqueness of individual authors, therefore, we can find contemporaries of Martínez Estrada, who, ideologically and stylistically, can be said to be "kindred spirits" of the essayist. To the list of cultivators of pessimistic intuitivism adduced by Sebreli, [26] we may add that of Scalabrini Ortiz, whose reflections on the country bear a remarkable resemblance to those of Martínez Estrada. Compare, for example, the following:

> La pampa abate al hombre. La pampa no promete nada a la fantasía; no entrega nada a la imaginación. El espíritu patina sobre su lisura y vuela. Arriba está la fatídica idea del tiempo... En cada rancho había un botellón de vino, un hombre melodioso y un acordeón. Pero, poco a poco, la tierra se fue recobrando: aplacó los bullicios extemporáneos. Volvió a imponer su despotismo de silencio y de quietud, volvió a quedar en suspenso y como en éxtasis. Manejando la tierra, el hombre fue allanado por la tierra. [27]

Similarly, just as Sebreli pointed to the recurring theme of the "eternal return" in Martínez Estrada, so too does Scalabrini Ortiz bear witness to the irresistable determinism of Nature:

> Al conjuro irrestible de esa metafísica de la tierra, la continuidad de la sangre se quebrantó. El hijo del colono ya solfea una burla cuando rememora los que fueron acucios del padre. Tras el gran sacudón inmigratorio que descompaginó su tono, la pampa se reafirma y los hombres recomponen su espíritu de siempre... El presente invisible les insufló a todos la idea del tiempo y de su fugacidad. En silencio, el hombre sorbe sus mates y mira cómo se van los días. [28]

Carlos Mastronardi provides another example of a basic sympathy towards the attitudes of Martínez Estrada, although the tone and style of his expression are quite different:

---

[26] See above, p. 75.

[27] Raúl Scalabrini Ortiz, "La tierra invisible," in H. Ernest Lewald, *Argentina: análisis y autoanálisis*, pp. 91-92.

[28] *Ibid.*, pp. 92-93.

> La tesis del desarraigo, que postula cierta inadecuación entre el hombre y su medio, posee sólida base. Su fundamento es el carácter desasido de aquellos habitantes que hacen de la tierra un mero lugar de explotación, no de inserción profunda. La naturaleza deviene un vasto instrumento manejado con desamor ... [29]

In this context, then, we may view the work of Martínez Estrada, — or rather his essays in particular — as a central contribution to the literature of the search for essence, as a fundamental component of an approach to analyse national reality in an historical/intuitivist way. Scalabrini Ortiz, Mastronardi and others [30] contributed to this literature, and a better understanding of Sebreli's criticism can be had by seeing, as we have pointed out, Martínez Estrada's work not only as representative of a highly gifted individual, but also as representative of a spiritual climate.

## The high priest of national renewal

The following quotation from his biography *Sarmiento,* probably more than anything else he wrote, successfully constitutes a broad summing-up of the rather complex personality of Martínez Estrada:

> Las imprecaciones de Sarmiento tienen siempre un acento religioso, porque surgen de sus entrañas encendidas en el horror de un espectáculo que lo ofende y le muestra la intensidad de los vicios y ceguera de sus contemporáneos. Su campaña no era religiosa, pero en definitiva respondía a las mismas determinantes morales que levantaron el furor de Tomás Moro, de Savonarola o de Robespierre. [31]

---

[29] Carlos Mastronardi, *Formas de la realidad nacional* (Buenos Aires: Ediciones Culturales Argentinas, 1961), p. 133.

[30] Apart from the feasibility of attempting to list all those writers who admit to having been influenced by the work of Martínez Estrada — and those who do not —, such concerns are without the confines of this study. However, in order to accentuate one of the principal targets of Sebreli's criticism — the whole *genre* of *fatalismo telúrico, intuitivismo pesimista,* etc. — I have chosen Scalabrini Ortiz and Mastronardi since they are of the same generation as Martínez Estrada, or very close to it. (We have already referred to similarities in Eduardo Mallea in this regard). In a more detailed examination of this theme, one would have to take into account, among others, Carlos Astrada, Murena, Kusch, Mafud, Canal Feijóo, etc.

[31] Ezequiel Martínez Estrada, *Sarmiento* (Buenos Aires: Deucalión, 1956), p. 204.

If we substitute his name for that of his avowed *maestro*, [32] we can appreciate that it becomes a remarkable self-comment. In effect, there is an unmistakable moralistic tone running throughout the work of Martínez Estrada, bathed, very often, in religious language. In an interview published in *Cuadrante del pampero* (1956), for example the essayist stated how he conceived of his duty in society:

> Creo que tengo el deber de contribuir con mi aporte, valga mucho o poco, a la tarea común de reconstruirnos o, como decía Echeverría, de regenerarnos, o como ya podemos decir, de purificarnos. [33]

Again and again we encounter the words "purificar," "moral" or "purificación," all of which inevitably cast the essayist in a role similar to that of an "exterminating angel." Moreover, many of his essays and articles bore religious names; "Nueva epístola a los romanos," [34] *Exhortaciones*, [35] "Segunda epístola a los romanos," [36] etc. This of course, was entirely in keeping with the type of ills that he diagnosed for his country:

> Resumiendo mis ideas, que son muy complicadas, y ya conocidas a este respecto, le diré que pienso que la causa de nuestros males es orgánica, constitucional. . . . No pueden suprimirse esos viejos y recientes males orgánicos por retoques parciales, o calafateo, de las partes periféricas que se descomponen y deterioran por la acción mecánica del transcurso del tiempo histórico. Hay que reestructurar y no enmendar, rehacer y recrear, purificar y regenerar más que reconstruir política o económicamente, lo cual se refiere a las glándulas y no a la piel. [37]

Here we have, then, not a sociologist, not a political economist, but rather a self-appointed diagnostician, convinced that the country's ills, social ills, were not to be solved by "conventional" means; these

[32] Ezequiel Martínez Estrada, *Meditaciones sarmientinas*. Compiladas por Enrique Espinoza (Santiago de Chile: Editorial Universitaria, 1968), p. 106.

[33] Ezequiel Martínez Estrada, *Cuadrante del pampero* (Buenos Aires: Deucalión, 1956), p. 162.

[34] *Ibid.*, pp. 143-147.

[35] Ezequiel Martínez Estrada, *Exhortaciones* (Buenos Aires: Burnichón Editor, 1957).

[36] *Ibid.*, pp. 84-87.

[37] Ezequiel Martínez Estrada, *Cuadrante del pampero*, pp. 119-120.

would only affect the superficial features of society. Defending his use of religious vocabulary, Martínez Estrada states:

> No os extrañéis de este lenguaje insólito en mí. No tiene nada de misticismo, ni de teosofía: es que simplemente, necesito emplear metáforas y un lenguaje figurado en cuanto me es posible para expresarme con más veracidad, exactitud y sencillez. [38]

And again, in an open letter to Argentina's judges, he explains:

> ...empleo la palabra purificación, tomada del vocabulario místico, pero con un sentido positivo, con preferencia a la palabra organización o regeneración, que se relaciona más bien con una perturbación mecánica... [39]

In broad terms we may safely affirm that Martínez Estrada was concerned fundamentally with what can be called the larger questions of life and existence as they impinged upon his conception of Argentinian reality. Rarely do his essays reflect an effort to come to grips with *purely* pragmatic goals, and inevitably, the presence of such concerns in his work are invariably linked to a more profound concept in the background. [40] Almost in anticipation, then, of Sebreli's objection that he created a type of ideological "smoke screen" with his preoccupations of "telluric fatalism" and other concepts, which effectively obscured the real obstacles to Argentine progress — all of a political/economic/oligarchic nature —, Martínez Estrada rejects *a priori* what the Marxist critic would have him do. Referring to the vital interests he shared with "brother Quiroga," he states,

> Interesábannos a ambos los problemas sociales sin política, sin sociología y sin economía política. Nos interesaba el ser

---

[38] *Ibid.*, p. 83.

[39] *Exhortaciones*, p. 12.

[40] We have noted in a previous chapter how the essayist wrote to the President of the Republic, General Pedro Eugenio Aramburu, on the specific problem of "saving Buenos Aires from itself," but even here his attitude is explained by his concept of the city, the giant metropolis, as discussed at length in *La cabeza de Goliath*. Nonetheless, we shall consider later how, towards the end of his life, and particularly in his voluminous *Diferencias y semejanzas entre los países de la América Latina* of 1962, he was quite capable of organizing and analysing a myriad of data and statistics.

humano y su destino, libre de sus expoliadores, y de los expoliadores de los expoliadores. Los dos teníamos un concepto
libertario de la libertad del hombre, y tanto él como yo lo
hemos expuesto en nuestras obras . . . Abominábamos de los
agitadores y demagogos de la acción y del pensamiento, quienes, al decir de Péguy, convierten la mística en política. [41]

We may observe here that there is clearly no attempt at self-apology,
no attempt to justify this position, but merely a statement of a
sipiritual/social posture that would appear to spring from a *temperamental* reality, as opposed to an ideological expedient. Martínez
Estrada, in all honesty, therefore, could have answered Sebreli's criticism by saying that his reluctance to see in economics the source of
national problems, may ultimately be questionable, but that it was
certainly not a case of *peccatum omissionis*. [42]

## El dolor de todos

While we have pointed to the recurring use of religious language
in Martínez Estrada, one searches in vain for an unequivocal statement
of theological/doctrinal positions that such language would ordinarily
warrant. Nonetheless, the absence of a concrete profession of religious
faith, did not preclude a religious experience, and the essayist at
various points in his life expressed a development in his attitude
towards belief in a God, not as a theological abstraction, but rather
in terms of personal meditation, and motivation. Running parallel to
this reality of a personal religiosity, is the role that he took upon
himself to carry out: that of constituting, by himself, the spiritual
conscience of Argentina and of America. In this context, optimism

---

[41] *El hermano Quiroga,* pp. 80-81.

[42] As far as can be established, Martínez Estrada never saw fit to make
a public reply to Sebreli's criticism, nor is there any evidence, through correspondence or innuendoes, that he took note of, or was disturbed by the
critic's views. Generally, personal attacks or replies in reaction to critics was
not characteristic of the essayist. Rather one encounters cases of generic
attacks, on groups of people or ideas. His *Exhortaciones* is a good example
of this, in which several groups are singled out for what the author considered
monumental shortcomings. There were exceptions, as our later discussion of
his uneven relationship with Borges will illustrate. In his private dealings,
however, and due frequently to his difficult personality, there are multiple
examples of tensions, irascibility and broken friendships.

or rather an attempt at optimism, may require a great deal of personal courage:

> No creáis que este dolor de todos que yo siento me arrastre a la desesperación, aunque me invade una congoja semejante a la muerte. He visto países y gentes, he aprendido mi lección estoica en la vida de nuestros próceres; algo sé de la historia de mi pueblo y tengo fe en el hombre y en la civilización. Desde hace algún tiempo, y por no sé qué necesidad de compensaciones, os confieso que he vuelto en cierto modo a recuperar mi fe en el dios que es Dios. [43]

This "dolor de todos" was to remain with him all of his life, and there is little doubt that the material and psychological consequences of such a vision of himself, caused him great personal suffering. This may be exemplified by the self-imposed exile he undertook in Mexico in 1960. At the annual dinner offered by the magazine *Cuadernos americanos*, he gave an impromtu speech and attempted to justify his departure from Argentina:

> Pues ocurrió primero que por haber revelado la índole hereditaria y crónica de los males que a mi juicio aquejan a mi país y denunciando luego a quienes creí que debiéramos culpar de ellos, vine a encontrarme como extranjero en mi patria, perdidos algunos amigos ilustres y ganados, otros apenas alfabetos; cerradas las puertas de diarios y revistas y señalado por índice de los amos de la patria. Arrojado, digo, a las ergástulas del pueblo ... [44]

Certainly, as we have pointed out, there were those who, so to speak, were on a different ideological wavelength from Martínez Estrada from *Radiografía de la pampa* onwards, and as if there were any doubt as to the motive and target of his social protest, the essayist became quite explicit in later works. In *Exhortaciones* (1957) for example, there is a Quevedo-like parade of *vendepatrias* that includes teachers, judges, soldiers, clerics and others, and most of whom are the target of a highly rhetorical vituperation. Again and again he felt constrained to repeat to all, his motives, his interpretations,

---

[43] *Cuadrante del pampero*, pp. 79-80.
[44] Ezequiel Martínez Estrada, "Los escritores frente a una actitud," *Atlántida*, Buenos Aires, LIII, 1123 (September, 1960), p. 22. The *Cuadernos Americanos* speech was reproduced here.

and his priorities. The essential message of *Radiografía de la pampa* suffered little change down the years, little development, and hence we find him saying in *Exhortaciones* (1957) what he had always been advancing:

> ¿Tendré que pasarme el resto de mis días repitiéndome como un disco rayado? No tenemos arraigo en la tierra (ni en el cielo); no sentimos amor, simpatía o afecto por el prójimo desconocido; no sabemos admirar, respetar ni estimular; no sabemos darnos, entregarnos, dejarnos llevar... no sentimos que somos un pueblo, una misión, una tarea, un deber, un destino. Somos cualquier cosa mostrenca...[45]

There is abundant evidence to point to a gradual hardening in Martínez Estrada's ideological position over the years, which, as we have noted, did not constitute to any appreciable degree a true development, in spite of the occasional optimistic note that we have also observed. It was a hardening in the meaning of a deepening sense of anguish and *desengaño*, of feeling himself destined to be the perpetual *malentendido*, and destined, too, to forever carry that "dolor de todos" in the face of hostility, when not a discouraging apathy. This, as we shall consider in more detail elsewhere, gradually engendered a pariah complex; in the lives of saints it is often referred to as a martyr complex; the difference is negligible.

Yet, paradoxically, this feeling of isolation was in great measure attributable to what one critic has very pertinently alluded to as the "ateísmo civil" of Martínez Estrada.[46] The words are well chosen; "civil" to the extent that he had no particular, obsessive vendetta against religion or Church, as such, but rather to the extent to which the Church had engaged in politics and had lost sight of its social mission (clearly evidenced by "Sermón en el desierto" in *Exhortaciones,* and an increasing mania, as we shall see later, against the Jesuit Order); and "ateísmo" in the sense that the points of his attacks ultimately constitute a *raison d'être* as they enter into the whole complex need of the essayist to denounce. In a somewhat sympathetic article that nonetheless cedes nothing to objectivity, the critic in question, César Fernández Moreno, perceptively points to the cultural

---

[45] *Exhortaciones,* p. 28.
[46] César Fernández Moreno, "Martínez Estrada frente a la Argentina," *Mundo Nuevo,* Paris, I (July, 1966), 41.

parallel to Sebreli's objection to Martínez Estrada's studious neglect of economic factors: [47] "...en su afán ejemplarizador, Martínez Estrada critica lo universal en lo argentino, es decir, ataca como defectos locales los que son defectos generales del hombre." [48]

"Ateísmo civil" also is a successful term in that it points to the belligerent, combative spirit in Martínez Estrada that was to leave him with very few friends. Consequently we find the essayist unaligned ideologically, and least of all, politically:

> ...Tengo sesenta años y estoy doncella, sin que siquiera haya pensado ninguna concupiscencia de poder, haber o saber. Aun siendo muy pobre y habiendo tenido que trabajar mucho, mucho, mucho para vivir, no he claudicado jamás con los radicales, ni con los conservadores, ni con los nacionalistas, ni con los comunistas (que todos me han cortejado). Preferí la persecución y la pobreza... ¿Qué tengo que ver con las putas, los sodomitas, los espías, los gangsters y los fascistas, para eliminar de mi ataque al peronismo a los gestores anónimos del peronismo? No soy nazi, no soy antisemita, no soy nacionalista, ni soy siquiera antropófago. ¿Por qué no he de tener amigos con quienes dialogar? Sí, lo mejor será que me calle otros cuantos años y que no estorbe a los denodados arquitectos de la Nueva Argentina. [49]

We observe, therefore, a gradual, yet continual self-isolation and almost pathological conviction of the essayist that he was destined to suffer for the path that he had chosen. And while the last two lines are not literally true (his most polemical essays, *¿Qué es esto?*, *Las 40* and *Exhortaciones* were written after the above statements taken from *Cuadrante del pampero* of 1956), the attitudes expressed remained essentially unaltered at the end of his life. What we see evolving, fundamentally, is a hardening anarchism of a very personal type. The following year, in *Exhortaciones,* and in reply to a letter from one

---

[47] It should be noted that Sebreli's position raises one serious objection, despite some valid arguments: its selectivity. While a reading of *Exhortaciones* and *Las 40* most probably would not have altered his central thesis, at least it would have offered evidence of the growing persecution complex in the essayist, together with other personal attitudes. These essays, both published in 1957 (Sebreli's work in 1960) are the only pre-1960 essays not openly cited by the critic.

[48] César Fernández Moreno, p. 41.

[49] *Cuadrante del pampero*, pp. 106-107.

of the very few individuals he called "brother," Martínez Estrada leaves no doubt as to his thoughts on the corrupting influence of power upon man:

> Todos los que ejercen algún poder, político, económico, religioso o sapiencial están al servicio de nuestros enemigos, son accionistas de ese gran Ingenio Azucarero que es el mundo capitalista, lo que en el lenguaje de Dante, San Juan de la Cruz y Marx es el mundo del sufrimiento, de las sombras y del despojo. [50]

"Nuestros enemigos," then, come to represent, all manifestations of authority, and in the same volume he issues a strong invocation to judges that they not allow themselves to be corrupted by the power that they wield, nor should they be influenced by "pressures" from political sectors. [51] Significant, too, are the three figures he uses as examples. Here we have, then, not a clear-cut ideological position, not even a doctrinaire anarchist of the Bukanin or Garibaldi type, but a very emotional, very personal eclecticism.

## In search of the Elusive

Yet there is something disquieting for the reader of Martínez Estrada in this continual neglect of political economy, of political institutions in favor of an interpretation that ultimately sees the solutions to Argentina's ills in terms of the individual, of the human dimension. Certainly, as a contemporary of Martínez Estrada had observed, intellectuals as a group, are generally averse to discipline, to programmes and systems, possessed as they are by an individualist psychology and heterodox attitudes towards thought; and probably in them more than in any other group the sense of individualism is excessive, accompanied by a tendency to put their intelligence above ordinary rules. [52] But it is indeed difficult to find any consistent manifestations of such attitudes in Martínez Estrada. No doubt the increasing tendency to withdraw within oneself, to see oneself as almost stigmatized by a manifest destiny, could be interpreted, as

---

[50] *Exhortaciones,* p. 90 ("Carta a Espinoza").

[51] See "Exhortación a los jueces," in *Exhortaciones.*

[52] Juan Carlos Mariátegui, "La revolución y la inteligencia," *La Escena Contemporánea* (Lima: Amauta, 1925), p. 196.

Sebreli has already put it, "au dessus de la mêlée" but a very conspicuous absence in Martínez Estrada is the cultivation of the superiority of the intellect; in other words, there is no great sense of intellectual pride (in the sense of a "natural" superiority) in the essayist (and in this sense one could make a clear parallel with Manuel Gálvez, who undoubtedly suffered from such excesses). Quite clearly Martínez Estrada stated,

> Mi vocación ha sido más la de aprender que la de enseñar... Declaro que nunca tuve interés por esa clase de venerable artesanía [saber profesional, utilitario y pragmático]. Yo prefiero la inquietud de seguir ignorando y averiguando, mucho más que la satisfacción delusoria de haber encontrado la verdad. Contra la ambición insensata de Raimundo Lulio estoy junto con Lessing, quien prefería la búsqueda de la verdad a su posesión segura. [53]

In other words, Martínez Estrada opted for the *flechazo* ("la búsqueda") in place of the *blanco* ("la verdad"), since the true value for him appears to reside in the striving itself, and not necessarily in the questionable possession of truth. This affirmation, of course, also has a dialectical corollary, as one critic has pertinently observed, [54] the actual attainment of truth/success, consequently becomes suspect, and ultimately corrupting. Thus we have the situation of the essayist striving after what must result, necessarily, according to the dialectic, in the act of possessing it, a *desengaño*.

*Existential stirrings*

Another facet of Martínez Estrada's personality that we touched upon in a previous chapter was the existential position, of a conscious-

---

[53] Ezequiel Martínez Estrada, *Meditaciones sarmientinas*, pp. 170-171.

[54] Martin S. Stabb, "Ezequiel Martínez Estrada: The Formative Writings," *Hispania*, 49 (March, 1966), pp. 54-60. In this perceptive article, Stabb traces the development of certain attitudes in the essayist, taking three articles published in *Nosotros* from 1917-1918 as his starting point, and touching briefly upon his poetry. The final section of this chapter reveals a somewhat similar method but treating an important theme untouched by Stabb in this article, and dealing with different sources. Another good corroboration of this constant in the essayist's ideology is to be seen in "Reflexiones acerca del error," first published in 1928. See, *Leer y escribir*. Ed. and arr. by Enrique Espinoza (Mexico: Joaquín Mortiz, 1969), pp. 53-60.

ness of the absurdity of life, occasionally evident in his work. Given the dialectic that we have just referred to, this position becomes increasingly more clearly motivated. While we first alluded to such a position in an analysis of themes in *Radiografía de la pampa,* an examination of Martínez Estrada's poetry from this thematic stand-point [55] will illustrate that *Radiografía de la pampa* did not exemplify, as one critic affirms, [56] an anguished outburst expressing a deep disillusionment born of the socio-economic conditions of the end of the 1920's and the military take-over of 1930. Rather, the existential position that we noticed in the 1933 work had clear precedents in the poetic phase of the essayist's literary career, and should be seen

---

[55] There has been no attempt to trace exhaustively the development of the feeling of the absurd in the poetry of Martínez Estrada, since, as we have mentioned in our introduction, that while of interest to the study of the personality of the essayist, his poetic creation will only be referred to obliquely and as an additional source to confirm attitudes evident in his essays, particularly when these are subject to controversial interpretation by critics. Valuable contributions to the study of the poetry of Martínez Estrada are, Adelaida Gigli, "La poesía de Martínez Estrada: Oro y piedra para siempre," *Contorno,* 4 (Dec., 1954), pp. 17-19, and Berta Lejarraga, "Aproximaciones a Ezequiel Martínez Estrada, poeta," *Cuadernos del Sur* (Universidad Nacional del Sur), 8-9 (julio 1967-junio 1968), pp. 89-96. The collections themselves are: *Oro y piedra* (1918), *Nefelibal* (1922), *Motivos del cielo* (1924), *Argentina* (1927), *Humoresca* (1929), and a brief return to poetry again in 1959, with *Coplas de ciego.*

[56] Aníbal Sánchez Reulet, "El problema de la identidad argentina en la obra de Ezequiel Martínez Estrada," unpublished public lecture given at the University of Illinois, Urbana, on 30th April, 1970. Adopting a rather similar position, Rodolfo Kusch in his "Lo superficial y lo profundo en Martínez Estrada," *Contorno,* 4 (Dec., 1954) states that "la *Radiografía* nace alrededor del juego político de 1930" (p. 1). Similarly, many critics have been at pains to see various turning-points in the essayist's work, which owe more to their own (often prodigious) imaginations than to true thematic considerations. Thus Kusch considers *Muerte y transfiguración de Martín Fierro* as the measure of *lo profundo,* which he sees developing since *Radiografía* (*loc. cit.*), while Ricardo Mosquera, in his "Martínez Estrada en la lucha por una Argentina contemporánea," *Homenaje a Ezequiel Martínez Estrada* (Bahía Blanca: Univ. Nacional del Sur, 1968) holds that the true turning point in the essayist's career was really his *Sarmiento* (p. 9). Understandably, the varied and complex nature of Martínez Estrada's work invites speculation of this type, and also the date of Kusch's affirmation — 1954, with only eight essays (out of a total of twenty-eight) published — would necessarily restrict its overall relevance. Nonetheless, in very few cases, if any, do such speculations ever take into account the essayist's own view of his "turning-points," which we shall consider later. While these need not constitute the last word on the subject for the critic, they at least provide a sense of proportion for such considerations.

as a continuation of established attitudes and not the engendering of new ones.

In *Oro y piedra,* published in 1918, we encounter the basic pessimism so evident in later works and in itself a mainstay of the poet/essayist's existential attitude. In "Ecce Homo," and in a clear reference to himself, the poet laments,

> Este privilegiado ser suieto a un estigma
> carnal, a inexplicables influencias, a un
> alto designio, debe descifrar el enigma
> de la funesta Esfinge que lo persigue aún.

> Su vida es como el rápido fulgurar de un cometa
> que atraviesa la noche desde un oscuro origen;
> sus esperanzas frágiles, su alma ansiosa e inquieta,
> ocultas e inflexibles las fuerzas que lo rigen.

> Mañana un soplo frío extinguirá la brasa
> que encendió su lujuria, su virtud y su guerra,
> y habrá sido la sombra de una nube que pasa,
> de una sombra sombría sobre la blanca tierra. [57]

The last line of the second stanza, and the first line of the third stanza, point to the whole fragility of life, how precarious life is faced with "ocultas e inflexibles... fuerzas que lo rigen," and eventually constituting "una sombra... que pasa." The collection *Nefelibal* also provides numerous examples of this *pesimismo vital,* as expressed in 1922, and also the dialectic of striving/disillusionment we have referred to:

> Mi conciencia carece de puntos de contacto
> El centro cosmológico es mi actual emoción.
> En mí comienza el móvil y en mí termina el acto.
> Mi conciencia carece de puntos de contacto.

> La tierra está desierta y el cielo está vacío
> En un Sahara pálido muere mi corazón.
> Vano es decir "hermano", vano es clamar "¡Dios mío!"
> La tierra está desierta y el cielo vacío. [58]

> ("Así es")

[57] Ezequiel Martínez Estrada, *Poesía: Oro y piedra, Nefelibal, Motivos del cielo, Argentina, Títeres de pies ligeros, Humoresca* (Buenos Aires: Argos, 1947), p. 44.
[58] *Ibid.,* p. 94.

By discarding any hope of religious consolation, the pessimism experiences a deepening as the terrible solitude of man imposes itself, an emotion still evident two years later (in *Motivos del Cielo*) in poems like "Al Dios desconocido" and "Paz." From the same collection we observe the poet's incomprehension of optimism in the circumstances. In "La noche" he affirms,

> No comprendo al diurno, al feroz optimismo,
> cuando es dolor la vida y en torno hay tanta pena.
> (El mar oscuro viene a morir en la arena
> y el silencio es la sombra tendida hacia el abismo.)
>
> Levantaré mi frente humillada, ofendida,
> con la marca del látigo, al cielo ultramarino,
> y la estrella que antes me alumbraba el camino
> me enseñará la forma de maldecir la vida. [59]

The deepening of emotion is accompanied, as we notice, by an increasing complexity of imagery, particularly in the first stanza, "el silencio es la sombra tendida hacia el abismo."

*Humoresca,* published in 1929, was, with one exception, [60] the poet's last incursion into poetry and one may observe the feeling of intense pessimism that we have traced flow into a full awareness of the absurdity of existence. In "Variaciones sobre un tema de Baudelaire," Martínez Estrada proclaims,

> Caí en un cuerpo efímero y busqué la manera
> de abrir brechas para irme de allí con la mirada,
> y para que la luz llegara desde fuera.
> Abrí cuatro ventanas que daban a la nada.
>
> Soy una isla abrupta en un mar inviolable,
> inviolable a sus ímpetus e infinita como él.
> ... ... ... ... ... ... ... ... ... ... ... ...
> Voy rodando hacia el fondo de un abismo.
> Tal vez no tenga fin esa caída,
> porque ese precipicio soy yo mismo.

---

[59] *Ibid.,* p. 136.
[60] *Coplas de ciego* (Buenos Aires: Sur, 1959). Another edition of his poetry was published in 1966, comprised of selected poems from previous collections. See *Poesía*, selection and introduction by Juan José Hernández (Buenos Aires: E.U.D.E.B.A.).

Sólo me cuesta, ese traspié, la vida.

... ... ... ... ... ... ... ... ... ... ... .

Soy un juguete absurdo, pero la maravilla
consiste en cierto fraude, porque lo soy de modo
que, por dar un sentido a esta atroz pesadilla,
cuando tiran del hilo que mueve mi rodilla
(Dios me perdone), a veces lo que muevo es el codo. [61]

The vocabulary used bears witness to the evolving consciousness of being caught up in a series of absurd relationships with life, reality, one's fellow man: "Cuerpo efímero," "ventanas a la nada," "abismo," "isla abrupta," "juguete absurdo," "atroz pesadilla." These, in turn, attest to the complexity of character possessed by Martínez Estrada, and immediately suggest an intriguing parenthesis to our discussion. Given such an existential position, coupled with the dialectic of the striving as opposed to the actual success of achievement, why did it not produce, as similar sentiments have done in countless other cases, the feeling that perhaps the only solution is that of suicide? [62]

## The purification of society

Yet it should also be observed that Martínez Estrada was not a confirmed existentialist in the sense of being a convinced follower of Kierkegaard, Heidegger or Sartre. His concept of the absurd drew more on Kafka than on anyone else, although, as we have proceeded to illustrate, Martínez Estrada had a temperamental disposition towards many existential themes. [63] Not unexpectedly, such attitudes

---

[61] *Poesía* (1947), *op. cit.*, pp. 279-281.

[62] It is pertinent to note that the one-time poetic mentor of Martínez Estrada, Leopoldo Lugones, and Horacio Quiroga, his veritable soul-mate, both committed suicide, as did one of the essayist's uncles. The young Martínez Estrada was fortunate to enjoy the patronage of Lugones, unquestionably the dominant figure in Argentine poetry of his day, and his appreciation of the poetic talent of the young poet can be seen in his "Laureado del gay mester," *La Nación*, 18th August, 1929. The essayist's admiration for him was quite clear. In 1959 he wrote, "Ningún autor ha provocado en mí, por la lectura de sus obras, un efecto de tal modo fascinador." See *Leopoldo Lugones, retrato sin retocar*, compiled by Enrique Espinoza (Buenos Aires: Emecé, 1968), p. 21. These words were first published in an article bearing the same title which appeared in *Cuadernos Americanos*, CII, I (Jan.-Feb., 1959), pp. 211-223.

[63] For a good consideration of the early stirrings of this disposition, see "Carta a Victoria Ocampo," *Sur*, 295 (July-Aug., 1965), 3-7. This letter was reproduced in *Leer y escribir* (1969).

can offer many psychological barriers to an attempt to translate them into some degree of social action, even if, as we have pointed out, the essayist was ultimately convinced that reform, in his terms of "purification" of society was well-nigh impossible to achieve, and that all attempts to alter social reality in Argentina were really cases of, *plus ça change* ... This temperamental reality was, as we shall consider later, of great importance in attempting to trace the extent of the essayist's impact and influence on later generations of Argentinians.

At this point, the fundamental contradiction may be expressed in terms of the targets of much of Martínez Estrada's criticism, which he shared with very many groups in the Argentine political spectrum, and in broad terms, with most of the Left (with the exception of the orthodox Marxists). But ultimately, to restrict oneself merely to an exposition of the sickliness or even to an acerbic, vitriolic attack on its causes and roots, could not hope to satisfy other generations whose concepts of political commitment demanded a concrete, pragmatic plan of action if Argentina were to be "cured." One can, in fairness, object that Martínez Estrada never envisaged himself in terms of a political leader, and as we have seen, rejected all power as ultimately corrupting, preferring to withdraw into himself, to meditate and analyse. If we were to put the situation in ecclesiastical terms, later generations were in search of a Cardinal Cisneros, and Martínez Estrada saw himself as a type of Savonarola. On the other hand, to see the essayist's whole work as Sebreli does, as the aberrations of,

> ... un intelectual argentino, perteneciente a la pequeña burguesía, aterrorizado por la crisis económica, decepcionado y escéptico. [64]

is to ignore the complexities of the personality of Martínez Estrada, that owe little to economic crises, and substantially more, as we have seen, to attitudes acquired, developed, and experienced in vital fashion, years before the worsening economic situation in Argentina at the end of the decade of the 1920's.

---

[64] Sebreli, p. 21.

## Chapter III

THE LITERARY ESSAYS AND THE ROLE OF THE WRITER:
MARTÍNEZ ESTRADA AND THE GENERATION OF 1945

LITERARY AND AESTHETIC MANIFESTATIONS, together with literary genres themselves, have offered to the critic of literature, and particularly the critic of Spanish American literature since the 1920's a disconcertingly complex panorama of classification. The dividing line between post-Modernism and pre-Vanguardism, the place of Futurism within Ultraism, to quote two examples, bear witness to a conceptual confusion shared also by the creators themselves, in those cases when they admit the relevancy of literary "labels." Consequently the critic increasingly has recourse to "generational" descriptions, that situate authors in general cultural manifestations operative at a given moment without necessarily restricting them to a definite aesthetic stance.

This tendency — to situate artists according to generational considerations — is nowhere more evident than in the Spanish American essay. While the critic can, with a large degree of exactness, talk in terms of the Romantic essay or the Modernist essay, the genre in the last thirty years or so will not submit easily to any attempt at clear literary/ideological definition. To mention but two examples, no adequate classification exists for the *Siete ensayos de interpretación de la realidad peruana* (1928) of José Carlos Mariátegui or José Vasconcelos' *La raza cósmica* of 1925. While it should be admitted that the essay as a genre has often exhibited a susceptibility to difficulties of classification, there can be little doubt that it shared those difficulties with other genres since the end of Modernism itself. Thus it would not appear an exaggeration to affirm that the critic of Spanish-American literature, in order to feel himself within a clearly definable and internally logical aesthetic has to go back as far as Modernism itself.

Generationally, then, Martínez Estrada (1895-1964) is related to Jorge Luis Borges (1899), Eduardo Mallea (1903), Leopoldo Marechal (1900) and Raul Scalabrini Ortiz, among others, but in keeping with the ideas outlined above, enjoyed a spiritual affinity with few of them and a temperamental relationship with virtually none. [1] The essayist, in fact, had no clear relationship with a particular literary aesthetic or epochal ideology, although the occasional critic has attempted to characterize the poetic phase of his career, 1918-1929, as post-Modernist with regard to certain themes and the use of particular language. [2] As far as can be established, Martínez Estrada,

---

[1] Martínez Estrada maintained a rather extensive correspondence with a large number of his contemporaries, very little of which has been published as yet. Despite a mutual preoccupation with the interpretation of Argentine life, Martínez Estrada and Eduardo Mallea appear not to have had a great deal of contact, much less friendship. Nonetheless, Martínez Estrada respected the author of *Historia de una pasión argentina*. See Emmanuel Carballo, "Tres radiografías de Ezequiel Martínez Estrada," *Casa de las Américas*, no. 33 (Nov.-Dec., 1965), p. 39. Relations with Jorge Luis Borges were often stormy. In his *Antología poética argentina* of 1941, Borges termed him "nuestro mejor poeta contemporáneo," although Martínez Estrada, with his poetic career far behind him at that point, interpreted this as a slight by Borges on his worth as an essayist (in conversation with Borges in East Lansing, Michigan, March, 1976). Their principal areas of friction, it would appear, were their respective attitudes to the first Peronist régime and the early years of Cuba under Castro. See Borges' "Una efusión de Ezequiel Martínez Estrada," *Sur*, 242 (Sept.-Oct., 1965), pp. 52-53. While close to the circles of the "grupo *Sur*," the essayist was never really a part of it, and that despite his long association with Victoria Ocampo. Contacts with Leopoldo Marechal and Scalabrini Ortiz appear to have been minimal, although the former and Martínez Estrada shared a fundamental concern for the dehumanizing effects of the great metropolis in works such as *La cabeza de Goliat* (1940) and *Adán Buenosayres* (1948). Similarly, Scalabrini Ortiz displayed a somewhat parallel preoccupation for the problems of national identity in his play *El hombre que está solo y espera* (1934). Given his complex of being an outsider in his own society that we have traced in the preceding chapter, a lack of abundant friendships would not be surprising. This situation notwithstanding, Manuel Pedro González referred to a conspiracy of silence against Martínez Estrada. See "Cómo se debe amar a la Patria," *Suplemento de Siempre* (México), 23 Dec., 1964.

[2] Critical attempts at placing Martínez Estrada within a particular literary aesthetic are very rare. An interesting one, if spoiled by an ideological interpretation that distorts the essayist's achievements, is Roberto Fernández Retamar, "Razón de homenaje," *Casa de las Américas*, no. 33 (Nov.-Dec., 1965), pp. 5-14. Adolfo de Obieta, in his "Ser, no ser y deber ser de la Argentina," *Sur*, 295 (July-Aug., 1965) saw the essayist as constituting a type of generation

while embroiled in polemics almost all his life, did not indulge in controversies over the literary orientation of his work. His principal preoccupations were conceptual and spiritual, and in a rather wide sense, ideological.

A somewhat little-known book review, however, published in 1956, gives a good indication of how he saw the imperatives of the age, both aesthetic and social, in the context of the vestiges of a persistent Modernism, in the figure of José Enrique Rodó. Commenting on the publication of the latter's complete works, he evokes with gentle irony the literary priorities of the turn of the century:

> Los discípulos que rodeaban a Rodó cuando al caer las tardes, en una luz de oro, platicaba con ellos transitando los jardines propincuos a la playa Carrasco, no aspiraban sino a escuchar su clara y melodiosa voz modulando preceptos dignos en verdad de Marco Aurelio y Walter Pater... Después de dos mil quinientos años parecía Sócrates redivivo en el Egeo rio-platense. Yo escuché a distancia su voz y le debo un homenaje de gratitud y de respeto. [3]

Despite the irony, Rodó's contributions were seen as valuable, as far as they went, and in their day:

> En una época de melena y chalina, de escribanía "sans souci" y "sans façon", Rodó vino a poner orden, a exigir pulcritud, a imponer armonía, simetría y decoro. Su filosofía es pues, ordenada, pulcra, armoniosa, simétrica y decorosa; su estilo como prosista lo es mucho más. [4]

Yet this is not a rejection, or at least not a total rejection, of Rodó's well known cult of the polished phrase. Contrasting the tastes of the contemporary reader, Martínez Estrada goes on to clarify:

> Quiero significar que el lector de hoy exige del escritor que diga algo que le interese personalmente... exige que el ave

---

by himself, a generation of "exploradores del ser." César Fernández Moreno, on the other hand, and in keeping with his fine insight into the essayist's life, quite clearly affirmed that Martínez Estrada wrote his books "fuera de toda órbita generacional." See "Martínez Estrada frente a la Argentina," *Mundo Nuevo*, Paris, I (July, 1966), pp. 37-47, especially p. 41.

[3] Ezequiel Martínez Estrada, "Yo escuché a la distancia su voz," *La Prensa*, 10 June, 1956.

[4] *Ibid.*

canora, además de hermoso plumaje y dulce voz, tenga sabrosa pulpa ... Por reacción contra el exceso de orden, pulcritud, armonía, simetría y decoro, es un ente antisocial, aunque se diga y se crea antiacadémico y antirretórico. Más que incrédulo, es iconoclasta. Yo mismo, de tener que confesarme en alta voz, diré que quizá simpatizo con el partidario de la rueca y la cabra contra el propagandístico del avión supersónico y del dictáfono. [5]

Expressing, in this way, his predilection for the bucolic, rural life, Martínez Estrada finally makes a rejection of the relevancy of Rodó's message to the 1950's, and as we can appreciate, the rejection is not without some nostalgia:

Rodó fue y es todavía un gran escritor y un amable filósofo que nos ha guiado durante buena parte del camino en busca de nosotros mismos; ahora, con una genuflexión que bien merece, debemos separarnos. Nuestra tarea es otra. Celebremos de nuevo y siempre, con ramos de laurel, al tallista, al cincelador, al camafeísta que ha labrado con tanto primor obras duraderas, sin inquirir qué materiales utilizó ... Se debe probar su arte como objeto de arte y no de joyería. [6]

Hence we appreciate a rejection of form in favour of content on the part of the essayist, although nor does he attempt to hide his taste too for the instruments of aesthetic communication. Basically (as he points out in the same article) the modernist aesthetic is inadequate ("el ideal de academia y ateneo") for the youth of his day. Yet one cannot overlook that this does not constitute a total rejection of Rodó's idealism; rather it is a recognition of its merits — as far as they go — while denying that they have the same relevancy in the 1950's as they had fifty years previously.

This, in turn, brings us to the rather complicated relationship between Martínez Estrada and youth over the years. Complicated because it was not entirely uniform, and for not always clearly discernible reasons. Moreover it should also be affirmed at this point that the discussion of such a relationship in no way contradicts the foregoing concerning the generational aspect of much of post-Modernist eras. Precisely the generation that followed Martínez Estrada's — that

---

[5] *Ibid.*
[6] *Ibid.*

of the so-called "generation of 1945" — was fundamentally concerned with *literatura comprometida* against the wider spectrum of society itself, and not with any narrowly defined aesthetic position. Generationally, Martínez Estrada belonged to the previous generation of the *martinfierristas* (that of 1925) but — and here we see our thesis of the generational, as opposed to "literary school" concept brought out — he was opposed to the platform, literary and social, of his generation, as were these of the generation of 1945: Referring to the *martinfierristas*, he stated:

> Fue un movimiento espasmódico, de incomodidad de los jóvenes frente a los viejos maestros de la literatura argentina, particularmente contra los pedagogos y los autores de manuales de preceptiva. Esos jóvenes tenían noticias del movimiento de búsqueda de novedades que se producía en Europa, pero no pasaron de ser muchachos descontentos con los padres que querían emanciparse sin saber para qué. Faltaba en el país un estado de conciencia acerca de los valores de la cultura y de la literatura nacionales como para intentar una reforma provechosa inspirada en la necesidad de darles un sentido ajustado a la realidad. Ignoraban que la historia había sido tan sofisticada como la literatura, pero como no se propusieron ninguna tarea seria al demoler las casas solariegas, no supieron construir y, en verdad, lo único que vale de esa aventura fue lo que desprestigiaron. [7]

Similarly — and this can be clearly inferred from the above — Martínez Estrada had very definite views why Borges (one of the principal *martinfierristas* of his day) and Mallea failed to constitute models for the following generation, as a whole, which of course did not preclude that certain individuals should consider them as mentors. [8] In answer to a question on the extent of Borges' influence on the present generation, Martínez Estrada replied:

> No puede hablarse de una influencia directa de Borges sino de las literaturas que él representa — las de los paraísos arti-

---

[7] Emmanuel Carballo, "Tres radiografías de Ezequiel Martínez Estrada," *Casa de las Américas*, núm. 33 (nov.-dic. de 1965), p. 39.

[8] The generation of 1925, and principally Jorge Luis Borges, Eduardo Mallea, Leopoldo Marechal and Martínez Estrada attracted many individuals to themselves. To talk in terms of disciples, we may mention two examples, those of Ernesto Sábato (Borges) and H. A. Murena (Martínez Estrada) and Mallea has enjoyed the admiration of many critics, among them Canal Feijóo and Francisco Ayala.

ficiales cuya flora edénica son las "flores del mal". Borges es el producto nativo de esas corrientes literarias. Recientemente, los hechos políticos le han demostrado que tiene otra tarea que cumplir, además de la de elaborar textos suntuosos y exquisitos.... Mallea se ocupa de temas de la vida argentina, pero no escribe desde dentro de la propia vida argentina: ve sus temas y personajes a distancia, como los puede ver un observador inteligente y extraño. El escritor joven encuentra que la preocupación principal de Mallea es la de escribir una buena novela con tema argentino. [9]

This, as we shall soon consider, constitutes a striking case of irony in that, the generation of 1945 accused Martínez Estrada — among others — of precisely the same type of "extrañeza" of which he accused Mallea. Yet the accusations have a very similar tone to those of Martínez Estrada. The 1945 generation in Argentina, composed of young writers such as H. A. Murena, Jorge Abelardo Ramos, David Viñas, Ismael Viñas, Adolfo Prieto, Rodolfo Kusch, to a great extent followed the example of the essayist in that they too were totally opposed to the traditional concept, held by the previous generation of Argentinians in possession of "una cultura maravillosa a la que sólo tenemos que estirar la mano para poseer en su integridad" [10] or as Martínez Estrada himself put it on many occasions, the idea of "una nueva y gloriosa nación." One critic sums up the situation as follows:

[A David Viñas] los *martinfierristas* le parecen una generación de traviesos muchachos, de gente que no llegó a superar la adolescencia emocional e intelectual, que a pesar de su tono revolucionario eran (parafraseo y hasta agrego) unos señoritos que jugaban a la revolución literaria y la conmoción estética del ambiente. Por eso, contaminaron de literatura hasta la política. [11]

Certainly this was not the case with Martínez Estrada. By 1948 the essayist had published considerably, including several essays that stirred a great deal of controversy: *Radiografía de la pampa, La cabeza de Goliat: Microscopía de Buenos Aires, Sarmiento* and *Muerte y transfiguración de Martín Fierro*. Clearly, while Martínez Estrada

---

[9] Emmanuel Carballo, *op. cit.*, p. 39.
[10] Emir Rodríguez Monegal, *El juicio de los parricidas* (Buenos Aires: Editorial Deucalión, 1956), p. 17.
[11] *Ibid.*, p. 27.

generationally belonged to the era of the *martinfierristas,* he could not be included among the "señoritos que jugaban a la revolución literaria." Similarly, one could not say, as did a rather youthful Enrique Anderson Imbert in 1933 referring to Borges, that "la realidad está ausente en sus obras" [12] or León Rozitchner, of Mallea, that he indulged in "ideologías abstractas para no arriesgar su vida." [13] Rather, as we suggested in a previous chapter, the highly moralistic tone of much of Martínez Estrada's prose, coupled with an attitude also alluded to earlier — that of his failure to offer concrete solutions to his (admittedly) fatalistic denunciations of Argentine reality — strongly engendered the impression of "distance," of "detachment" from what the essayist was attacking. Hence the irony that we pointed to above with reference to Martínez Estrada's opinion of the attitude of the 1945 generation towards Borges and Mallea.

In addition, then, to the naive cult of Futurist "fads," the generation of 1945 equally rejected the concept of the intellectual, of the professional writer, as the cultivation of a literature that did not emanate from a personal commitment to one's social milieu, the *contorno.* [14] Yet what distinguished that generation from the aims of the *martinfierristas* in Argentina, or the *estridentistas* in Mexico (who attacked those who practised a then decadent Modernism, all included under the heading of "lamecazuelas retóricos") [15] was that one must begin the analysis and reconstruction of the national reality from within (as opposed to the americanization of Marinetti's Futurist platform) and, more importantly, that one's primary commitment should be to that reality.

Certainly Martínez Estrada's spiritual and literary formation included the study of a host of non-Argentinian (mainly European) authors but there was never the question of his attempting to superimpose a crudely digested foreign "solution" to an Argentine situa-

---

[12] *Ibid.,* p. 60.

[13] *Ibid.,* p. 48.

[14] The principal literary organs of the generation of 1945 were *Ciudad* and *Contorno,* both of which dedicated special numbers to commentaries on the impact of Martínez Estrada on Argentine literary circles (1955 and 1954, resp.). The name "contorno" itself bears witness to the wider, sociological interest of the founders.

[15] This is the term used by List Arzubide, one of the original *estridentistas,* in his book, *El movimiento estridentista,* 2nd ed. (México: Secretaría de Educación Pública, 1967), p. 7.

tion. [16] The instruments, then, of the essayist's denunciation — the intuitive approach, intensified, no doubt, by his reading of Spengler, the geographical determinism, also adumbrated by Spengler, and later by Keyserling, as we have seen, to name the principal ones — were not the real point of the younger generation's criticism. The principal objection was the *attitude* of the essayist's attacks, and equally importantly, the single focus of his analysis. Summing up the attitude of the younger generation, Raquel Weinbaum (pseudonym of Ismael Viñas) stated:

> Se presiente que el autor apenas si se ha deslizado desde el plafón al lado del órgano, porque el mundo de los hombres sigue bullendo ahí abajo... contra las losas, entre la perrada hedionda, sobre los bancos mugrientos. En el valle de lágrimas puerco y visible como el fresco gigantesco. El mundo es lo que está *ahí. Ahí abajo.* Muy por debajo del escritor puro que describe... El universo se ha atornillado allí, y nada más. Únicamente Martínez Estrada sabe del adentro y del afuera. Sus ojos zahoríes y casi divinos le permiten alejarse del aliento y del hedor de los hombres. [17]

The last sentence of the above strongly suggests that Martínez Estrada's fundamental attitude in his criticisms was that of self-righteousness and detachment with reference to the country. Yet there is an evident danger of overstatement in Weinbaum's affirmation; moreover, his views have much in common with other critics of his generation who rejected the cultural relevancy of writers whom they considered representative of patrician attitudes, which is what he also implies with regard to Martínez Estrada. There is a real risk of misunderstanding here, however. If there is an attitude in Martínez Estrada that can be termed "purist," it is not in the sense of one

---

[16] This is generally true for the writers of the younger generation — that of 1945 — although as we have alluded to in the previous chapter, there were those like Víctor Massuh, who rejected *a priori* the whole concept of geographical determinism as an analytical instrument for the investigation of the cultural roots of Latin America.

[17] Raquel Weinbaum, "Los ojos de Martínez Estrada," *Contorno*, Buenos Aires, 4 (Dec., 1954), p. 1. Similarly, César Fernández Moreno held that, "la generación del 50, y Sebreli en particular, atacan a Martínez Estrada por ser un denunciante profesional, un intelectual de todos modos encaramado a su torre, un hombre que no se juega, que no actúa." See "Argentina frente a Martínez Estrada," *Mundo Nuevo,* 2 (Aug., 1966), pp. 31-42.

who is "above the fray," but rather one who is convinced of the veracity of his interpretation. In both cases, naturally, there is a real possibility of a resulting intransigence, but the motives are clearly different. [18] More typical of the generation's position vis-a-vis the essayist is that of Ludovico Ivanissevich Machado who stated that "La historia de la sociología argentina se dividirá en antes y después de Martínez Estrada." [19] Even more so is that of Rodolfo A. Borello, who sees the essayist's role in Argentinian literature as fundamental:

> No es exagerado afirmar la importancia y el influjo que ejerce hoy la obra de Ezequiel Martínez Estrada. La *Radiografía,* su magistral estudio de Buenos Aires, sus interpretaciones de Hudson y el agotador trabajo sobre *Martín Fierro* justifican una vida dedicada voluntariamente a los problemas de nuestro país y a la delucidación de sus aspectos esenciales . . . Si hoy nos enfrentamos una realidad erizada de interrogantes, si hoy nos preguntamos por las causas de un sinnúmero de hechos es él quien los planteó y señaló con honda agudeza. [20]

Borello's objections, on the other hand, rest on the rejection of the "fuerzas ocultas" thesis that is central to *Radiografía de la pampa,* although in essence he is in agreement with many of Martínez Estrada's conclusions. [21] Starting from a firm mistrust of the intuitive approach, Borello points to a basic objection, and that of those committed to a multi-faceted view of the milieu — the all-pervasive telluric fatalism of Martínez Estrada:

---

[18] This question — that of the basic attitude of Martínez Estrada towards Argentine society — is obviously of fundamental importance to an understanding of his personality, to say nothing of his impact on Argentine letters of his day. The facets of his personality that we have traced in the preceding chapter would certainly support the idea of a writer *temperamentally* destined to cultivate an essentially lonely existence, a condition further exacerbated by an almost pathological need to proclaim his vision of Argentina's ills, no matter the cost in personal terms. But this need not include a tendency towards an intellectual arrogance or smugness, as Raquel Weinbaum suggests. For a quite different (and pathetic) vision of the man, see Arnaldo Orfila Reynal, "Nada más que un recuerdo," *Casa de las Américas,* núm. 33 (nov-dic. de 1965).

[19] Ludovico Ivanissevich Machado, "El puritanismo en Martínez Estrada," *Ciudad* (Buenos Aires), I (Primer trimestre, 1955), p. 23.

[20] Rodolfo A. Borello, "Dos aspectos esenciales de la *Radiografía de la pampa,*" *Ciudad* (Buenos Aires), I (Primer trimestre, 1955), p. 24.

[21] *Ibid.,* p. 27.

Señalar una misteriosa influencia del viento de la pampa sobre las estructuras de la nación, o sus costumbres, no es dar con el factor clave sino engañarnos con una seudo solución, con una seudo ciencia. Es convertir en sistemáticas las fallas que vemos como odiosas, y erigir en orgánico lo que carece de claro sentido... Partió a comprendernos con la derrota en el alma, y sintiéndose vencido por esta infinita soledad de las extensiones deshabitadas de nuestro suelo, nos vio sin salvación.

No creemos en la presencia de esas fuerzas invisibles, tampoco podemos aceptar como arma para la lucha ese estado de ánimo que nos lleva a la resignación antes que a la callada conciencia de nuestros males, y al estudio de sus posibles soluciones... Hundirnos en el infierno no es la mejor forma de empezar a salir de él. [22]

Here then, instead of the reasons summarized by Rodríguez Monegal, is the root of the problem of Martínez Estrada's relevance to the new generation of writers. The problem is not so much that of "moralistic posture" (Weinbaum) or that of "alienation" (Rodríguez Monegal) but rather that in the last analysis Martínez Estrada's fatalism cannot provide "arma para la lucha"; if indeed the essayist's diagnoses are correct, then the endemic fatalism of his essential message virtually constitutes a deeply nihilistic position: those who would follow Martínez Estrada would ultimately find themselves to be "herederos de la nada." Ismael Viñas also underlined the situation succinctly:

Ese estudio, [*Sarmiento*] si provisto de armas analíticas previas, no podrá ser nunca frío: el moralista devendrá más fácilmente predicador y profeta que profesor; lo que no podrá ser nunca es un observador objetivo, un descriptor claro de la realidad. [23]

---

[22] *Ibid.*, pp. 29-30. Ismael Viñas, a contemporary of Borello, reached very similar conclusions about this aspect of Martínez Estrada:

...su obra es la declaración constante de una desilusión, y la energía profética con que la proclama tiende a aplastar en él mismo toda posibilidad, ahogándolo en la jeremiada apostrófica, y a nublar en nosotros la apostura crítica libre, no sólo con respecto a él, sino también, lo que es más grave, con respecto a la realidad. ("Reflexión sobre Martínez Estrada," *Contorno*, Buenos Aires, 4 [Dec., 1954], p. 2.)

[23] Ismael Viñas, "Alrededor del *Sarmiento*," *Ciudad* (Buenos Aires), I (Primer trimestre, 1955), p. 31.

Those who looked for the teacher, found only the moralist and preacher; those who would look for ammunition for the struggle to evolve a far greater degree of commitment to the problems of their social reality found a virtually untransferable personal philosophy.

## The mistrust of science and the anti-rationalist attitudes

In describing Martínez Estrada's attitudes towards Modernism as exemplified by his comments and general evaluation of the impact of José Enrique Rodó on the American intellectual tradition, we have noted that the essayist saw himself obliged (if somewhat reluctantly) to deny the relevancy of the bucolic niceties of the Modernist aesthetic to the problems of contemporary Argentina. At the same time it is also abundantly clear that his rejection was not, say, that of the Marxist critic who would consign the whole movement to the final stirrings of a decadent bourgeois class totally oblivious to the needs of an oppressed proletariat. Martínez Estrada, in short, saw the Modernist movement as largely irrelevant to the needs of his day, but that the laborious cultivation of highly ornate lyrics and prose — like the figure of Rodó himself — appeared to enjoy some degree of historical justification. To that extent, then, Martínez Estrada — writing this in the 1950's — appears to occupy a mild post-Modernist position, which, broadly speaking, rejected the hollow imitations of Darío, but not necessarily (or at least not wholly) Darío himself. [24]

On the other hand, the essayist's concept of relevancy did not include any "approximation" between the arts and sciences, which in essence was a primary concern, as we have considered, of the various Futurist movements in the continent in the 1920's, and to this extent, Martínez Estrada is in harmony with the generation of 1945 that also attacked the "señoritos que jugaban a la revolución literaria." On the contrary, one of the constants running throughout the essayist's work is a deep-seated distrust of the impact of science on culture, and the attendant dangers — as he saw it — that such an impact created. Be it "la cultura *kitsch*," "la cultura mecanizada" or "la cultura de fábri-

---

[24] This in fact was the case with Enrique González Martínez, whose famous poem "Tuércele el cuello al cisne" of 1910, stressed not so much a rejection of Darío but rather a rejection of his *preciosista* imitators. Accordingly, González Martínez is widely accepted as initiating the post-Modernist phase.

ca," these terms denoted the progressive dehumanization of Western culture that Martínez Estrada continually warned against. Thus, in his discussion of various outstanding literary and philosophical authors, he rarely neglected an occasion to remind the reader the extent to which the author under discussion was far removed from succumbing to such dehumanization. We may also note in passing that the essayist's consistency in this matter gives rise to the question of to what extent his predilection for certain authors was governed by such considerations or that the fact that these personalities, to the extent that they were exceptional creators, of necessity, displayed gifts and qualities that would automatically place them far above the effects of the encroaching cultural mechanization that Martínez Estrada saw about him. In his study of one of his principal spiritual mentors, William Henry Hudson, we see a clear example of the essayist's attitudes:

> El libro de Lewis Mumford, *Técnica y Civilización* es elocuente a este respecto: la *tekné* es el instrumento de deshumanización que arrastra al hombre a la esclavitud de sus creaciones. Es preciso, pues, adoptar una posición firme desde los comienzos de la serie de desarrollo de una de ambas direcciones: perfeccionamiento moral del hombre o perfeccionamiento mecánico de las cosas. [25]

Not unexpectedly, such attitudes, as we shall gradually appreciate, form part of an evolving world-view that includes a rather pessimistic vision of the evolution of culture. In the same work we find a broader statement of Martínez Estrada's position:

> El mundo ha cambiado fundamentalmente y el alma ha sido desalojada hasta de los textos de psicología. En tan pocos años, y aunque permanezcan en pie los artefactos de la civilización, el mundo ha sido poblado por una nueva raza de invasores y conquistadores que no en todos los casos declaran su odio al ser humano ni manifiestan su brutal misión por la violencia; esa raza triunfante es la de los antiguos bárbaros que se tomaron una tregua para reaparecer con los atavíos completos de la supercivilización... La más mortífera de esa conquista ha sido la técnica, nueva divinidad infernal, y la sabiduría del hombre se ha puesto al servicio de la antigua, antiquísima impiedad. [26]

---

[25] Ezequiel Martínez Estrada, *El mundo maravilloso de Guillermo Enrique Hudson* (México: Fondo de Cultura Económica, 1951), p. 275.

[26] *Ibid.*, pp. 279-280.

And not without a hint of condescension on the part of the essayist, he proceeds to reassure that:

> También puede el hombre de ciencia ser considerado como un artista, en tanto separa el saber metodológico del saber intuitivo, el saber que sabe que sabe del que comprende. En las mayores alturas de la ciencia una ley estética rige las leyes de la verdad. [27]

The reply to our speculation concerning Martínez Estrada's apparent predilection for authors that are far removed from any "compromise" with "mechanized" values gradually suggests itself. The principal human or artistic attribute that really sets man apart from the barbarous encroachment of the *tekné* culture is that special faculty called intuition, and the other authors that Martínez Estrada chooses to study all possess this attribute in considerable measure. Turning to his essays on Frank Kafka, we encounter the concept of the intuitive expanded, in that it is seen in opposition to all ordered or structured knowledge:

> De todos modos es correcto considerar en la obra literaria de Kafka tres aspectos: el de una teodicea negativa, que al suprimir la necesidad de Dios suprime al mismo tiempo la necesidad de un orden normativo para el acontecer y para la conducta pública y privada del hombre; el de una sociología en que es indispensable separar el orden convencional, institucionalizado, del proceso "incardinable" del acontecer caprichoso dentro de aquel diagrama teórico; y el de una psicología de acciones y reacciones puramente mecánicas, sin conciencias ni pautas de volición que autodeterminen nada. Porque el hombre obligado a pensar conforme a un canon, es mero "robot" del canon que se impone y no vigía del proceso tumultuoso de la realidad. Y todo esto equivale a decir: la quiebra del concepto clásico de causación o determinismo. [28]

While we are tempted to see a large measure of exaggeration in these affirmations, it is convenient to remember that a most cohesive and

---

[27] *Ibid.*, p. 303.

[28] Ezequiel Martínez Estrada, *En torno a Kafka y otros ensayos* (Barcelona Seix Barral, 1967), p. 31 (Compilados por Enrique Espinoza). While this volume was published posthumously, most of the material previously appeared in periodicals.

articulate statement of the dehumanization of society, George Orwell's *Nineteen Eighty-Four* (1948) was written around the same time as *El mundo maravilloso de Guillermo Enrique Hudson* (1951) or *En torno a Kafka,* published posthumously in 1967, but the above material first published in 1950. [29]

Similarly, Martínez Estrada sees Montaigne as essentially a non-scientific thinker:

> El mundo en que vivimos tiene una estructura literaria, estética si la tiene matemática y biológica. Para Montaigne la verdad del mundo, su realidad real se parece más a un ensueño que a un sólido geométrico. En vez de interesarle la ley del péndulo, le interesan las hipotéticas leyes del vivir del hombre en el mundo, entre seres y cosas afines y seres y cosas incompatibles. [30]

Likewise, Honoré de Balzac is seen as embodying the creation of a perfectly recognizable world that owes very little to a scientific "pre-ordering" but proceeding, rather, from an intuitive ability to penetrate reality:

> La sociedad no tiene "un sistema" como tampoco lo tiene la naturaleza — tiene formas y funciones — y cualquier filósofo de la vida que siga un método científico de exposición y se atenga a su propio sistema como la sociología y la historia académica ha de falsear forzosamente el fluído y contradictorio curso de la vida humana... Sólo se exige la condición de que obedezcan a las reglas del juego de la vida misma; y en posesión de esa clave le fué posible a Balzac crear, imaginativamente, un mundo tan cierto como el nuestro, una historia apócrifa que inclusive puede reemplazar a la historia auténtica con una legalidad igual. [31]

Not unexpectedly this open hostility to scientific method, particularly with regard to the ordering of life itself, this deep mistrust of systems, of structures, also found an echo of sorts in his evocation of his great mentor, Frederick Nietzsche:

---

[29] "Acepción literal del mito de Kafka," *Babel* (Santiago de Chile), 11, v. 13, no. 53, Primer semestre, 1950, pp. 24-28.

[30] Ezequiel Martínez Estrada, "Montaigne, filósofo impremeditado," *Heraldos de la verdad* (Buenos Aires Editorial Nova, 1957), p. 71.

[31] "Balzac, filósofo y metafísico," *Heraldos de la verdad,* p. 104.

Una cosa hay cierta: es que Nietzsche coloca al hombre en el centro de los problemas gnoseológicos y lo examina en función de todas sus conexiones, con el mundo ambiente, con su historia y con sus posibilidades en el futuro. Supone haber sido el primero que descubre (como verdad o como problema) que la ciencia es una máscara que se emplea cubriendo el mundo para no reconocer la verdad. [32]

Implicit in this rejection of scientific values as a basis for living, for life, is the corollary that the truly, authentically human dimension is to be achieved through some type of return to a primitive existence, or rather to a primordial existence. [33] Martínez Estrada never gives a coherent description as to how this reintegration is to be achieved, although in his analysis of Kafka's artistic world he suggests that such authenticity is to be arrived at through the use of myth:

El mundo de Kafka, en resumen, no es el de los restantes seres humanos muy contentos con cualquier rutina que los libere de la angustia y la responsabilidad de pensar; tampoco es el mundo del filósofo ni del campesino: *es el mundo real*, y sólo puede ser expresado por el mito, por la metáfora, por el lenguaje de la intuición que hablamos cuando estamos dormidos, es decir, cuando nos reintegramos al sentido nocturno y orgánico de la vida. [34]

This rejection of any degree of "systematized" thought raises the question of a basic anti-rationalist dimension in Martínez Estrada's thought, literary and philosophical. Naturally this is not a question of organized thought as such; nor are we really faced with questions as to the discipline of the artist; such anarquism *reductio ad absurdum* would leave the artist completely sterile, and Martínez Estrada is one of the most disciplined of writers. [35] Rather, it is a re-

---

[32] "Nietzsche, filósofo dionisíaco," *Heraldos de la verdad*, p. 190.

[33] The influence of Jung and Freud is evident here and in the following quotation from the essayist's work on Kafka. For a good description of how Jung saw the artist as in communication with a primordial netherworld and as possessing a primordial vision, see the chapter "Psychology and Literature," in *Modern Man in Search of a Soul* (London: Routledge, 1962), pp. 175-199. The work was first published in 1933.

[34] *En torno a Kafka*, pp. 32-33.

[35] "Más bien la producción es laboriosa. Antes de nacer, las ideas suelen combatirse entre sí, como en no recuerdo qué drama de Maeterlinck, los seres

fusal to allow any systematized method to intercalate itself in the course of the creative process. Thus the intuitive faculty in the artist becomes close to a formulation as the principal literary/creative virtue. In a later study on Balzac, Martínez Estrada again reiterates the primacy of intuition:

> No poseía Balzac ningún método científico con que trabajar en el campo de los conocimientos empíricos — en esto tiene razón Croce —, no lo necesitaba, pues declaradamente la fuerza de su inteligencia se manifiesta por la intuición, como en todos los genios, y no por el raciocinio. Tenía el instinto de cómo se deben saber las cosas aunque no las supiera: por encima y más allá de la razón. [36]

Reality, or "real reality" as the essayist has expressed it, is penetration of the ordered universe to the vision of a primitive world beyond, through the use of the faculty of intuition, and the use of myth as the instrument. These channels of artistic creation must be preserved, affirms Martínez Estrada, from the structured (and hence anti-intuitive) approach of the scientific method.

### The mission of the writer

Fundamental, too, in Martínez Estrada's view of the artist is one aspect of the artist's view of himself. The great artists that he discusses — Balzac, Montaigne, Hudson, Nietzsche — all possessed a clear consciousness of a personal categorical imperative that impelled them to write: a sense of vocation, of an inner drive to creativity, or as Ortega put it, as clear sense of mission. [37] This in fact comes very close to the Jungian concept of Creativity, or the Muse, as taking possession of the man, with or without his volition, and converting him into the artist. [38] Balzac is quoted as an example of this:

---

se despiden para nacer, o como los cromosomas. Hay capítulos de *Radiografía de la pampa* que rehice hasta diez veces." *Cuadrante del pampero*, p. 171.

[36] Ezequiel Martínez Estrada, *Realidad y fantasía en Balzac* (Bahía Blanca: Universidad Nacional del Sur, 1964), pp. 41-42.

[37] See José Ortega y Gasset, *Libro de las misiones* (Madrid: Espasa Calpe, 1965).

[38] Martínez Estrada saw his own literary production as proceeding from the same situation. Asked if he believed in the "misión rectora, directriz, orientadora del escritor," he replied: "Creo que el escritor es uno de los instrumentos de que se vale la 'fuerza superior misteriosa, incognoscible e

Desde sus primeros ensayos Balzac considera que cumple una misión, la de revelar el alma de la sociedad en cuyo rostro sonriente ha leído su destino tremendo. Un don de penetrante intuición es lo que caracteriza su genio, y este aspecto del saber que podemos llamar gnóstico, tiene importancia fundamental en todas sus novelas. [39]

With reference to Argentinian letters, Martínez Estrada, too, was very conscious of the mission that destiny had mapped out for him, and also to what extent he had complied with it; not surprisingly, his comments are very often tinged with his subjective appraisal that inevitably appears to oscillate between arrogance and pathos:

> Quizá toda mi obra causídica en prosa... pueda definirse como investigación, análisis y exégesis de la realidad argentina. Con *Radiografía de la pampa* yo cancelo, no del todo pero casi definitivamente, lo que llamaría la adolescencia mental y la época de vida consagrada al deporte, a la especulación o al culto de las letras. *Radiografía de la pampa* significa para mí una crisis, por no decir una catarsis, en que mi vida mental toma un rumbo hasta entonces insospechado. Diré que fuí enrolado en las filas del servicio obligatorio de la libertad de mi patria... *Radiografía* es, pues, un apocalipsis, una revelación o puesta en evidencia de la realidad profunda. [40]

These sentiments, taken from the prologue to his *Antología* of 1964, contrasts sharply with the sentimentality and pathetic quality of feelings expressed in a letter to Victoria Ocampo, around 1946 ("poco después de terminada la segunda Guerra"):

> Confieso que me reconozco incapaz de fraguar una niñez apócrifa ni de hacer literatura sobre la verdadera. Bastante tiene de absurdo y de trivial. Al fin y al cabo, cuanto aconteció en mi existencia tiene poca relación casual, lógica, conmigo. Parezco ser un ente que atravesó ileso e inmune los

---

ineludible'... Todo lo que vive, y hasta lo que se mueve, está sometido a esa realidad suprema que, según Heráclito, no vemos porque tenemos ojos. El escritor, el artista, el científico, el santo — Dostoiewski creía que también el criminal y la prostituta — la obedecen y la sirven, porque son moléculas luminosas del cosmos que los ojos no nos dejan ver." (*Cuadrante del pampero*, pp. 169-170).

[39] *Heraldos de la verdad*, p. 105.

[40] *Antología*, pp. 12-13.

hechos que constituyen su existencia terrestre, humana, dia-
ria, documental. Nada tengo que ver con mi biografía. Repasando el texto, siento que vivir y ser son dos realidades
distintas ... Repasando mi vida, veo que sólo he sido yo el
culpable de una valoración pesimista, y que prolongar la
existencia más allá de la pubertad es un funesto error que
se paga con la misma supervivencia. [41]

The deep pessimism, not without a strong element of bitterness, reveals the stark discouragement that his mission was to occasion; in
short, it is almost in terms of Baudelairian spleen, although we should
not overlook the possibility of a medical condition contributing to
such a state of mind. [42] The "servicio obligatorio" is a rather concrete
statement of his awareness of his mission. Given this situation, then,
of an "internal imperative" the applause of society, in so far as it
offered its seal of approval in the shape of literary prizes, could not
really impress the essayist. Quite the contrary, the "laureles de oro"
as Martínez Estrada often referred to them, had quite the opposite
effect. Not without reason he once stated, "Entre nosotros el elogio
y el panegírico son letales." [43] Martínez Estrada came to realize that
prizes such as the Premio Nacional de Letras and Premio Municipal
de Buenos Aires (among those awarded to him) eventually came to
signify a degree of collaboration with the "Establishment" that he
had set himself against. Moreover, he found that literary awards only

---

[41] "Carta a Victoria Ocampo," 3-4.

[42] While Victoria Ocampo dates the letter as "poco después de terminada
la segunda Guerra," it is possible that this particular mood in Martínez Estrada was partially motivated by the onset of the very painful skin disease
that was to keep the author bedridden for years. The early 1950's are thought
of as the actual period of illness (and confirmed by correspondence) although
it may well have begun to manifest itself in the late 1940's. On the other
hand, the great similarity in tone between the preceding citation from the
*Antología* and the highly demagogic style of *Las 40* (1957) might suggest a
possible chronological relationship between the tone expressed in various
essays. A closer examination of the essays, however, does not warrant a view
that would restrict essays of a particular tone to a concrete period, or still
less, that the mood of certain essays was occasioned by a set of events that
were not to apply later.

[43] Ezequiel Martínez Estrada, *Antología*, p. 14. Another example of his
mistrust of the applause of the literary establishment was his affirmation
that: "En mi país sólo han pretendido y pretenden sofocar mi voz, sean
cuales fueran los homenajes que me hagan." (José Bianco, "Escritores y amigos recuerdan a Don Ezequiel Martínez Estrada," *La Gaceta* [México], XI,
no. 124 [Dec., 1964], p. 6).

served to dissuade artists from their chosen path and to seek society's praise as an end in itself.

## The applause of the literary Establishment

At this point it is well to remind ourselves that despite affirmations (including many by the essayist himself) to the effect that his real center of interest — his mission — were the social sciences, Martínez Estrada did not really see himself in that light. In view of our previous considerations of the essayist's deep-seated distrust of "cultura mecanizada" this comes as no surprise. Nonetheless, it is necessary to make a basic distinction between the *poetic sensibility* that guided all his work — to varying degrees, and the *free-ranging nature of the genre of the essay itself*, which included, very often, sociological or semi-scientific facts and theories. To ignore this is to run the risk of seeing contradictions where there are none. Lanuza González, for example, referring to *Radiografía de la pampa* in 1958 (twenty-five years after its first printing) states:

> Se la premió [a *Radiografía*] como obra literaria, lo que fue en cierto modo fatal porque equivalió a desconocerla como lo que ante todo es: un antecedente de patología sociológica. [44]

Martínez Estrada, on the other hand, as we have pointed out above, described his work as "una apocalipsis, una revelación." On the one hand, the vocabulary of the social science, on the other, a virtually religious vocabulary. No doubt the essayist would have agreed that the literary prize exerted an "institutionalizing" effect on the work that went contrary to its being considered as a fundamental point of departure in the history of Argentine literature. Yet it is also evident that the words "patología sociológica," while not a totally inaccurate description of the effect and subsequent interpretation of the work, is out of step with its intention, which as we have noted earlier with reference to the essayist's attitudes towards the sciences, could not be formulated in such a way, without incurring a flagrant contradiction. On the other hand, the author himself has given more

---

[44] E. Lanuza González, "A 25 años de *Radiografía de la pampa*," *La Nación* (28th Dec., 1958).

than one affirmation as to how he saw himself, with reference to this situation. The author is quoted from time to time as terming some of his work (particularly *Radiografía de la pampa*) as "sociología psicoanalítica" [45] or "trabajo sistemático de demolición," [46] and we are again in the realm of the effect of the work and not in that of the temperamental attitude of the author. Speaking in 1953 at a ceremony commemorating the twenty-fifth anniversary of *Radiografía de la pampa*, Martínez Estrada is quite unequivocal in his reply to the introduction made by Jorge Luis Borges:

> Hizo usted bien en recordar, Borges, que yo soy un poeta...
> Es exacto, soy un poeta y no un sociólogo o un economista.
> Pero tenía que hablar y decir lo que tenía que decir porque
> estaban gritando los gansos, y yo tenía que hacerlos callar. [47]

*The essential poet*

Moreover, he went on to say that Lugones was also due the homage that he was receiving, together with Paul Groussac and Horacio Quiroga — "los dos maestros que me ayudaron a encontrarme a mí mismo." There can be little doubt, therefore, that despite the enormous range and variety of his reading, which included, admittedly, history, philosophy, sociology and economics [48] — to name but a few — Martínez Estrada himself was convinced of his fundamentally literary temperament.

On the other hand, as we alluded to earlier, the essayist occupied a rather peripheral position with regard to literary movements and

---

[45] "Radiografía de una *Radiografía de la pampa*," *La Nación* (11th Dec., 1958). This is a report of a tribute offered to Martínez Estrada in the "Casa del Escritor" on the occasion of the anniversary of the publication of his famous work.

[46] Emmanuel Carballo, *Casa de las Américas, op. cit.*, p. 39.

[47] "La 'Sociedad de Escritores' celebró los 25 años de *Radiografía de la pampa* de Ezequiel Martínez Estrada," *La Prensa* (4th Dec., 1958). In contrast to this clearly serious view of himself, Martínez Estrada occasionally referred to his role in life in much more lighthearted terms. In a letter to Rodríguez Urruty (18th Feb., 1957) he calls himself a "curandero social." See Carlos Adam, *Bibliografía y documentos*, p. 187.

[48] The vast amount of material read by Martínez Estrada is well-nigh impossible to catalogue, and really only of speculative value as it cannot be accompanied by extensive comments of the author. However, it is interesting to note, in connection with Sebreli's earlier imputation that the essayist was unaware of economic causes and effects, that in *Las 40* (p. 77), he refers to the fifty specialists in economics that he had consulted since his youth.

polemics, excepting, of course, the early poetic phase of his career. Once asked whether his literary stance coincided or differed from that of the *martinfierristas,* he answered:

> Lo que yo he hecho es un trabajo sistemático de demolición de los valores falsos y caducos para crear una nueva conciencia de la nacionalidad. Yo he trabajado siempre como si no hubiera existido ese movimiento, y algunos otros; nunca les he dado importancia. Y si escribiera una historia de la literatura argentina no los mencionaría siquiera, a no ser como un trastorno infantil, digamos el sarampión o la viruela boba. [49]

This, however, was not always the situation of the essayist, as we have referred to previously, in that until the early 1930's the young Martínez Estrada appeared destined to become a very promising poet. He admired Lugones, unquestionably the leading Argentinian poet of his day, and while we have noted in his poetry the seeds or origins of a deep disillusionment that was to manifest itself much more strongly throughout his prose work, the break with the Argentinian literary establishment did not come formally, until *Radiografía de la pampa.* His deep spiritual relationship with Horacio Quiroga was instrumental in forcing him to sever the literary umbilical cord that had previously connected him with Argentine literary circles. Figuratively, Martínez Estrada referred to the change in terms of that he would now write a book with his right hand [50] but it was Quiroga who contributed most to the change from the "left hand":

> Hacia 1930... yo había decidido no escribir más poesía, coronado de laureles de oro y amortajado de silencio por mis cofrades. Progresivamente, él [Quiroga] y yo llegamos a la certeza de que nuestra Campaña del Desierto había terminado... El me inició en la lectura de obras desagradables, que había considerado yo de menor cuantía y fuera de los cánones del gran estilo, y extinguió en mí la lámpara mortecina de la poesía que había iluminado los lóbregos senderos de mi juventud... Barrió en mí los últimos residuos de una educación deficiente y académica, y la credulidad ignorante y escolar en la palabra de los críticos engañosos...

---

[49] Emmanuel Carballo, *op. cit.,* p. 39.
[50] José Bianco, *op. cit.,* pp. 5-6.

Hudson, de su devoción, completaría la deseducación en la que, buena o mala, me encuentro satisfecho. [51]

## The rootlessness of the Argentine writer

Writing with the "right hand," of course, went accompanied by a whole reappraisal of Argentinian literature, and it is pertinent to remember that the ostracism of the essayist from literary circles — brought about by himself — continued not only for the iconoclastic nature of his own creative writings, but also for his extreme opinions concerning the literary tradition in Argentina itself. Just as he had pointed to the Argentinian's lack of roots in the land (*Radiografía de la pampa*) so too did the writer's situation bear witness to a basic artificiality that rendered sterile his creative attempts:

> El escritor argentino rehuye compromisos y obligaciones de *gens* aunque los acate de partido y de estamento. Perteneciente a la clase media y pequeña burguesía, refleja una vida burocrática que da espaldas al pueblo que no forma parte de la población de su parroquia. Cualquier escritor de raza advierte que es un desarraigado. [52]

In addition to this, the essayist sees the Argentine writer still suffering from an implicit censorship, dating from the nineteenth century that militated against alarming the newly-arrived immigrant or the banker, so eager were the leaders of the country to attract people and capital in order to overcome the barbarity of the interior. Hence, according to the essayist, writers — generally speaking — by their refusal to go against the current of the times — and Martínez Estrada here is clearly inferring a type of moral cowardice — indulged in a type of self-prostitution with an Establishment that preferred its writers to extol the country's extraordinary capacity to produce wheat and cattle. [53] Taking his point of departure, characteristically, to be the Conquest, or rather the Colony itself, the essayist traces the continuing divergency between history/politics/or national, social reality, and Argentine literature:

---

[51] Ezequiel Martínez Estrada, *El hermano Quiroga*, pp. 67-70.

[52] Ezequiel Martínez Estrada, *Para una revisión de las letras argentinas*, compilados por Enrique Espinoza (Buenos Aires: Losada, 1967), pp. 14-15.

[53] *Ibid.*, p. 17.

Si el trauma de la Conquista fija un complejo de ocultación
y pone en vigor una crónica administrativa, el de la Revolución fija otro de narcisismo patriótico; el de la Reorga-
nización, el de la grandeza por bula pontificia; los de la Era
del Oropel y la Era del Fraude, el de la "tierra arrasada," en
la que no se siembra y no se esquilma. [54]

Naturally, there were exceptions to this, such as *Martín Fierro* or
*La Gringa*, but Martínez Estrada very perceptively points out that
Argentine literature did not reflect the national events that produced
a deep cultural shock, such as the "aluvión inmigratorio." [55] Although
the essayist does not formulate it, the implications that this has had
on the growth of social institutions and political ones in particular,
appear to suggest themselves: in submitting to such a sterile role,
Argentinian literature lost the opportunity of contributing to the
critical evaluation of several myths, principally, one deduces, that of
the "nueva y gloriosa nación."

The most cursory reading of Argentinian literature would support Martínez Estrada's basic thesis. Whereas North America possesses a prodigious amount of literature devoted to Reconstruction
after the Civil War or of the great expansion westward, Argentine
literature has not, in general occupied itself with its own corresponding
themes. The average Argentinian might, in justifiable self-apology
reply that quantity does not necessarily imply quality, but this objection even if it were true would not really counter Martínez Estrada's contention that the intelligentsia in the country virtually prosti-
tuted itself by not turning its attention to phenomena of fundamental
importance as the waves of immigration, the impact on the country
and culture of the "vacunocracia."

Not unexpectedly, such a "sell-out" on the part of writers tended
to engender, historically, the development of a guilt-complex that has
persisted to the present day:

La traición a nosotros mismos es el problema central y radical de nuestra vida en todas las manifestaciones de su real
existencia: el problema del existir histórico de un pueblo,
de una gran nación desgobernada y esquilmada, pero sin
conciencia del mundo en que vive ni de las gentes que con-

---

[54] *Ibid.*, p. 19.
[55] *Ibid.*, p. 17.

viven en él, ni siquiera de la realidad, a la que no ha ter-
minado de resignarse y adaptarse. [56]

The essayist quotes Ricardo Rojas as one of the few who had any
consciousness of this historical "betrayal" [57] but it should be empha-
sized that Martínez Estrada's whole literary activity comes to signify
an attempt to awaken a consciousness of the phenomenon in Argentina. In other words it is a call, as in *Radiografía de la pampa*, to
authenticity. But it is here, precisely, that the critic begins to appreciate the great impatience and rancour that the work of Martínez
Estrada gave rise to. In short, the reader who is willing to accept the
basic premises of the essayist and accompany him in the search for
a solution to the conditions and realities of the "real" Argentina, is
ultimately left in a *callejón sin salida*. After awakening the individual
to his vision of his country, to the need to face up to the painful
reality, he proceeds to affirm that since the symptoms are either congenital or consist in "hidden forces," he virtually precludes the real
possibility of solution to the situation described. This, broadly speaking was the procedure adopted in *Radiografía de la pampa*, in *Muerte
y transfiguración de Martín Fierro* and *La cabeza de Goliat*. In *Para
una revisión de las letras argentinas* the pattern persists:

> Entre nosotros es inútil e invalioso remontar el pasado, es
> decir, ejercer el ministerio de la historia, y ninguno de nues-
> tros historiadores ha podido vencer esa censura tácita, esa
> inhibición inconsciente con todo acto fuera de lo conven-
> cional, pese al hombre que piensa. ¿Por qué hemos tenido
> aprensión a la verdad histórica y a la veracidad literaria?
> ¿Por qué nos es tan fácil la literatura de evasión y de ara-
> besco y tan difícil la verista? Aunque el escritor personal-
> mente sienta en su conciencia la necesidad y hasta el deber
> de ser veraz, aquellas fuerzas latentes que en él mismo exis-
> ten, lo desvían a cierta altura de su investigación o de su
> meditación, para desfigurar su razonamiento y su propósito
> convirtiéndose en observador desdeñoso. [58]

At the same time the author does not offer any concrete method of
exorcism against the "fuerzas latentes" merely stating that "cuando

---

[56] *Ibid.*, pp. 34-35.
[57] *Ibid.*, p. 37.
[58] *Ibid.*, p. 45.

tengamos conciencia de nosotros mismos, esos fantasmas se desvane-
cerán por su propia inconsciencia." [59] This is virtually the parting
concept of *Radiografía de la pampa,* and equally, the pessimism im-
presses itself much more than the solution. The dark pessimism of the
diagnosis, however, gives way occasionally to consideration of those
few exceptions who have produced "real" literature, and what Martínez Estrada understands by "real" literature is one that has visible
roots in a social reality and reflective of the glories and tragedies of
everyday life. [60] Again and again Quiroga is used as an illustration:

> El gran Horacio Quiroga, mi maestro y hermano, que a us-
> tedes y a nosotros pertenece por igual, escribió una clase de
> cuento característico suyo, con el mensú de Misiones por
> protagonista... Ahí la vida de la selva misionera, terrible
> como sus animales y sus plantas, se nos ofrece con toda la
> crudeza de su amarga y tajante realidad... Esa es literatura
> auténtica... Pertenece a una gran literatura porque es copia
> veraz y sin retoques de lo real y cierto, feo y rudo, cruel y
> torpe, tal como viven la mujer, el hombre y el niño de la
> selva... Es buena literatura porque no traiciona ni desfi-
> gura la realidad, y la realidad siempre es supremo artífice
> de belleza, de verdad y de simpatía. [61]

### Authentic literature

In the context of the writer's *labor,* as outlined above, such a
view of literature is readily understood, but it must be admitted that
as a viable literary aesthetic it is lamentably restrictive and amazingly
simplistic, more so since Martínez Estrada was well versed in literary
historical styles and tastes. Realism, then, or at least a mixture of
realism/naturalism becomes the chief literary virtue.

Clearly Martínez Estrada is advocating the institution of a concept of literature that has roots, first and foremost, in the masses as
opposed to a literature for élites. Accordingly, one may be tempted
to see some degree of relationship between such a concept and the
Marxist concept of "socialist realism" that manifestly has roots in

---

[59] *Ibid.,* pp. 113-114.

[60] Horacio Quiroga, William Henry Hudson, the early English Voyagers,
the Salón Literario de Marcos Sastre, José Hernández, and Florencio Sánchez are the examples most quoted by the essayist. It is not unusual that
half are not Argentinian, given Martínez Estrada's thesis.

[61] *Para una revisión de las letras argentinas,* pp. 148-149.

"una realidad tajante," and its known goal of approximation to the *lumpenproletariat*. But Martínez Estrada will have none of it:

> Voy a poneros un ejemplo bien conocido de literatura política, de la causa del ser humano al servicio de un programa de gobierno, de literatura dirigida. Es de los escritores de la Rusia soviética ... He leído indignado ... "El trabajo del escritor". Eso es una desfachatez; y si os parece poco diplomática la palabra, una felonía. Es traicionar la situación humillada y ofendida de la inteligencia libre a un plan quinquenal de servicio obligatorio. [62]

It is at this point that we realize that Martínez Estrada's attitude towards "popular literature" is slightly more subtle than at first consideration. His previous affirmation concerning the role of the writer as a true reflection of the social milieu — and not of selected interests — appeared to circumscribe to some extent the individual liberty of the writer. His rejection of the Marxist position, however, reveals a view of the artist that does not tolerate interference with the artist's individual role. In other words, the essayist is against art at the service of interests, elite interests or proletarian interests. Hence we arrive at a fundamental distinction in Martínez Estrada's view of serving the interests of the people: that between *pueblo* and *proletario*. The former alludes to a national/cultural reality and the latter to a narrowly political conception. In reflecting the "real tangible" of society, Martínez Estrada also gives to the writer a role of unifier, of one who contributes to the texture of the fabric of society. In a lecture given at the Argentine embassy in Montevideo in 1956 he stated:

> De ninguna manera he venido a lisonjearlos ni a lucir mi voz de sirena ... Les hablo así porque tenemos que mar-

---

[62] *Ibid.*, pp. 153-154. Moreover, in an earlier work, it was clear that the essayist rejected an altogether photographic realism in literature:

> ¿Cómo puede haber realismo en literatura si no hemos creado una realidad? Una realidad existe cuando está organizada, ordenada no sólo dentro de un territorio y un siglo, sino dentro de un sistema de valores. El *Martín Fierro* y el *Facundo* están ordenadas dentro de una realidad que expresa valores, y son reales no por lo que copian como copia, sino por lo que extraen de la realidad para que sirva a una reconstrucción amplia, total, de la realidad ... La realidad es el panorama, no las cosas que hay dentro de él. (*Muerte y transfiguración de Martín Fierro*, p. 298.)

char juntos, y debo advertirles que el paraíso del escritor, el que les señalo, es el de Gólgota. Literatura para el pueblo, pero no proletaria ... Los escritores que se apartan del deber de consagrar su inteligencia ... están al servicio, sin saberlo, de los enemigos de la redención verdadera, de los ignorantes, de los humillados y de los afligidos ... una literatura alcanza la transcendencia universal cuando refleja la vida y el medio ambiente de un pueblo, de un país. O como ha dicho más o menos, nuestro excelente Borges, una literatura nacional no tiene que ser forzosamente una literatura nacional ... la literatura debe ser no sólo reflejo de la vida de un pueblo sino el órgano de penetración en las entrañas de la tierra y del habitante, el vínculo de solidaridad y simpatía, la argamasa de la solidaridad humana que empieza por la solidaridad familiar. [63]

The danger of inconsistency here rapidly becomes apparent. How can Quiroga's reflection of reality — "sin retoques, copia veraz" — be reconciled with a writer such as Borges, whose art is far from being realist? If Quiroga is used as an example of great literature, because of his realism, how can a writer such as Borges, who doesn't *obviously* reflect "el medio ambiente" nor whose work can be considered to be an organ of "penetración en las entrañas de la tierra"? Martínez Estrada does not show an awareness of the problem. Naturally, if the critic wishes to indulge in matters of definition (what is reality? what is a true reflection of it? etc., etc.,) then he will doubtless encounter ways of reconciling the apparent inconsistencies. On the other hand, if we restrict ourselves to the spirit and tone of the lecture, (from which the references to both Borges and Quiroga are taken) we find a probably more satisfying answer. Fundamentally, Martínez Estrada is against any interference with the artist and his artistic expression — be these interferences in the form of an implicit censure of certain topics, that we have discussed, or in the form of art serving the interests of small groups or large masses (the essayist's rejection of "socialist realism" [64] — and, incidentally — Peronist

---

[63] *Ibid.*, pp. 153-158.

[64] For an interesting discussion of the essayist's personal experience with the concept of "socialist realism" and his rejection of it, in conversation with Russian students at the University of Moscow, see "Lo real y el realismo" in *En torno a Kafka y otros ensayos*, pp. 11-20. This article was first published in *Cuadernos Americanos*, 18, v. 100 (jul.-oct., 1958), pp. 258-264.

realism). In this light, then, words such as "retoques" and "desfiguración de la realidad" refer to the intercalation of non-artistic/non-aesthetic interests between the artist and his artistic vision. In this way the artist will be true to himself ("la consagración de la conciencia") and by the act of expressing himself he automatically reflects his environment as he freely conceives it. Consequently one does not have to be Argentinian to faithfully reflect Argentina (cf. the example of Hudson) or write about *gauchos* to be a *criollista* writer (the case of Borges). This, of course is a virtually relativist position, and the fact that Martínez Estrada nowhere espouses an absolutist view of art — with regard to aesthetics — would tend to bear out its validity. [65]

Nonetheless, the question was never given a definitive clarification by the essayist himself, and a few years later, at a lecture organized in Bahía Blanca and referred to as "Mensaje a los escritores," Martínez Estrada again appeared to advocate a rather direct communication with the masses:

> En síntesis, mi opinión coincide con la de quienes creen que la literatura, para que no se malogre en ejercicio calisténico o en entretenimientos de paciencia y habilidad, debe transcender de las élites a la masa, sin perder categoría, para que adquiera su real carácter de literatura. Y, por ende, de literatura nacional. [66]

---

[65] Martínez Estrada's concept of reality was in fact relative and multiple. This is very obvious from his essays on Kafka in *En torno a Kafka y otros ensayos*. As early as 1945, however, — and with this we again bear witness to the evolution in the essayist's conception of "real" literature — there was evidence that this concept was not restricted to a "photographic" realism. In a letter to his friend Gregorio Scheines dated 2nd June, 1945, he wrote:

> Jamás pensaré que la literatura realista, la humana, la buena sea un error; pero creo que es una limitación, no la real, ni la humana, ni la buena de verdad. Una limitación agradable desde Homero, y todavía desde mucho antes... Pero si quiero comprender, sentir y saber, no puedo conformarme con la crónica periodística, con el relato policíaco, con aquello que me cuenta el espectador ocasional. Yo sé que hay algo mucho más serio, terrible y complicado. (Carlos Adam: *Bibliografía y documentos de Ezequiel Martínez Estrada*, p. 142.)

[66] *Para una revisión de las letras argentinas*, p. 181. This essay, entitled "Mensaje a los escritores," was first given as a public lecture on Día del Escritor, 13th June, 1959, and organized by the Colegio Libre de Estudios Superiores de Bahía Blanca.

Yet the key phrase here is really, "sin perder categoría." In this way the integrity and liberty of the individual writer are respected. In other words, the writer should find his inspiration in the people without following any political or ideological philosophy or the naked interest of others ("sin retoques"). This is virtually what the essayist has in mind as he adds later, (in the same lecture) in what is as close as he ever came to formulating unequivocally his aesthetic stance:

> Bien sé que la emancipación de los individuos y de los pue-
> blos se opera por otros medios, pero el conjunto de los fac-
> tores coadyuvantes a ese fin, la misión de la literatura es
> ésa, precisamente, de identificarse con el pueblo, de tener,
> aunque sublimadas, su alma, sus pasiones, sus ideas. [67]

Again the really important phrase is "aunque sublimadas." In this way Martínez Estrada avoids the severe limitations of a realist-naturalist position. And it is in this way, too, that his view of a national literature can embrace such disparate creators as Borges, Quiroga, Mallea and Hernández.

## The writer and the State

Fundamentally, and not surprisingly in view of the above, Martínez Estrada conceived of literature as a liberating force (just as he considered himself to be such a force) which was to free Argentina not only from the suffocating influence of selfish minority interests, [68] but also from the huge historical burden of a culture that was really a pseudo-culture. Just as we have traced a temperamental, if not a pathological distrust of the highly-structured — and in his terms of reference, dehumanized and dehumanizing — organization, the logical conclusion to this attitude is an inevitable deep mistrust of the State itself. Tracing the development of the modern state from the time of Aristotle, the essayist notes how the modern bureaucracy has assumed the stabilizing powers of the old aristocracy but sees no radical change in the relationship between governors and governed:

---

[67] *Ibid.*, pp. 192-193.
[68] With reference to the *catilinarias* hurled at various groups within Argentina (in a manner at times reminiscent of Quevedo), see his *Cuadrante del pampero* (1954).

> La aparición del Estado democrático, calcado en los precep-
> tos del *Contrato Social* de Rousseau, ofreció desde el primer
> momento el inconveniente de establecer una nueva relación
> entre los gobernantes y los gobernados, sin modificar los fun-
> damentos elementales del Estado monárquico y absolutista . . .
> Tampoco los territorios nuevos como los de América ibérica
> dieron lugar al establecimiento de verdaderos Estados demo-
> cráticos; por sus antecedentes de colonización y mestizaje
> fueron mucho más favorables aun para el desarrollo de go-
> gobiernos unipersonales bajo las más fervientes proclamas de
> libertad, igualdad y fraternidad. [69]

Basic, too, to his understanding of the State is the conviction that
since the substitution of the "normative" function of the State (up
until the nineteenth century) by the State becoming its own end
(from Napoleon onwards), the gradual movement towards the Fascist
State is inevitable. [70] Yet even more important to an appreciation of
Martínez Estrada's concept of the state is the impossibility of coexistence, as he sees it, between the State as an *instituto de fuerza*
and an *instituto de derecho,* which inevitably gives rise to an enormous amount of tension, in the worst of cases converting the whole
concept of Law into a thinly disguised agency of force. [71]

Consequently the writer, if imbued with a sense of mission, and
also if conscious of a need to resist any attempt on the part of others
to subvert his art (and by this Martínez Estrada really means the
subversive interests of the State, among others) then it becomes
implicit that in truly reflecting the *pueblo* in his work, the writer is

---

[69] Ezequiel Martínez Estrada, "Anverso del Estado," *La Nación*, 15th
Aug., 1954.

[70] *Ibid.*

[71] *Ibid.* Consonant with this view, of course, was the belief, often expressed by Martínez Estrada that the impossibility of such coexistence was
due to the historical perpetuation of the barbarity, exposed by Sarmiento,
in the guise of the State — or *Nación* — itself. Consider, for example, the
following:

> La perennidad de lo facúndico — palabra legalizada por Saúl Ta-
> borda [the famous Argentinian pedagogue] — está en el funciona-
> miento de las instituciones, en los poderes del Estado, en la con-
> ducta de los gobernantes. Y en verdad hay que comparar a Facundo
> con la Nación y no con el pueblo ni con la civilización de las
> ciudades, según el consejo de Sarmiento. Mejor dicho, hay que
> tomarlo en su siguiente avatar, Rosas, y compararlo con el Estado.
> El Estado es él. (Ezequiel Martínez Estrada, *Los invariantes his-
> tóricos en el Facundo* [Buenos Aires: Viau, 1947], p. 8.)

thereby cooperating in the construction of a new concept of *pueblo-estado-cultura*, that has roots in the people themselves and not in any monolithic structure. Later, in fact (at least by 1956), the essayist in a letter to a friend, came very close to the formulation of the above:

> Tampoco se le ha suministrado a mi pueblo una cultura de clase, una cultura humana y cívica, de su situación en la sociedad, en el Estado y en la familia, como la literatura y el arte han cumplido en otros países más adelantados que el nuestro (porque los hay). Por cultura de clase no solamente entiendo, mi amigo, una cultura proletaria, con todas las acepciones de esta palabra dogmática, sino de una calidad que, sin aspirar a ser excelente, tampoco sea ruin. Nuestra vida espiritual de las "élites" no merece reproches menos severos... Me limitaré a decir que cualquier intento de culturación de las masas en nuestro país debe partir del principio de que somos huéspedes trashumantes de nuestra propia patria... [72]

The fact of his self-imposed exile in Mexico (1959), then later in Cuba (1960-1962) is no doubt a monument to the depth of disappointment at the failure of people, and writers among them, to accept his diagnosis of the country's ills. Nonetheless, very few commentators [73] of the work of Martínez Estrada have given sufficient notice to the immense personal courage that such a mission demanded of him, and probably none at all to that courage that preferred exile to suicide.

## Martí and commitment

In the context of the above, however, it would appear practically inevitable that Martínez Estrada should have warmed to the populist roots, and the whole liberating character of the Cuban Revolution, so much so that the rumor abounded that he had become a Cuban

---

[72] *Cuadrante del pampero,* pp. 115-116. This letter comes from a section entitled "Cartas sueltas de un mazo" and gives no indication as to whom it was addressed.

[73] Two exceptions are E. González Lanuza, "A 25 años de *Radiografía de la pampa*," *La Nación* (28th Dec., 1958), and Emir Rodríguez Monegal, "Escritores y amigos recuerdan a Don Ezequiel Martínez Estrada," *La Gaceta* (México), XI, núm. 124 (Dic., 1964).

citizen, despite his clear denial of this. [74] Yet also in the context of the discussion of the essayist's views of literature and the artist's role in society, it becomes evident that problems of how he was to avoid the question of "socialist realism" and still remain at the service of the Revolution, were bound to arise. On the other hand, the Cuban régime realized the prestige to be gained from having one of the leading intellectuals of Latin America at its disposal and as far as can be established, made no attempt to persuade him to write favourably about Cuba. [75] In reality, there was no need for such persuasion. In 1961 a group of leading Argentinian intellectuals (Borges, Mallea and Bioy Casares among them) denounced publically the increasingly communist orientation of the Cuban régime. Not unexpectedly, Martínez Estrada sprang to the defence of Cuba:

> Piensan ustedes como los lectores de historias fantásticas y de periódicos de la prensa en cadena, y tienen del socialismo una idea de curas párrocos. Es increíble que algunos de los buenos escritores argentinos sean crédulos lectores de los infundios elaborados, concienzudamente, en los laboratorios de la Agencia Central de Inteligencia. Esta palabra, fascinante de por sí, los ha ofuscado, pues pertenecen ustedes a la "intelligentsia" de la oligarquía, o sea al despotismo ilustrado, y hallan inteligente lo que ese organismo de perversión espiritual prepara como barbitúricos para los esclavos libres del fascismo imperialista. [76]

The essayist's commitment to the concept of a culture that has deep roots in the traditions of the people, is, as we have seen, central to his whole conception of literature and its functions. The antithesis

---

[74] The matter of his Cuban citizenship is reported as a fact in "Posición del escritor E. Martínez Estrada," *La Nación* (16th Jul., 1961), and in a letter to David Tiefenberg dated 10 August, 1961, the essayist affirms his Argentine citizenship. See Ezequiel Martínez Estrada, *En Cuba y al servicio de la Revolución Cubana* (La Habana: Ediciones Unión/Ensayo), p. 90.

[75] "Tanto aquellos trabajos en México como los que realizo ahora en Cuba, han sido hechos con absoluta libertad de opinión, ajustándome al estudio imparcial de los hechos históricos y a las conclusiones que a mi juicio se infieren lógicamente de ellos... En México y aquí he tenido completa libertad en la ordenación de las piezas documentales a mi criterio de mayor autoridad, y en la interpretación que con buena fe creo correcta." *En Cuba y al servicio de la Revolución Cubana*, p. 90.

[76] *Ibid.*, p. 97.

of this, alluded to above, was a firm rejection of the "intelligentsia"
and "literary élites." Yet the central problem remained: how to
reconcile service to the Revolution with intellectual integrity. Before
proceeding to how Martínez Estrada approached the problem, however, it is necessary to see his commitment to Cuba, not only in the
context of his being inspired by the events in Cuba but also in
the light of his fundamental commitment to the personality and work
of José Martí. Basically the essayist was convinced that this revolutionary, *par excellence,* had not received the attention that he merited
from his fellow Latin Americans, or rather, that to restrict Martí to
the status of a pre-Modernist poet was to do him a great injustice.
Martínez Estrada notes that Martí, like himself, exhibited a contempt
for the "cultura de fábrica," [77] and pauses to reflect that the liberty
of peoples — fundamental in the Cuban — has never appeared as a
literary theme in Latin American literature. [78] But it was Martí's
mammoth struggle on behalf of the people, the common people, their
liberty and their future, that struck a responsive chord — one of
many — in Martínez Estrada. Slowly, but relentlessly, it becomes apparent that Martí, in turn, had a liberating influence upon the essayist. [79] As we have noticed in our previous discussion of his views
on the concept of a popular culture, Martínez Estrada made — or
attempted to make — a distinction between "popular literature" and
"proletarian literature" or literature "para el pueblo, pero no proletaria." Such an affirmation not only presupposed an aesthetic position
but also a certain distance, an uneasiness perhaps, with the wider implications of the "cultura de masas." But when he re-discovers Martí
— Martí the patriot, the revolutionary — and his immense love for
the common people, this uneasiness discernibly subsides, and in this
way Martí frees the Argentinian from this tension that he had never
fully resolved:

---

[77] *Ibid.,* p. 128.

[78] *Ibid.,* p. 137.

[79] While not confirming unequivocally such a "liberation," Martínez Estrada strongly hints at virtually such a situation in the prologue to his *Martí:
el héroe y su acción revolucionaria* (México: Siglo XXI Editores, 1966), p. 1:

> Puedo decir que Martí se me reveló por sí mismo en su dimensión
> universal de mito, quiero decir de existencia paradigmática que
> condensa y depura las virtudes inherentes a la condición humana.

Martí considera la cultura como una manifestación especí-
fica de las sociedades organizadas y no como expresión de
cualidades personales y precarias, patrimonio de un esta-
mento o de una clase. Como para los etnólogos, a su juicio
la cultura es el estrato profundo de la psique ecuménica, lo
último que puede ser removido por la revolución que es un
sismo en ese terreno. Está en la raíz y es su alma, por eso
pertenece a los pueblos y no a las épocas ni a las escuelas,
que es lo que antes se enseñaba en los libros de historia de
las civilizaciones. [80]

Martínez Estrada, as can now be gathered, underwent a strong emotional experience in Cuba that affected many of his hitherto established attitudes. While it would be somewhat exaggerated to speak
in terms of a Damascusian experience, the stay in Cuba (1961-62)
caused some important changes in emphasis, as we have noted in the
above example. In an attempt to characterize these changes, we may
say that, in general they embodied a hardening or a consolidation
of previous attitudes that now pointed, much more so than could
previously be construed, to a semi-doctrinaire position. We can appreciate this from some of his later pronouncements on the role of
the intellectual in society:

De la copiosa literatura polémica que se ha derivado de esas
discusiones [sobre literatura socialista comprometida] a mi
juicio los documentos más valiosos para formar conciencia
clara de los deberes sociales del intelectual, respetando la
libertad de expresión que es indispensable, son las interven-
ciones en los foros de los primeros ministros de Cuba y de
China, Fidel Castro y Mao Tse Tung. Ambos estadistas de-
mostraron haber entendido a fondo el problema de la cultura
como elemento vital y esencial de la sociedad, poniendo entre
paréntesis, como es debido, los aspectos formales y técnicos,

---

[80] *Ibid.*, p. 128. If one accepts the thesis of a rather vociferous *peronista*,
Martínez Estrada — or rather the Martínez Estrada of *¿Qué es esto?* — was
possessed of a very fundamental antipopulism, a view, as we have pointed
out, that is exaggerated not so much in its basic premise but in its scope of
application. See Agustín Ferraris, *Pido la palabra: respondiendo a Ezequiel
Martínez Estrada, Mario Amadeo y Ernesto Sábato* (Buenos Aires: Editorial
Capricornio, 1957), pp. 5-18. In a later essay, moreover, there is ample evidence of how Martínez Estrada had little patience with those educators who
equated ignorance with stupidity when treating the problems of mass education. See *Análisis funcional de la cultura* (La Habana: Ministerio de Educación y Casa de las Américas, 1960), pp. 91-100.

temperamentales y ideológicos, que competen más al creador que a su obra... Fidel Castro y Mao Tse Tung no
pensaron en una cultura abstracta, de gabinete y definicio-
nes, sino en una cultura viviente y concreta, de obras y va-
lores; ni en una sociedad de sociólogos, sino viva y concreta. [81]

Clearly there is a striving here, begun, as we have seen, before the
Cuban experience, for a *functional* conception of culture, as opposed
to the culture of the "intelligentsia" but the words "libertad de expresión" are important in that there is a clear residue, in this change
of emphasis, of his previously expressed opinion concerning intellectual integrity, which, implicitly, he sees endangered by a too-
doctrinaire interpretation of "literatura comprometida." For all the
appearance of assurance, Martínez Estrada (the praise of the socialist
leaders, etc.) was unable to make a full reconciliation of socialist
cultural thinking and his own, very deep awareness of the writer's
role in society and the unalienable right to self-expression; the antithesis between commitment and integrity was never fully resolved
by the essayist. [82]

---

[81] *Ibid.*, pp. 138-139.

[82] Despite his frequent attempts to arrive at a coherent synthesis of the
writer's personal, intellectual integrity and a sense of mission towards the people, that is, a concrete sense of a social role, they all display an uneasiness
which was born, no doubt, from a strong desire to avoid the twin aberrations
of socialist realism and the intelligentsia. Even as late as *Análisis funcional
de la cultura* — which won the Cuban Casa de las Américas prize in 1960 —
the difficult balance is still evident:

> La tarea del escritor ha de ser, pues, conforme a su misión y
> deber, llevar al pueblo una obra por decirlo así aristocrática, como
> las grandes culturas populares de Grecia y Roma sin bastardear el
> principio de la democracia social y de los prejuicios de los instruc-
> tores de cuartel y de los líderes de partido (p. 75).

CHAPTER IV

## THE RADICALIZATION OF THE CUBAN PERIOD
## AND THE ENCOUNTER WITH JOSÉ MARTÍ

DESPITE THE TITLES of many of his earlier essays — *Radiografía de
la pampa, Ensayo de interpretación de la vida argentina* (the subtitle
to *Muerte y transfiguración de Martín Fierro*) — there is ample evidence to point to a fundamentally American preoccupation behind
the more obvious Argentinian applications of Martínez Estrada's
meditations and imprecations. Moreover, if we stop to consider the
essayist's whole career in terms of a personal odyssey, in terms of a
strongly American awareness, then we are able to discern a recognizable line of development that begins with *Radiografía de la pampa*
and finds its climax in *Diferencias y semejanzas entre los países de
la América Latina* and the work on José Martí. Apart from the interest that such a focus engenders, it is important in another sense.
The years in Cuba (1960-62) in this light, can then be conceived as
a climax to the whole of the essayist's work instead of a somewhat
idiosyncratic hiatus ascribed to an encroaching senility, as some critics
virtually suggested. [1]

---

[1] This should not necessarily be taken as indicative of bad faith on the
part of critics, although there were some obvious examples. The opinion poll
taken by the *porteña* magazine *Atlántida*, 1123 (Sept., 1960) and entitled
"Martínez Estrada y el país" attempted to survey the opinions of some
leading Argentine intellectuals on the topic of the essayist's self-imposed
exile in México — and eventually Cuba — and offers a good case in point.
Jorge Luis Borges, for example, stated that Martínez Estrada, rather melo-
dramatically, saw himself given a choice between humiliation, suicide and
exile. Manuel Gálvez, together with Ernesto Sábato publicly declared themselves *enemistados* with the essayist. Particularly in bad taste is the view of

From the beginning, then, Martínez Estrada harboured no illusions about Argentina constituting a more or less "pure" European
enclave in an otherwise barbarous continent, as many of his com-
patriots would conceive it. [2] In *Radiografía de la pampa*, for example,
the reader is soon aware except in some specific instances (such as
the complex engendered by the Conquistador's failure to find an *El
Dorado* in the River Plate region — which was not the case in Mexico
or Peru) that the essay is essentially an American treatise. Even
further, it is occasionally apparent — in instances such as the description of the development of the *hijo humillado* complex, which
was the psychological weight of the *mestizaje* continued down the
centuries — that certain phenomena dealt with had really much more
application in other American countries of a more varied racial composition than Argentina, to say nothing of the modalities of the whole
colonial experience itself in the continent. Similarly, as we shall
consider later, the personal odyssey we have alluded to can also be
conceived, in parallel fashion, as the progressive radicalization of
Martínez Estrada.

Starting with *Radiografía de la pampa*, then, one can immediately
appreciate the American application of much of the essayist's vital
themes. Occasionally it manifests itself by implication:

> Ni antes ni después el pueblo que flotaba en las colonias
> tenía que ver con el territorio. Un pueblo vertido dentro de
> inconmensurables perímetros, que no se han ampliado pro-
> gresivamente por exosmosis, cediendo al crecimiento en área
> según el crecimiento en número y en energía, no puede
> tener fuerza ni unidad. Queda ondeando en sus términos, si

---

Delmiro Saenz that the author was indulging in a gigantic lie. On the other
hand, the impartial observer cannot help but suspect that in many of the
basic attitudes and public statements that he made, Martínez Estrada left
himself exposed to a lot of adverse criticism. On page 23 of the same issue
of *Atlántida*, in a speech conceived as a farewell to Argentina he declared:
"Adiós, opulenta nación de ganados y mieses, que honras con magnificiencia
y estrépito de clarines a tus héroes y mártires muertos en el destierro." As
can readily be appreciated, such statements could well be construed as indicative of a mental or psychological abstraction from the country even prior to
the essayist's physical absence.

[2] As we have noted in a previous chapter, essayist José Edmundo Clemente espoused a rather rigid "European" position with respect to the authentic traditions of Argentina, as did Víctor Massuh, in rejecting the "telluric"
concept of America, although to a somewhat lesser extent.

el territorio ha sido originariamente mucho mayor que el pueblo ... No tiene forma, porque no tiene unidad interior; habrá crecido para ocupar hasta el borde su recipiente, y todo lo que dentro ocurra se parecerá más a la aglomeración de un pólipero que a la gestación de un cuerpo en el vientre de la madre. Aislarse y contemplarse con recelo es el gran mal de la soledad y de la ignorancia, y la clave para interpretar los enigmas de Suramérica. [3]

The final lines of the above clearly express an American preoccupation, but it is equally evident that the people involved is that of the whole continent and that the solitude engendered by the immense geographical dimensions could also be found in Brazil, Peru or Venezuela. On other occasions there can be no doubt of the main focus of the essayist's attention:

Suramérica es todavía un episodio subsidiario de Europa, pero tiene un alma americana, cerrada, muda, solitaria. Su historia de fuste se limita a unas cuantas páginas de estadística, y no ha pensado aún cómo sepultar a los muertos en la tierra de nadie, que luchan constantemente contra lo extranjero y quieren quedarse solos con su nada. [4]

Similarly, the work of that most Argentinian of Argentinians — Domingo Faustino Sarmiento — in many respects is seen by Martínez Estrada to relate to many continental situations:

Facundo es una autobiografía, y una sociología, una obra literaria y un fragmento de historia, una acusación de defensa de los pobres y ausentes y un capítulo de la antropología americana. También era una tentativa para la investigación de la historia más que una simple galería de personajes y pintura de ambiente ... [5]

The above citation, from Sarmiento, if compared with the previous one can attest to a change in tone, if not to a change in attitude, from the basic premise of Radiografía de la pampa. Martínez Estrada's fundamental conviction that the Conquista was nothing less than a

---

[3] Ezequiel Martínez Estrada, Radiografía de la pampa, p. 79.
[4] Ibid., p. 92.
[5] Ezequiel Martínez Estrada, Sarmiento, p. 146. For a more strictly Argentinian application of Sarmiento's attitudes, see Ezequiel Martínez Estrada, Los invariantes históricos en el Facundo (Buenos Aires: Viau, 1947).

wholesale pillage and virtually a historical leap into a primitive and primordial past[6] never really left him, even admitting changes in tone and expression, and as late as his *Diferencias y semejanzas entre los países de la América Latina* (1962) he denounces the conquest of America as nothing less than a mere financial adventure and that money was the ultimate *sine qua non*.[7] Accordingly, the critic occasionally encounters considerable difficulty in reconciling the defence — even if a very rare defence — of the Mother Country, with the above views of its achievements, or "non-achievements" as the consensus of the essayist's opinions would have it in Latin America:

> La obra y la vida de Sarmiento, pues, son una crítica a la conquista y a la colonización de España en América, pero ¿qué pueblo, aun los más avanzados en la cultura y en la civilización estarían exentos de graves culpas si se los enjuiciara con el mismo rigor? Italia, Alemania, Francia, Inglaterra tienen en sus historias páginas no menos sombrías y abyectas que España. El progreso de las naciones y los pueblos se realiza a través de monstruosas infamias, de todo género de injusticias y brutalidades, y si los historiadores no seleccionaran con un arte que participa tanto del género de la historia como de la perfidia, todos merecerían una condenación no menos severa a los ojos del filósofo.[8]

*An increasing chauvinism*

Statements of this type are indeed rare in the span of the essayist's work and certainly we may consider as much more typical the previous citations from *Radiografía* and other works, above. However, even within this line of mistrust and rejection of Spain and above all, of the inheritance, cultural and political, that it bequeathed to America, the critic gradually discerns a development, in the sense

---

[6] "Cada día de navegación, las carabelas desandaron [*sic*] cien años," *Radiografía de la pampa*, p. 75.

[7] "La conquista de América se hizo con el *in hoc signo vincit* del dinero, o sea de la riqueza representada por él. Tanto la empresa de los conquistadores y colonizadores, acaparando las tierras y obligando al indígena y al negro a trabajos de esclavitud, cuanto los filibusteros y contrabandistas, no tuvieron otra finalidad que la de enriquecerse por la violencia y a ultranza." Ezequiel Martínez Estrada, *Diferencia y semejanzas entre los países de la América Latina* (México: Escuela Nacional de Ciencias Políticas y Sociales, 1962), p. 324.

[8] Ezequiel Martínez Estrada, *Sarmiento*, p. 198.

of an increasing arbitrariness that is lacking in the earlier discussions of America in the essayist's work and which reaches a high point in *La poesía afro-cubana de Nicolás Guillén* (1966):

> América no significa nada para España, menos de lo que España significa para nosotros; y muchísimo menos de lo que le significan Europa, la ciencia y la filosofía contemporáneas, la música y el teatro. Sus filósofos, sus ensayistas; casi sin novelistas y cuentistas, sin dramaturgos y con sólo ocho poetas realmente grandes — Valle Inclán, Jiménez, Machado, García Lorca, Díez-Canedo, Pedro Salinas, Miguel Hernández, Rafael Alberti —, muchos agrupados en cofradías o peñas, ¿qué pueden representar para España, Guillén, Vallejo, Neruda, Pedroni, A. Eloy Blanco? No tiene modo de incorporarlos siquiera a la historia de la poesía castellana, ni de considerarlos pertenecientes a la misma área de cultura. [9]

And even earlier along this course of what is virtually a rampant cultural chauvinism, Martínez Estrada felt constrained to issue some rather gratuitous remarks concerning relations between Spaniards and Americans that the critic has difficulty in incorporating into any effort for a greater understanding of Nicolás Guillén:

> Lo que nos separa y nos separará por muchas décadas a los americanos y a los españoles es lo mismo que los separa a ellos entre sí: de una parte, los que son amantes de la libertad y refactarios a cualquier dogma de sumisión y teoría; de otra parte, los que son amantes de esclavizar, atemorizar y señorear, sea por las armas o por el pensamiento. [10]

*The increasing radicalization*

The harshness of this simplistic approach is not without antecedents in the work of Martínez Estrada, [11] but at least the critic had no difficulty in appreciating the point or what is more important, the appositeness of such judgements. It is here — in the attempt to motivate, to some extent at least, the many examples of an apparently

---

[9] Ezequiel Martínez Estrada, *La poesía afrocubana de Nicolás Guillén* (Montevideo: Editorial Arca, 1966), p. 33.

[10] *Ibid.*, p. 31.

[11] Most of his polemical essays include a large measure of "anathemas" cast at various sectors of society. For the best examples of this, see *Cuadrante del pampero* (1956) and *Exhortaciones* (1957).

curious arbitrariness, in tone and content, of many of the nine essays associated with the "American" period of Martínez Estrada [12] — that one approaches the central problems of the latter part of his life. We have noticed in the previous chapter how the essayist put forward Fidel Castro and Mao Tse Tung as leading authorities on the role that writers and intellectuals ought to adopt in society, and there can be no doubt that in the light, not only of his own literary creation, but also in that of his various literary biographies, [13] such a judgement appears quite out of character. At the same time, and in the face of the speculation resulting from such incongruities, it must be stated that there is no reason to doubt the sincerity of such affirmations and that Martínez Estrada was emphatically not a person to be bought or sold, nor to dishonestly enlist his services in favour of anything. We have already suggested above that the essayist's career may be measured in terms of a parallel development of a progressive "americanization" and radicalization. We have given examples of how both tendencies existed in the essayist long before the Cuban period, and it would appear irrefutable that these tendencies received considerable additional fertilization within the whole phenomenon of the Cuban Revolution. A good example of how such a radicalization (and as regards the Cuban Revolution, a "cubanization") carried over into areas which were not political in a strictly ideological sense, is the following view of Martí which clearly appears modelled upon the "official" view of the patriot in present-day Cuba:

> El nuevo derecho que anuncia Martí, es el derecho corporativo, derecho sindical y social. El derecho para consagrar la posesión de bienes por el más fuerte y el más astuto, no tenía razón de ser, pues estos no lo necesitaban siéndoles privativo el uso de la fuerza. El derecho aparece cuando se tiene conciencia de que es necesario compensar una clase de privile-

---

[12] *Familia de Martí* (1962), *Diferencias y semejanzas entre los países de América Latina* (1962), *El verdadero cuento del Tío Sam* (1963), *En Cuba y al servicio de la Revolución Cubana* (1963), *El nuevo mundo, la isla de Utopía y la isla de Cuba* (1963), *Antología* (1964), *La poesía afrocubana de Nicolás Guillén* (1966), *Martí: el héroe y su acción revolucionaria* (1966) and *Martí revolucionario* (1967). *Mi experiencia cubana* (1965) is a re-issue of *En Cuba*, above.

[13] Consider, for example, *Realidad y fantasía en Balzac* (1964), *Heraldos de la verdad* (1958) and *En torno a Kafka* (1967).

gios con otra, un razón de poseer y detentar con otra de mayor legitimidad. [14]

On the other hand, it is equally unquestionable that Martínez Estrada was in a very favourable situation, morally and artistically, and above all with particular regard to his morale, as regards his susceptibility to the invitations he received from the Mexican magazine *Cuadernos americanos* and the Cuban magazine *Casa de las Américas* in 1960 and 1961, respectively. Even prior to the essayist's famous farewell speech in Mexico in 1960, [15] there was abundant evidence to attest that his disenchantment with Argentina was reaching an intolerable level. In an article of late 1959 entitled "Lectura de la actualidad argentina," he wrote:

> Tanto la naturaleza de nuestros males materiales como la índole de nuestros vicios morales son endémicos. Todas las crisis se configuran por una misma etiología y presentan idénticos síntomas. La terapéutica, en síntesis, consiste en dejar hacer a la naturaleza, que providencialmente repone con cada cosecha y cada cría los bienes que se sustraen... Nuestro pueblo no tiene ningún privilegio sobre otros mejor organizados y con mayor espíritu de solidaridad que fueron y son abatidos. No ha sido educado para la libertad; y su formación cosmopolita ha hecho de él una masa boyante, sin arraigo en la tierra, sin ideales por los cuales vale la pena vivir y morir. [16]

Two years later, and in Cuba, he was to describe in more poignant terms the depth of his despair with his life-long efforts to bring his country to a consciousness of its fundamental malaise:

> Hay cosas que he podido hacer y cosas que no pude y que jamás haré. Entre ellos unirme a los que crían sebo allí donde yo he quemado mi vida en una hoguera de pasión encendida para alumbrar un camino en la noche, pero que hasta ahora sólo ha dado humo y cenizas. [17]

---

[14] Ezequiel Martínez Estrada, *Martí revolucionario*, Vol. I, one volume published. (La Habana: Casa de las Américas, 1967), p. 121.

[15] Ezequiel Martínez Estrada, "Un año más de *Cuadernos Americanos*," *Cuadernos Americanos*, v. 109, n. 2 (March-April, 1960), pp. 51-55.

[16] Ezequiel Martínez Estrada, "Lectura de la actualidad argentina," *Cuadernos Americanos*, 6, 107 (Nov.-Dec., 1959), pp. 13-16.

[17] Ezequiel Martínez Estrada, *En Cuba y al servicio de la Revolución Cubana*, p. 93. Although this volume was published in 1963, the quotation

It is in this context, then, that the critic is obliged to attempt an interpretation of the increasingly iconoclastic (the proper adjective is most probably, "revolutionary") tone of much of the content of the later essays. The self-imposed exile in Mexico and Cuba now appears as a refuge and a solace, even a relief from the atmosphere in his own country. Yet it would constitute an exaggeration to visualize such an atmosphere — around the end of 1959 — as one of heated controversy and debate with regard to the work of Martínez Estrada. It becomes evident to the critic, that, reading between the lines — principally of the essayist's correspondence — that the deep frustration of the period came not so much from feelings reflective of a persecution complex but rather quite the opposite: that the true frustration arose from a fundamental *neglect* of his work, and this, to any artist, is most probably the final discouragement. This can be adequately brought out by a letter from Martínez Estrada, soon after his arrival in Mexico, to Carlos Albarracín Sarmiento:

> Estamos en México y pienso quedarme, si es posible, el resto de mis días. Aquí me quieren y me respetan los desconocidos, y allá sólo mis fieles amigos de antaño. Estoy cansado de trabajar en una empresa imposible, contribuyendo a que se diga que en la Argentina hay gente de valer, pero no que se los obliga a ir a ganarse el pan en el extranjero. [18]

The final two lines of this clearly hint at a lip-service paid to the essayist's work, while the real implications of what he considered his *labor* remained effectively ignored. And while the critic must be aware of the possibility, in writings of this type — the self-justificatory type of literature — of a pathological sensitivity to criticism of any kind, there is also evidence, some years prior to his exile, that Martínez Estrada did not want to be thought of as "persecuted" by society, [19] nor that he rejected criticism out of hand. [20]

---

is taken from one of the items included, entitled, "Mensaje de la Liga Argentina por los Derechos del Hombre ante la Conferencia latinoamericana por la soberanía nacional, la emancipación económica y la paz" and dates from 1961.

[18] Carlos Adam, *Bibliografía y documentos de Ezequiel Martínez Estrada*, p. 175. The letter is dated 10th Dec., 1959.

[19] In a letter to Hugo Rodríguez Urruty (18th Dec., 1957), Martínez Estrada wrote: "Mi amigo: no me gustaría que me considerara usted un perseguido, ni mucho menos. Mis dos últimos libros de polémica me han

Psychologically, then, it would appear that the invitations to Mexico and Cuba, constituting as they did a virtual re-call to arms, this time in a wider, American service, came at the correct moment, and in the context of his advocacy of Fidel Castro and Mao Tse Tung involved important changes of emphasis, which are best seen in his work on José Martí and in *Diferencias y semejanzas entre los países de la América Latina.*

Changes of emphasis, yes, but not fundamental departures from established positions. With regard to the increased radicalization of the essayist under the influence of the Cuban experience, it may be safely affirmed that, as in the case of earlier Americanist attitudes on the part of the essayist, it, too, had clear antecedents in his work. As early as 1947, in an article entitled "Imperialismo y buena vecindad," Martínez Estrada traced the nefarious relationship, as he saw it, between fascism and capitalism:

> Creó el fascismo el clima y la psicosis para el dominio del mundo, que no había sabido crear el capitalismo, y en ese sentido lo perfeccionó ... si el fascismo es la etapa ulterior del imperialismo económico, el imperialismo es su antecedente natural, y ninguno de los dos puede ser juzgado sino dentro de una concepción filosófica, más amplia que los abarque y los identifique. [21]

Evidently there is no great attempt at any "dialectical" interpretation here, and while there is the implicit criticism of the United States in the very title ("Good Neighbour"), there is little to lead the critic to suppose that such radicalism was anything other than the rather commonplace expression, inevitably Leftist, of the average politically unaligned Latin American intellectual. Nonetheless, there is evidence in the same article of a recurring theme in the essayist's later radical

---

traído amargos sinsabores, y necesito un poco de tiempo para reparar mis fuerzas." Carlos Adam, *op. cit.*, p. 186.

[20] In a letter to Arnaldo Orfila Reynal (30th May, 1947), for example, the essayist's reaction to a recent criticism of his *Sarmiento* by Carlos Alberto Erro, another famous Argentine essayist ["Un Sarmiento ahistórico," *Realidad* (Buenos Aires), v. I, no. 2 (March-April, 1947), pp. 267-275.], displays a clear firmness of opinion, but certainly no dogmatic rejection of Erro's views. See Carlos Adam, *op. cit.*, p. 153.

[21] Ezequiel Martínez Estrada, "Imperialismo y buena vecindad," [part of *a mesa rodante* under this title], *Cuadernos Americanos*, 5, XXXV (Sept.-Oct., 1947), pp. 81-82.

development: an obsession with the role of the Jesuit Order in Latin America, which Martínez Estrada saw as fundamentally Fascist, and the instigator of certain mental and social traits that have conditioned the ways of thinking of so many people. Fundamentally, he held the Jesuits personally responsible for creating a psychosis — notably in Paraguay — for the better efficiency of Spain's colonial enterprise in America; in other words, that the Jesuit order constituted the ideological arm, as it were, of the Conquest. And later he saw the British West Indies Company as basically perfecting the Jesuit economic and social policies, [22] and affirming that the Order was one of the biggest shareholders in the International Bank in Brussels. [23]

This in fact brings us to an approximation of the characteristics of this later radicalization of Martínez Estrada. On the one hand it is born of a broadening and widening of an extra-Argentine situation that promised a definite attempt on the part of the essayist to reach beyond himself; on the other hand this process of radicalization in many instances became reduced to the level of a rather crude propaganda in favour of the Cuban régime, and also to the level of a political naivety that the critic has difficulty in reconciling with the depth and sophistication of earlier pronouncements. His two works of 1963 offer striking examples of this, *El verdadero cuento del Tío Sam* and *En Cuba y al servicio de la Revolución Cubana,* the former constituting nothing more than a rather crude propagandistic tract. Commenting, in the second work, on the Cuban Revolution, the essayist blandly states:

> En fin, se trata de aceptar la marcha incontenible de la civilización o tomar partido por las fuerzas que han demorado y ensangrentado la historia de la humanidad. [24]

and slightly later he adds,

> Aunque no gobernada [la Argentina] por caudillos de látigo y sargentos de péñola, sí lo ha sido por camarillas oligárquicas o por lacayos sin librea que pusieron sus riquezas naturales y el trabajo de sus compatriotas en manos de sus enemigos más peligrosos, las buenas naciones benefactoras...

---

[22] *Diferencias y semejanzas entre los países de la América Latina,* p. 236.
[23] *Ibid.,* p. 200.
[24] *En Cuba y al servicio de la Revolución Cubana,* p. 47.

Expongo esta situación meramente a título ilustrativo, porque quiero significar que la libertad o soberanía de los pueblos americanos se divide en dos categorías, según los grupos de naciones que no la disfrutan: el que sabe que le ha sido usurpado, y el que lo ignora. [25]

While the tone of such simplistic affirmations can find certain antecedents in part of Martínez Estrada's earlier "polemical" literature, [26] the *content* of the above "disquisitions" lead the critic to see an implicit abandonment of sophistication, which, if not tantamount to the abandonment of his intellect, is at least an affirmation of a primitivism [27] that appears quite untypical of the author of *Radiografía de la pampa, Muerte y transfiguración de Martín Fierro, Sarmiento*, etc.

## The disciple of the maestro

Side by side, in a type of parallel development to the markedly primitive radicalization of Martínez Estrada, as a result of his Cuban experience, ran that of a personal liberation, an opening out from years of what was national introspection, the turning in upon oneself, as a result of his experience of Martí. To say that Martínez Estrada went a great way towards finding himself through his encounter with Martí would be to affirm some type of "conversion" that we have earlier discounted. Nonetheless, there can be no doubt that the Cuban patriot produced in the Argentinian a reaction as fundamental as Sarmiento, in an ideological sense, and as far-reaching as Horacio

---

[25] *Ibid.*, pp. 59-60.

[26] All of the essays published in 1956 and 1957, including *El hermano Quiroga*, reveal the depth of the author's apocalyptic sense of the aberrations of much of Argentine institutional life.

[27] In a perceptive article, Peter G. Earle speaks in terms of a *primitivismo sobreviviente* in Martínez Estrada, in the sense that the essayist saw the essential afflictions of humanity in man himself, and this vision, accordingly, influenced all his work. While one can find some evidence for such a focus of the essayist's work (as Earle does, particularly with reference to the short stories of the author) the critic is still faced with the problem of reconciling such a view with the undeniable enthusiasm with which Martínez Estrada undertook his Cuban enterprises. Moreover, as we have already suggested, it was precisely the study — the encounter — with José Martí that, during a crucial time in his life, imbued him with a sense of human solidarity and optimism, that he had rarely experienced previously. See Peter G. Earle, "El perspectivismo narrativo de Martínez Estrada," *La Nación*, 6th July, 1969.

Quiroga, in a personal, human sense. Even a cursory reading of his works on Martí reveals glimpses of how the Cuban seemed to fulfill, to embody, the best qualities of American man — and for that matter — all men:

> El instinto de la dignidad humana tanto como el sentimiento entrañable de la justicia determinan su actitud revolucionaria, y lo repite frecuentemente en diferentes tonos y circunstancias, lo cual inviste a su misión libertadora de una responsabilidad que no es común en los teóricos puramente racionalistas partidarios de la lucha armada por la libertad..
> Concretamente, Martí fue un revolucionario para lograr un ideal más que un fin concreto, el de la independencia de Cuba y Puerto Rico, la de la América sometida y la de todos los pueblos tratados injustamente con despotismo y humillación. [28]

Martí, as it were, was transfigured by the need to pursue and realize this ideal, so much so that even his family did not understand that he was "accionado, poseído por una divinidad terrible." [29] In the eyes of Martínez Estrada, then, José Martí is lifted above and beyond the purely Carribean implications of his life's work [30] to become the Revolutionary Supreme, the Redeemer, and it is this universalist aspect of Martí, among others, that is irresistible for the Argentine essayist. In a passage rather moving for its relevance to Martínez Estrada's own life experiences one can appreciate the extent of the Cuban's appeal:

> ¿Qué motivos pueden determinar a alguien a asumir la representación de una comunidad, inclusive el pueblo de un país, para exigir en su nombre un cambio de la estructura social, una revolución? El mandato no existe, la representación es cuestionable, acaso la mayoría de los individuos ignoran la existencia y la representación que ese alguien invoca. Sólo un gran ideal, una fe fanática puede decirlo... No vivimos razonando nuestros actos sino dentro de una línea de conducta y de un modo de ser y de actuar que rige cada uno y todos nuestros actos. Tampoco vivimos por entero para

---

[28] Ezequiel Martínez Estrada, *Martí: el héroe y su acción revolucionaria* (México: Siglo XXI Editores, 1966), pp. 10-11.

[29] Ezequiel Martínez Estrada, *Familia de Martí* (La Habana: Casa de las Américas, 1962), p. 12.

[30] *Martí: el héroe y su acción revolucionaria,* p. 138.

nosotros, sino, en gran parte, para los demás, no siempre
para nuestro bien sino para el ajeno y para la felicidad de
los otros. Así piensan los redentores y los revolucionarios. [31]

Yet this fundamental, essential attraction to the life and personality
of Martí on the part of Martínez Estrada was in no way an escape
from the reality of Argentina. Far from isolating him from a "dis-
agreeable" milieu, the immense qualities that he saw in Martí only
served to confirm him in his previous diagnosis of his country's ills,
or rather of the correctness of his desire to expose them. Not long
after his return to Bahía Blanca in 1963, the essayist replied to the
question, put to him earlier, concerning the continuing relevance of
*Radiografía de la pampa*:

> Sí; creo que, a decir verdad, todavía no ha adquirido su
> total vigencia (ni mucho menos), pues para ello se requiere
> adquirir conciencia de la anatomía y fisiología del país, y no
> sólo de su mapa. Hasta hoy los hechos han ido poniendo de
> relieve zonas que se perciben confusamente en razón de no
> tenerse visión cabal del conjunto... en tanto la historia ar-
> gentina obedezca a las mismas fuerzas modeladoras del pa-
> sado; en tanto no se renueve de raíz el instrumental que se
> maneja en el hacer histórico de cada día, y las mismas manos
> con la misma técnica elaboren la misma materia prima, no
> habrán cambiado los elementos constituyentes de la realidad,
> ni la vigencia del diagnóstico, si en su momento fue exacto
> (o aproximadamente). [32]

Clearly, then, Martínez Estrada did not return from Cuba "trans-
formed," but that some degree of change occurred may be inferred
from the very tone of the above, and if we recall the moral situation
of the essayist before he left for his self-imposed exile, we cannot
dismiss such a tone as merely coming from that serenity which old
age regularly brings with it. Moreover, there is also evidence available
to point to a realization in Martínez Estrada that his work on Martí
was in fact to be the crowning achievement of his life, and that the
final months of his life were marked by the obsession that he might
die before seeing his *Martí revolucionario* in print. In a letter to
Roberto Fernández Retamar on 20th March, 1964, he wrote:

---

[31] *Ibid.,* pp. 11-12.
[32] Carlos Adam, *Bibliografía y documentos de Ezequiel Martínez Estrada*,
pp. 200-211. The letter is to Dr. Julio Sager, and dated 8th Nov., 1963.

A mi juicio, es lo mejor (en calidad y en fervor) que yo he producido ... Yo estoy absolutamente seguro del pensamiento social y político de Martí; pero no creo que esa "vera efigie", como las otras, sea reconocida como auténtica. Si nos mostrasen fotografías de Moisés, Cristo y Mahoma, nos horrorizaríamos. Puedo mandar capítulos, anticipadamente, para discutir y ganar tiempo. Me horroriza pensar que puedo morir sin ver impresa esa obra. [33]

And three months later, in correspondence again to Roberto Fernández Retamar, he wrote:

Los cuatro últimos años de mi vida consagrados a Martí han sido para mí el tiempo mejor aprovechado. Me he purificado y he aprendido a estimar la sabiduría, la santidad, el heroísmo, la abnegación, todos los tributos esencialmente humanos en él ... Piense en la edición en Montevideo. ¿No se demorará todo? ¿No se crearán nuevas dificultades? Quiero ver mi obra antes de irme. [34]

The allusion to "irme" is a premonition of his impending death, [35] and he in fact died six months later, without seeing his *Martí revolucionario* in print, which was not to be published until 1967. Martínez Estrada had studied Martí as early as 1946, [36] but the whole personality of Martí was not to take hold of him until the Cuban experience, and there can be little doubt that the very recent phenomenon of the Cuban Revolution, the anti-North American campaign, contributed to give the life-long struggle of Martí a new

---

[33] Roberto Fernández Retamar, "Razón de homenaje," *Casa de las Américas,* 33 (Nov.-Dec., 1965), p. 14.

[34] *Ibid.,* p. 12. Not everything was quite as pleasant as this, however. Despite the invitation of the Casa de las Américas to work in Cuba, the essayist himself records that his initial experience with Cuba was not altogether a source of satisfaction. See the correspondence with Samuel Feijóo and Roberto Fernández Retamar (especially the letter to the latter dated May 3rd, 1960) in "Para un epistolario cubano de Don Ezequiel Martínez Estrada," *Islas,* Santa Clara, Cuba, 7, no. 2 (July-Sept., 1965), pp. 69-83.

[35] Martínez Estrada often talked of his own death in terms of a journey, and he frequently referred to it as "esperando el coche." See, for example, his letter to Carlos Adam (10th Nov., 1963), in Carlos Adam, *Bibliografía y documentos de Ezequiel Martínez Estrada,* p. 196.

[36] For example, see "Sarmiento y Martí," *Cuadernos Americanos,* 4 (July-Aug., 1946), pp. 197-214.

relevance, even if, as the essayist once observed, not even the Cubans had a proper understanding of the patriot. [37]

## Re-encounter with America

The other fundamental work to come from Martínez Estrada's Cuban period (it was actually partially prepared in Mexico) is the prodigious *Diferencias y semejanzas entre los países de la América Latina,* virtually a survey of the essential political, social and sociological reality in Latin America from the Conquest to the present day. Such a description is clearly reminiscent of *Radiografía de la pampa,* and in fact the real (and only) antecedent the work has in the long and varied path of Martínez Estrada's essay is indeed the 1933 work, if we conceive of "antecedent" in terms of a work with rather obvious continental applications. Yet, on closer examination, the critic readily discerns some fundamental differences, principally in tone, but also in content and conception. But so different is the tone that only a certain continuity of themes convinces, ultimately, that both works are of the same author. Inevitably, the whole phenomenon of the Conquest (which constituted the very cornerstone of *Radiografía de la pampa*) continues to be conceived in very condemnatory terms, but the critic cannot but notice how different in approach, how much more balanced (without losing any of its force of argument) are the essayist's descriptions in comparison with the work of almost thirty years previously:

> Es innegable que la Conquista sacó a los pueblos del estancamiento en que habían caído, agotadas las fuerzas dinámicas de superación y hasta de innovación, pues no puede negarse que se trataba de civilizaciones en decadencia. Empero, todas ellas, aún aquellas más alejadas del tronco étnico de las razas superiores, y del ejercicio de la vida social de alto nivel, conservaban sin mayor deterioro los códigos morales, de la industria privada y pública, la integridad del carácter, el honor o, si se prefiere, la honra que se había erigido en tribunal que castigaba sin indulgencia los delitos y las transgresiones que afectaban más que a la propiedad de bienes materiales, al patrimonio espiritual que rayaba en las alturas de lo sacro. Esas fueron las civilizaciones decaden-

---

[37] Letter to Carlos Adam (10th Nov., 1963), in Carlos Adam, *op. cit.,* p. 196.

tes que la Conquista sumergió en la miseria y la desespera-
ción; ésas las gentes que sometieron a la esclavitud, ultra-
jaron y dejaron esparcidas y desamparadas por todo el territorio dominado. Reivindicar una empresa predatoria llevada
a cabo por individuos en su mayoría desclasados, con saña
y codicia criminales, no puede favorecer ni a las naciones
que en esa aventura de malhechores participaron. Y menos
a los sentimientos piadosos, si se puede hablar así, nobilia-
rios, de raza, de magistraturas, estamentos o profesiones,
como se estila generalmente. [38]

Virtually, at this point in the development of Martínez Estrada's
essay, we can determine a synthesis of the historico/sociological work
(such as *Radiografía de la pampa, Muerte y transfiguración de Martín
Fierro*) and the more obviously polemical essays (*Cuadrante del pampero, Los invariantes históricos en el Facundo*, etc.). Certainly the
relentless incision, the marshalling of strongly emotive vocabulary, all
culminating in a burgeoning conclusion, point to some rather obvious
antecedents in his first incursion into the essay as a genre, but the
development is also equally obvious. Gone is the apocalyptic tone,
the incessant hurling of anathemas, the bottomless pessimism of *Radiografía de la pampa*. Admittedly, the denunciatory attitude still
accompanies the essayist, as evidenced in the above quotation, but
the distinct impression of a consciousness of other interpretations,
that the first four lines provide, is quite alien to the unrelieved iconoclasm of *Radiografía de la pampa*. [39] Literally absent, too, from the
1962 work is that veritable cornerstone of the earlier essay, "las fuerzas telúricas." Certainly there is the occasional mention of "la realidad
telúrica" [40] and the re-affirming of the general role played by geo-

---

[38] *Diferencias y semejanzas entre los países de la América Latina*, pp. 91-92.

[39] Asked on one occasion why he put no bibliographical notes or only
the briefest mention of sources in *Radiografía de la pampa*, Martínez Estrada
retorted that, "no puse citas ni hice transcripciones, porque la índole del
estudio no lo requería," adding that, "¿Estaba yo escribiendo un libro de
texto de sociología para ganarme unos pesos? ¿Escribía yo para lectores a
quienes había que explicarles historia, economía y política argentinas porque
las ignoraban? Mucho más tarde me di cuenta de que escribir sobre la verdadera Argentina, después del gran fraude nacional de los impostores, era
de Shangri-La." Letter to Dr. Julio Sager (8th Nov., 1963), in *Bibliografía
y documentos de Ezequiel Martínez Estrada*, p. 200.

[40] *Diferencias y semejanzas entre los países de la América Latina*, pp. 5-22.

graphical determinism in the forging of present-day Latin American societies, but there is a distinct lack of the mystical and mythical overtones of the 1933 work. [41]

### Martínez Estrada comprometido: the qualified fatalism

An even more striking difference between the two studies is the extent to which Martínez Estrada shows a willingness to grapple with the pragmatic, concrete difficulties of socio-economic problems, such as land reform, often with a fine sharpness of analysis:

> Las luchas por la distribución de la tierra entre quienes la trabajan o sobre cualquier otro principio de justicia distributiva, tiende a dar acceso a la pequeña propiedad, al campesino, pero de ninguna manera altera la estructura del sistema ni de los fundamentos jurídicos de la propiedad privada. Es un cambio de dueños, por expropiación o confiscación, que multiplica el número de propietarios, lo cual, en sí, no significa ni que el rendimiento de la explotación sea mayor ni mayor el beneficio del campesino. [42]

This type of detailed examination of a concrete sociological reality is extremely rare in *Radiografía de la pampa,* which preferred an attempt at the penetration of "la realidad profunda." Clearly the audience, or rather the readership, is more than the Argentinian public, as he goes on to discuss the meaning of the land for various Latin American countries. [43] At the same time, it gradually becomes evident that much of *Diferencias y semejanzas entre los países de la América Latina* is imbued with a certain prosyletization which manages to stop short of outright propaganda. It should be added that this is not indicative of any political alignment in the essayist, but rather that the willingness to enter into socio-economic controversies stems from the process of radicalization that we have referred to

---

[41] Consider, for example, the following:

> La inhistoricidad del paisaje, la enorme superioridad de la naturaleza sobre el habitante y de las fuerzas ambientes sobre la voluntad, hacen flotar el hecho [of the *Historia* of Mitre] con la particularidad de un gesto sin responsabilidad, sin geneología y sin prole. Técnicamente en estas regiones, no hubo nadie ni ocurrió nada. (*Radiografía de la pampa,* p. 91.)

[42] *Diferencias y semejanzas,* p. 231.

[43] *Ibid.,* p. 217.

previously, and in turn given particular impetus from the essayist's Cuban experience.

New *manías* are also to be observed, in comparison with the 1933 essay, and chief among them are the Jesuits, who, as we have already noticed, came to embody the more heinous aspects of the Conquest by virtually educating the Indians in what Martínez Estrada called Fascist principles. A rather strange development, however, in *Diferencias y semejanzas entre los países de la América Latina,* is the repeated insistence upon the greater social and geo-political proximity of Latin America to Africa as opposed to Europe, a curious position reminiscent of that of Spanish essayist Angel Ganivet with regard to Spain and Africa in his *Idearium español* (1897). Of course, from the contemporary perspective of third-worldism as an economic and geo-political concept, this is not new, but in 1962 no other major Latin America writer was seriously proposing it. Whatever the significance of the idea (Martínez Estrada did not pursue it elsewhere), the most probable target of it was Argentina, concretely those *porteño* intellectual circles, "more European than the Europeans," that had made cosmopolitanism a way of life, or an end in itself. Hence the radical nature of his affirmations:

> Es indispensable adoptar un nuevo criterio de valorizaciones, y admitir la relación tectónica y orgánica de América con África para aquilatar justamente la menos honda y cuasi superficial con Europa. No somos europeos sino en los abonos artificiales, o en las zonas corticales, mientras el resto del organismo responde al mismo sistema nutritivo y muscular del África. [44]

In the same way, the greater discipline, finer analytical method, and well-documented reasoning that characterizes *Diferencias y semejanzas entre los países de la América Latina* (as compared with *Radiografía de la pampa*) occasionally gives way to the reiteration of what are now established themes in the essays of Martínez Estrada. From time to time in this work the essayist appears to revert to the almost pathological need, as we have noted in earlier chapters, to *cantar las cuarenta,* to mercilessly pursue the implications of certain matters until the fibers of the true reality are laid bare. Naturally, the com-

---

[44] *Ibid.*, p. 23.

monplace, the so-called "sacred cows" of Latin American society are brought under attack. Hence, as we have seen, the essayist expressed a large degree of skepticism with that principal panacea of social improvement — Land Reform; similarly the whole episode of Independence from Spain was virtually the result of the selfish interest of a small minority, which had no consciousness whatsoever of the masses. [45] The innate distrust of the State that we have witnessed in previous essays and articles again is adumbrated, and again in terms of the incompatibility that Martínez Estrada saw between the State's twin functions of *instituto de fuerza* and *instituto de derecho*; and when the principal representatives of these institutions fail to coordinate their resources (inevitably as Martínez Estrada would say) within the body politic, then the result is institutional anarchy:

> Cualesquiera sean los elementos que componen su terreno histórico, la raíz de los conflictos sangrientos en la vida de casi todos los pueblos hispanoamericanos, está en la colisión de las grandes fuerzas humanas primarias incompatibles y antagónicas por naturaleza; la astucia y la vigilancia, o el civilismo legalista y el militarismo dictadorial... De ahí que el abogado y el militar encabecen, más que dos fórmulas antagónicas de organizar la sociedad, dos temperamentos o dos tipos específicos de humanidad. [46]

In this way, then, through a general conception of the State, Martínez Estrada returns to his frequent, earlier comments on the human condition as the real, ultimate source of man's miseries. Yet once again the critic is struck by the absence of the great apocalyptic denunciations that to a great extent characterized *Radiografía de la pampa*. Certainly the fatalism is still there, but the effort made by the essayist to reach a more "rational" fatalism, or a more readily communicable fatalism, bears fruit as a result of the greater degree of conceptual discipline that relies less upon his intuitive faculty. This is well brought out in some very perceptive remarks about the militarist temperament and his view of its role in Latin American societies:

> El militarismo es en Hispanoamérica tanto una organización de casta cuanto una ideología profesional; es un estamento

---

[45] *Ibid.*, pp. 374-375.
[46] *Ibid.*, p. 462.

nobiliario allí donde no existe nobleza, que supone represen-
tar cierta jerarquía sacerdotal, cuya misión teórica consiste
en velar por el mantenimiento de los órdenes jurídicos y éti-
cos de la sociedad. A medida que decaen las instituciones
laicas y cívicas se ha creído investido de potestades caris-
máticas, puesto que no emanan de ningún estatuto sino de
un don, de una merced providencial ... En lo propiamente
político, el militarismo es, a su vez, consecuencia más que
causa, de un hecho de muy vasto alcance: el de la debilidad
orgánica o estructural de la democracia en nuestro continente. [47]

The greater discipline in analysis, the positive sympathy with
which he evokes certain *caudillos*, however, gradually lead the critic
to realize, that despite the pessimism in many descriptions, the earlier
pessimism, the endemic fatalism of *Radiografía de la pampa* that had
been the root of the concept of the *pecado original* of the continent,
is not in evidence. The principal reason for this is not difficult to
formulate. Fundamentally, the 1962 work is, in its own way, a call
to arms. It is, as we have noted, often argumentative, frequently
indulging in a type of proselytism, with the particular aim of con-
vincing, of inciting the reader, if not quite to revolution, at least to
the acquisition of an incandescent consciousness of the depth, both
human and historical, of the miseries of Latin America. But — and
this is of vital importance — where *Radiografía de la pampa* exhuded
dark fatalism and discouraged (virtually) the search for effective
solutions (which in 1933 the author would have strongly eschewed),
*Diferencias y semejanzas entre los países de la América Latina* argues,
cajoles and invites. And this change in Martínez Estrada is hardly
less than remarkable. If our thesis is correct, the experiences of his
temporary exile, the first-hand experience of the Cuban Revolution,
and above all the encounter with the intense human attributes of
José Martí, combined to effect this change. Almost modelling himself
on the patriot, Martínez Estrada again and again exposes the op-
pression of the masses in the continent:

Muchas de las atrocidades y perversiones que se presentan
como normales en la vida política de Latinoamérica, respon-
den al criterio de que sus pueblos están integrados en gran
proporción por razas inferiores, y que carecen de aptitudes

---

[47] *Ibid.*, p. 431.

para la vida social pacífica y ordenada. El desprecio al bajo pueblo campesino por los líderes, cualquiera sea su orientación ideológica, que en el mejor de los casos han hecho de su defensa un capítulo de la piedad hacia el desdichado cuya suerte está equiparada a la del animal de trabajo. Sentir a sus pies una población miserable daba al caudillo, de espada o de toga, la sensación de una superioridad que lo habilitaba para emplear medios impropios de una sociedad efectivamente civilizada. Gobernaron como bárbaros con el pretexto de que gobernaban a bárbaros y que la barbarie era la regla del juego. [48]

The cold, relentless analysis of the 1933 essay stands in clear contrast to the human compassion of the above lines. In contrast, too, to the earlier iconoclasm, almost pontification, on the essential ills of Argentina and America at large, the 1962 work offers essentially the redemption of the Continent through a *toma de conciencia*, that is portrayed as the first step to an ultimate political action. One thing is thus certain: the *parricidas* of the generation of 1945 in Argentina — even Sebreli himself — would have found little to quarrel with in the Martínez Estrada of *Diferencias y semejanzas entre los países de la América Latina*. The writer they saw as "au dessus de la mêlée" [49] has his feet firmly on the ground, rooted in a deep commitment.

Similarly, Sebreli could hardly complain at the progressive radicalization of Martínez Estrada as evidenced by his *Análisis funcional de la cultura*, and least of all with the basic attempt to form a culture with popular roots and the dismissal of most of Western culture as "mechanized." [50] While it chronologically belongs to the American period in Martínez Estrada's essays (published in 1960, and winner of the Casa de las Américas Prize of the same year), strictly speaking it represents the development and maturing of life-long preoccupations rather than a direct result of his Cuban experience as in other works that that we have discussed above. The principal parallel to the work

---

[48] *Ibid.*, p. 379. Very few critics have given sufficient critical attention to the effect of the work of Martí on Martínez Estrada. An exception is a recent penetrating article by Alexander Coleman, "Martí y Martínez Estrada: Historia de una Simbiosis Espiritual," *Revista Iberoamericana*, vol. XLI, nos. 92-93 (July-Dec., 1975), 629-641.

[49] See Emir Rodríguez Monegal, *El juicio de los parricidas* for a good account of those who saw Martínez Estrada in this light.

[50] *Análisis funcional de la cultura*, pp. 106-107.

in the essayist's productions is undoubtedly *Para una revisión de las letras argentinas,* where, as we have noted, one of the principal themes was that of the evolution of a genuine popular culture, as opposed to a more "elitist" conception, typical of the "intelligentsia." In the 1960 work, however, the attempt to distinguish between "cultura popular" and "cultura de masa" is much more evident; moreover, capitalism is seen as the principal bulwark of the latter, which was ultimately based upon a law of supply and demand:

> La cultura dirigida, que es lo que se entiende por cultura de masas dosificada científicamente, tiene ese aspecto, esa misión: perpetuar indefinidamente un status de necesidades espirituales standard en vista del más bajo precio y del mayor consumo. [51]

But equally, all totalitarian systems, together with capitalist ones, inevitably enslave the individual, and on this level at least, the differences between the systems are negligible:

> El trabajo de cualquier clase, si social, era para Marx una mercancía que entraba en las combinaciones del producto de mercado; en consecuencia, todos los productos del ingenio y la habilidad humana, como las ciencias, las artes y las letras ... Nada quedaba fuera de ese universo cerrado, y un solo mapa de intereses, precios y ganancias cubría el territorio de las actividades humanas. [52]

To a certain extent, then, *Análisis funcional de la cultura* — coming before the more recent events of Cuban history — represents a hiatus in the gradual process of radicalization that we have discussed with reference to the essays of the Cuban or American period. As yet Martínez Estrada had not voiced his praise of Fidel Castro and Mao Tse Tung as theorists in questions of the writer's role in society; the principal preoccupation at this point is "esa enfermedad de la cultura enyugada en el servicio de intereses económicos," which is symptomatic of the sickness of world society. [53] Hence the essayist was alarmed at the way culture had become a political instrument, instead of politics having become a cultural instrument, as he wanted

---

[51] *Ibid.,* p. 130.
[52] *Ibid.,* pp. 122-123.
[53] *Ibid.,* p. 48.

it. Discounting a neo-*arielista* attempt at the re-implantation of ancient Greek culture in its authentic form as unfeasible, [54] Martínez Estrada proceeds to praise Mexico as the only country that has known how to exploit "su patrimonio humano" in the sense that it has learned to benefit from "las fuerzas indígenas como sostén de una nueva cultura americana y de un nuevo régimen de vida basado en la identidad de origen y destino." [55]

Most other countries, according to the essayist, had capitulated as it were, to the commercial interests of modern civilization and the resultant culture reflected not a true autochthonous reality but rather a spurious hybrid that was intimately related to the needs of the burgeoning industrial state. Putting the problem in a wider perspective, Martínez Estrada affirmed:

> El orbe industrializado necesitaba para su prosperidad, de elementos propios de otras esferas de la vida social extra-económica. Necesitaba un arte y una ciencia, una forma de espiritualidad adaptada a sus sistemas. En tanto las inclinaciones estéticas, las vocaciones científicas y las infinitas formas de manifestarse la psique exigían por su parte, sin regimentación ni unidad, la satisfacción de esa clase de necesidades, se ahondaba la discrepancia entre un modo de ser y otro, entre el cosmos ordenado y unificado de la maquinaria y el caos de las propias, personales de ser. [56]

The "cosmos ordenado y unificado de la maquinaria" is in fact fundamental to the concept of "cultura *kitsch*" or mass culture that according to the essayist, offered a great danger to humanity, not only for its total neglect of the true roots of culture, but also of its dehumanizing function, inherent to a system that essentially served only commercial interests. Implicitly, then, the essay, like the entire direction of Martínez Estrada's essays, is fundamentally a call to authenticity, and a valuable instrument to the achievement of this is the realization that cultural authenticity, in the meaning of a popular culture with visible roots in the people, is the first step towards a cultural self-realization that is ultimately the greatest deterrent to the cultural levelling and dehumanization of mass-bound, mechanical culture.

---

[54] *Ibid.*, p. 91.
[55] *Ibid.*, p. 39.
[56] *Ibid.*, pp. 125-126.

CHAPTER V

## TOWARDS A SOCIOLOGY OF THE ESSAY IN MARTÍNEZ ESTRADA

IMPLICITLY, OUR STUDY OF Ezequiel Martínez Estrada up until this point has been principally concerned with the personal vision of the essayist to the extent to which his views displayed a highly personal, and therefore, subjective, concept of the vital essentials of what it meant to be Argentinian, and, in a wider context, Latin-American. And this uni-lateral conception of the essayist — seeing and evaluating the achievements of the author through the prism that he holds out to the reader — is evidently valid, as far as it goes. Nevertheless, it is also evidently deficient. One large area of concern to the critic which would be left virtually untouched by such a personal approach is that of the extent to which a synthetic effort would reveal an underlying view, or world-view, of reality, of existence, of history: in short the *Weltanschauung* [1] of Martínez Estrada.

Clearly this method of approach offers some dangers. Such a concept is of necessity circumscribed to the extent to which the artist carries over his world view into his work, and this need not always be a complete transfer. Moreover, *Weltanschauung* may be conceived as an accumulative phenomenon reaching its zenith with

---

[1] For a very good discussion of the many implications of the concept, see Karl Mannheim, *Essays on the Sociology of Knowledge* (London: Routledge & Kegan Paul, 1959). Mainly developed in the inter-war years (1919-1939), the concept of *Weltanschauung* — sometimes known as the "sociology of knowledge" — received signal contributions from German sociologists. Mannheim, although born in Hungary, lived and taught in Germany for many years.

the last work of the artist, or as explicit in every artistic, aesthetic creation of the author concerned. A third mode of conceptualization is that of reaching an understanding of the basic tenets of such an overview by examining its manifestations at various points, including the last work, without giving any one point more importance than another with regard to the formulation of the view. This is essentially a synthetic approach which regards the world-view implicit in the creative manifestations of the artist as worthy, in itself, of study and evaluation. This, in broad terms, is the method that shall be adopted for this chapter. In this way the critic is not taken up with the question of which works are more "representative" than others in an attempt to extract the salient features of such an over-view; on the contrary, as we shall proceed to illustrate, often the lesser-known works of Martínez Estrada offer more, in this sense, than the more famous ones.

Such an approach to the essays of Martínez Estrada ultimately purports to examine the extent to which some of the essayist's basic attitudes implied a subscription, if not always a conscious one, to much wider concepts of society and social reality, to what virtually may be called a "sociology of the essay."[2]

Despite the presence of thesis novels and plays, imbued with a strongly social (as opposed to aesthetic) aim, it may be readily accepted that the essay as a genre is generally more "compromised" by the pressures of the social circumstance in which it was produced. Thus Juan Marichal, in a parallel to our earlier affirmations concerning the difficulties of literary classification, places the essay squarely in a social setting:

> El contraste entre la novela (o cualquier otro género tradicional) y el ensayismo es particularmente significativo en esta relación de una forma literaria con la realidad humana representada por ella: se puede hacer una historia interna del género novelístico, aislado de su ambiente histórico, pero en cambio resulta casi imposible desprender de su ganga circunstancial al ensayismo.[3]

---

[2] With reference to the general orientation of this chapter, especially the latter part, I have relied on the perceptive article by K. E. Shaw, "Ángel Ganivet a Sociological Interpretation," *Revista de Estudios Hispánicos* (Univ. of Alabama Press), Tomo II, núm. 2 (Nov. 1968), pp. 165-181.

[3] Juan Marichal, *La voluntad de estilo* (Barcelona: Seix Barral, 1957), p. 13.

With its roots so deeply within society, then, the essay would appear to suppose a prior degree of involvement from the essayist himself. Certainly studies exist that trace a historical identification between society and its conscience (represented by the artist) in Latin America,[4] but practically none that has traced the particular relationship between artistic creation and the institutional strength and institutional growth in a given society. With even more perception Juan Marichal adds, with reference to the Spanish essay:

> ¿No es acaso visible que el porte ejemplarmente continuo del ensayismo británico expresa y se sustenta en la estabilidad interna de una sociedad y de la clase que la rige durante dos siglos y medio, entre Addison y Virginia Woolf? El dramatismo permanente de la historia española hace, por el contrario, que en el ensayismo hispánico se den constantes altibajos en el porte expresivo de los escritores y en sus formas de individualización humana: coexisten, y a veces alternan rítmicamente en nuestro ensayismo, el bufón y el "hombre de bien", el desahogo y la plática sermonaria, la confesión desgarrada y la reserva aristocrática.[5]

The latter sentiments have Spain as their point of reference, but it is clear that the cultivation of the essay in Latin America, historically speaking, has known the categories mentioned by Marichal. And following the parallel with Great Britain, it is to be inferred that the undoubted *altibajos* of the Argentinian essay both express and thrive upon *altibajos* of institutional life in that country. Doubtless examples may be found to support such a view, but many eminent exceptions may be adduced to question its general application. Thus writers like Borges, Mallea and Martínez Estrada hardly reflect or "express" the "ups-and-downs" of Argentine society, and periods of chronic instability of France in this century have done little to diminish the universal appeal of much of French literature.

Fundamentally, Marichal suggests the concept of a social determinism between artist and his *milieu,* his main interest being that of the formatory influence of society on the artist. If we are to approach a conception of the "global-view" of Martínez Estrada, then

---

[4] See, for example, "The Artist and Social Conscience" and "The Writer as Conscience of his Country," in Jean Franco, *The Modern Culture of Latin America: Society and the Artist,* pp. 1-13 and 205-235 respectively.

[5] *La voluntad de estilo,* p. 14.

an attempt to measure to what extent the principal mainstays of his thought drew upon his reaction to Argentine society has to be made. It should be clear that this view in no way affirms that artistic genius can be reduced to matters of determinism, as some of the cruder Marxists would have it. Originality in ideas evidently must arise from somewhere, but the influence of the milieu, even on this, cannot be ignored. [6] Nor does the concept claim, on the other hand, that all men are influenced necessarily in the same way by the environment. Nonetheless, as we shall consider, the extension of many of Martínez Estrada's views and concepts — that is, when they are given a wider context — reveal how a reaction to the environment entered into their original formation.

In accordance with our original tracing of the similarity of attitudes between Oswald Spengler and Martínez Estrada with regard to the concept of a certain recurrence of themes throughout history, it is evident that Martínez Estrada is fundamentally a historicist, like his German mentor. Historicism — whose most famous exponent was probably Arnold Toynbee — attempts to see in history the gradual unfolding of universal patterns or laws, the attempt to decipher some hidden "message" or latent meaning which will ultimately constitute a type of "key to the cosmos." Yet, as Karl Popper has pertinently suggested, historicism partly grew out of a reluctance to only see history as a progression of dates and lives of monarchs and other leaders; in short, that there is an irresistible *drama* inherent in history itself, and that it is this, we may add, that chiefly concerns the historicist:

> Historicism ... is a reaction against the naive method of interpreting political history merely as the story of great tyrants and great generals. Historicists rightly feel that there may be something better than this method. It is this feeling which makes their idea of "spirits" — of an age, of a nation, of an army — so seductive. [7]

There can be a little doubt that Martínez Estrada was basically oriented towards the idea of a historical spirit manifesting itself throughout Argentine, and at times, American history in general. Yet he is

---

[6] K. E. Shaw, "Ángel Ganivet: a Sociological interpretation," p. 166.
[7] Karl R. Popper, *The Poverty of Historicism* (New York: Harper and Row, 1964), p. 148.

very far from the conception of a neo-Fascist view of the gradual unfolding of the "manifest historical destiny" of Argentina. The essayist is clearly diametrically opposed to such a position in that — and in this way he departs from "orthodox" historicism which is basically optimistic in intention — he affirms the continued historical presence of a social and psychological stigma (which itself will receive extended comment elsewhere) that characterizes his concept of the whole phenomenon of the Spanish Conquest in America. Almost inevitably, such a concept sometimes acquires "mystical" overtones, that also are accompanied by an overriding fatalism, a fatalism that was the constant companion of Martínez Estrada, as we have previously affirmed. Consider, for example, the following:

> Pesa sobre ellos [los argentinos] la fatalidad de una sociedad mal constituida, fundada rutinariamente sobre la crueldad, la ignorancia y la injusticia. Pero dice lo bastante para que comprendamos que se trata de males orgánicos y constitucionales, de un estado infeccioso generalizado, pues en ninguna parte [de *Martín Fierro*] se dice a dónde se pueda acudir para remediarlos. También por eso, el Poema — traducido en la lectura bien o mal — habla al lector de verdades profundas, en el lenguaje secreto — humano y universal. [8]

Thus, these "males orgánicos" whose reality is conveyed by "lenguaje secreto" that ultimately communicates "verdades profundas" bears witness to an attempt to evoke — such "mystical" language as the above rarely attempts a direct description — an historical presence that cannot be sufficiently well arrived at by the more usual methods of historical investigation. Hence, inescapably, Martínez Estrada is obliged to increasingly rely upon an intuitivism that ultimately serves as a restrictive device to the dissemination of his ideas. It is best said at this point, moreover, that the critic has to be wary of accepting Martínez Estrada's implicit justification for resorting to such "lenguaje secreto" in that the traditional teaching of Argentine history is a total mis-construction of the truth. The danger for the critic here is evident: to admit such a premise is to accept that distortion and mis-construction justifies the "lenguaje secreto" of intuitivism.

---

[8] Ezequiel Martínez Estrada, *Muerte y transfiguración de Martín Fierro,* I, p. 385.

Such a premise views Argentine history, moreover, as admitting of virtually only one interpretation: that which will arrive at the "verdades profundas." But this is a pitfall that the critic must avoid, even if the essayist himself subscribed to it. As we have seen in a previous chapter, Jorge Luis Borges, referred to the large over-simplifications inflicted on Argentinian history in Argentine schools, but this view did not force him into the historicists' camp.

Of fundamental importance, too, to the historicist orientation of history is that once the structure, paradigm or "invariants" as Martínez Estrada called them, are "identified," then the subsequent flow of history is interpreted from this one view-point. Hence there is always an obvious danger of having facts "conform" to the established pattern, and this clearly constitutes a distortion. Yet it need not involve questions of sincerity or intellectual honesty; as we have mentioned above, the main obstacle to rational assent to such an intuitivist conception is the intuitive method itself. Hence a period of constitutional dynamism in the course of Argentine history is interpreted by the essayist as a time when the "constants" of the past went underground:

> La vida constitucional e institucional desde 1853 en adelante, tiene mayor dinamismo, una riqueza incomparablemente más variada en sus desarrollos melódicos y abarca más extensas áreas de la vida pública y privada. En cambio, a mi juicio, precisamente por esa diversidad de ornamentación los invariantes coloniales se profundizan y siguen su curso subterráneo como no podía menos de suceder, o se hospedan e inmovilizan encapsulados en los centros vitales de la vida constitucional. [9]

Naturally, the subsequent institutional lapse in Argentina would appear as a "justification" of the essayist's affirmation of the "curso subterráneo," but it is quite obvious that this is an *a posteriori* construction, that in turn responds to an earlier, "global" focus; and to that extent it inevitably constitutes a distortion. Yet as far as this

---

[9] Ezequiel Martínez Estrada, *Los invariantes históricos en el Facundo*, p. 24. An almost identical example is present in *Radiografía de la pampa*: "Lo que llamábamos barbarie no había desaparecido, sino que había refugiado en zonas neutrales esperando el momento propicio." (p. 174).

critic has been able to establish, the essays of Martínez Estrada have not been approached from this point of view. [10]

A clarification at this juncture, however, would appear pertinent. It is one matter to affirm the existence of certain aberrations or distortions in the historical method of Martínez Estrada, but it is quite another to deny that history or society can be conceived of in terms of patterns or structures. To do this would be to virtually deny existence to sociology and the philosophy of history. Basically the historical/sociological essays of Martínez Estrada may be conceived of in terms of an attempt to encounter and identify certain patterns that he intuitively viewed as existent in Argentine and Latin American history and societies. The excesses that he incurred in this attempt, as we shall proceed to discuss, arose from his intuitive method that increasingly identified historical tendencies with "universal laws," which is typical of the historicist method. [11]

Nonetheless, if one can identify certain deviations in Martínez Estrada's method, they are deviations from what sociology, at least, has considered to be a norm of procedure for the investigation of society. Thus Karl Mannheim states,

> That the causal and the interpretative approach to social events are equally important cannot be questioned once it is clear that given structures require particular causal agents

---

[10] Too often the critic, faced with the imaginative brilliance of the intuitive method used by Martínez Estrada is inclined to consign such manifestations to the realm of poetic inspiration, which incurs a distortion no less pardonable than that which we have ascribed to the essayist. Certainly, as we have pointed out elsewhere, the poetic dimension was important to Martínez Estrada and at many points in his non-poetic work there are clear examples of a poetic sensibility at work. Nonetheless, Martínez Estrada also had the pretensions of a thinker and an analyst and it would be wrong to see distortions at that level as constituting poetic "excesses." José P. Barreiro offers a clear example of this type of interpretation. Referring to *Radiografía de la pampa* he stated:

> Plétora de esbozos brillantes, muchas veces rayanos en la travesura dialéctica, con una policromía de esquemas paradójicos, que confirman el ingenio creador del poeta... las conclusiones que cincela sobre la psicología argentina y la realidad de nuestra evolución histórica, con una visible delectación de orfebre, resultan desconcertantes, escépticas y hasta demoledoras en aspectos que no merecían tanta crueldad exegética. (*El espíritu de Mayo y el revisionismo histórico* [Buenos Aires: Ediciones Antonio Zamora, 1955], pp. 156-157.)

[11] Karl R. Popper, *The Poverty of Historicism*, pp. 110-111.

for their existence and that a structural change cannot take place without a corresponding shift in the necessary motivations ... The causal method reconstructs events in their temporal sequence, while the structural interest focuses on the patterns which operate in a functional system. [12]

On this level, therefore, we can conceive of the distortion in Martínez Estrada's method as proceeding from the introduction of the heavily intuitivist dimension of his analysis at the causal level, producing a fissure, as it were, in the resulting structure. This penchant towards the intuitive faculty, however, is not merely an idiosyncracy of the essayist. Karl Mannheim also saw the structural approach to historical change as inevitably involving intuition to some degree:

It is only through this gradual progression towards concrete structures that we will equip ourselves for the business of dealing with historical configurations. For every intermediate phase of the typology which we may bypass, we ultimately pay the penalty of having to regress to the *ad hoc* attack, to improvisation in which intuition is likely to play a major role. One can, of course, always take historical facts at their face value and array them without the appropriate sociological apparatus, but such an impromptu venture, equipped only with common sense, will stop short of a structural grasp of the material. [13]

In effect, the structural attempts of Martínez Estrada are frequently spoiled by the intromission of concepts that rely heavily on an intuitive base. Further, the very formation of the typology mentioned above is seriously compromised by the intuitive faculty. As a result, the empirical basis of the essayist's affirmation often become obscured. Consider the following:

... el Poema es un poema de la realidad histórica más que de la realidad étnica, moral y psicológica. La realidad histórica es un concepto más amplio y central que cualquier otro; se forma con los invariantes que a través de los siglos perpetúan a un pueblo como tipo de raza, de misión, con su fisonomía y su némesis ... tiene un *ethos,* un rostro, un sino. Confundir en el Poema esos elementos invariantes con

[12] Karl Mannheim, *Essays on the Sociology of Culture* (New York: Oxford Univ. Press, 1956), p. 79.
[13] *Ibid.,* p. 87.

los episódicos, al Martín Fierro biográfico con el Martín Fierro histórico, la persona y el personaje, es desvirtuar el propósito expreso del Autor y el sentido de la Obra. [14]

Here we have the clear promulgation of the concept of historical constants that manifest themselves down the centuries, gradually unfolding the national "destiny," and at this point, at least, there is no attempt at a "causal" justification.

Another possibility of interpretation of the historicist method employed by Martínez Estrada is that of Karl Popper, who saw the appeal of historicism as,

> ... merely part of the vogue of evolutionism — a philosophy that owes its influence largely to the somewhat sensational clash between a brilliant scientific hypothesis concerning the history of the various species of animals and plants on earth, and an older metaphysical theory which, incidently, happened to be part of an established religious belief. [15]

On the one hand, Martínez Estrada is a confirmed evolutionist; and in fact we have traced elsewhere how he went much further with his telluricist affirmations that, as with all telluricists, go considerably beyond Charles Darwin. Yet in another sense, the Conquest of Latin America — and in particular the River Plate region — constituted a type of Paradise Lost in that the colonizers did not come to terms with Nature, continually violating it and thus ruining the unique possibility for the creation of authentic life and social structures; untimately, of course, this came to mean a coming to terms of man with himself against the background of American Nature. This, says the essayist, he has never done, continuing to create "seudoestructuras" and be at the mercy of formatory "fuerzas psíquicas" and "fuerzas telúricas" in perennial fashion. [16] Yet we have also seen how the essayist frequently used vocabulary like "purification" and "redemption" (which is the point of Popper's reference to "an older metaphysical theory") to describe the depth and the dimensions of the solution, of the "males orgánicos" of Argentina and America.

---

[14] *Muerte y transfiguración de Martín Fierro,* I, p. 299.
[15] Karl R. Popper, *The Poverty of Historicism,* p. 106.
[16] This, extremely *grosso modo,* is the basic theme of *Radiografía de la pampa,* the words quoted referring to chapter headings in the work.

But there also exists a fundamental difference between Martínez Estrada and the evolutionists. The latter system is open-ended towards the future within a continuous development or progression. That of Martínez Estrada is ultimately confined within a circle; a large and richly ornamented circle if one prefers, but nonetheless a circle. All progress in the sense of basic change in the essential human condition is virtually impossible, according to the essayist. We have already referred to how, inspired by Spengler, he saw Argentine history as a continual reoccurence of themes and movements — principally the whole spiritual, social and psychological failure of the Conquest — that in a multitude of ways continue to vitally affect the Argentinian. Redemption in this context does not imply a transcendence of the past (impossible in Martínez Estrada's view) but rather a coming to terms with the past in order to better live with it, thereby achieving some degree of authenticity in Argentine life, the only authenticity possible. But the circle is effectively closed. Occasionally one finds examples of how even this illusory movement is denied by the essayist:

> El ser humano ve en torno suyo que todo cambia velozmente porque cambia él. Pero ni aun él cambia, porque se lo vuelve a encontrar inclinado sobre la misma vasija y al pie del mismo telar mil años más tarde. El concepto de inmovilidad mental es indispensable ahora, como la ha fijado Boas, y el concepto de mística y magia de Lévy-Bruhl y Frazer. [17]

Thus the circle closes even further as does the fundamental pessimism of the author.

While the concept of historicism need not always terminate in the "closed circle" idea as developed by Martínez Estrada, it will always be open to grave objections — despite the undeniable appeal it directs towards the imagination — in that its force basically rests upon what are virtually non-rational premises, which history and sociology must eventually reject as non-scientific. The following is a useful summation of such objections:

> Most of the shortcuts to the dynamics of history suffer from the common maladies of abrupt and unpremeditated diagnoses. One of these maladies is the tendency toward un-

---

[17] *Los invariantes históricos en el Facundo,* p. 9.

reliable interpretations and unverifiable verdicts. The other is the temptation to hypostatize *ex post facto* the inner necessity of a past turn of events without prior examination of the alternative solutions which were potential in one phase or another of the development. This is how history has often been constructed in the grand sweep, as the realization of pre-existing ideas, as the resolution of epochal issues, or as the fulfilment of an inexorable destiny. Comte, Hegel, Marx and Spengler demonstrate these pitfalls of an abrupt and ill-equipped attack. [18]

Such vocabulary as "pre-existing ideas" or "inexorable destiny" find a strong echo, it will readily be admitted, in the essays of Martínez Estrada, and at this point we may recall the temperamental affinity that the essayist had with such a method of interpreting history. The marked tendencies towards fatalism and an innate feeling for the absurdities of life together with a clear penchant to withdraw into oneself that we have examined in previous chapters, would not, in retrospect appear as unnatural motivations for such a view of history. Yet the overriding irony of this situation is that Martínez Estrada was imbued with a desperate need to communicate, to dialogue, to begin a re-education of the country, of the continent, while the instruments he used ultimately communicated only with some kindred spirits and *entendidos*. [19]

On the other hand, Martínez Estrada was very far from the formulation of aristocratic attitudes or a view of art as the concern of minorities. Apart from his historicist procedure, the essayist also was deeply imbued, as we have discussed elsewhere, with a fundamentally

---

[18] Karl Mannheim, *Essays on the Sociology of Culture*, p. 87.

[19] It should be noted that except for a renewed feeling of human solidarity that he received from his studies on Martí in the latter part of his life, it is doubtful that Martínez Estrada ever entertained illusions about a direct communication with the masses, although it is clear that he strongly advocated a re-education of the masses, especially with regard to the re-interpretation of Argentine history and the whole idea of "una nueva y gloriosa nación" as expressed in the national anthem of Argentina. Rather his criticism and imprecations were directed at the principal centers of authority, the Church, Judiciary, Presidency, etc. (cf. *Exhortaciones*, 1957). As we have also previously mentioned, in a letter to Julio Sager (8th Nov., 1963) the essayist bears witness to the high level of culture of the average reader of *Radiografía de la pampa*. See Carlos Adam, *Bibliografía y documentos de Ezequiel Martínez Estrada*, p. 200.

moralistic conception of political and historical reality. [20] Previously, too, we have seen how Martínez Estrada had a deep mistrust of the State, as such, and of practically all manifestations of organized authority. [21] Important also, in this connection, is the equally deep antipathy that he had for "saber científico" or the mechanized aspects of the "cultura kitsch." [22] At the base of all these dislikes is a difficulty (or reluctance) on the part of the essayist to face up to the dehumanizing nature of the evolving industrial society. These attitudes, taken collectively, reveal what sociology (and principally Ferdinand Tönnies) [23] has designated as a *Gemeinschaft* view of society.

---

[20] There exists evidence to suggest, however, that Martínez Estrada's early writings, of the late 1920's and early 1930's, and produced against the political background of an incipient Fascism in Europe and increasing technological advances, partook of an epochal sense of uneasiness that the development of technical powers were fast outstripping man's moral development. In a lecture given in 1934, for example, Karl Mannheim warned about the dangers to society and to the individual of such a "disproportionate development in human faculties." See *Rational and Irrational Elements in Contemporary Society* (London, Oxford Univ. Press, 1934).

[21] It will be recalled how, in a letter to Enrique Espinoza the essayist affirmed that, "todos los que ejercen algún poder, político, económico, religioso o sapiencial están al servicio de nuestros enemigos." (*Exhortaciones*, p. 90).

[22] It is convenient to note here how very close to a moral view of life the whole concept of "cultura *kitsch*" finds itself, and thus it would fall into a *Gemeinschaft* conception. This in fact is one of the predominant experiences — that of a moral attitude — of *Análisis funcional de la cultura* (1960), where the idea of a mechanized culture or mass culture receives its fullest development. Yet the essay, in the background of a progression of essays from Martínez Estrada, communicates the strong impression that, despite the brilliance of analysis, of the expert synthesis of a host of sociological, ethnological and philosophical sources, Martínez Estrada saw the problems of culture principally in religious terms. The real problems that interested him were those "authentic" cultures as opposed to "false" cultures, of "right" and "wrong" attitudes. Essentially, in the view of this critic, such attitudes strongly suggest that the essayist plainly did not (and perhaps spiritually, could not) come to terms with the whole basis of modern society. Martínez Estrada's prodigious analytical powers in reality side-step one of the most aggravated issues that have faced intellectuals in the XXth Century: the need to entirely re-think the role of culture, the arts, and the whole humanistic tradition in a technological age. Instead of effectively coming to grips with these mammoth problems, the essayist didn't really join battle. For a less pretentious but very sensitive approach to the scope of the problems involved, cf. Jaime Rest, *Literatura y cultura de masas* (Buenos Aires: Centro Editor de América Latina, 1967).

[23] Ferdinand Tönnies, *Fundamental Concepts of Sociology: Gemeinschaft und Gesellschaft* (New York, American Book Co., 1940). Tönnies is held to

This view — which is really a "world-view," so encompassing is it
in nature — conceives society on the basis of community relationships
(as opposed to an emphasis on association or contractual relationships which are seen by Tönnies as representative of a *Gesellschaft*
view of society) together with a strong emphasis on the "traditional"
virtues of neighbourliness, inter-dependence, charity, etc. This orientation, implicit in *Radiografía de la pampa,* becomes more and more
pronounced in the subsequent essays. An admissible over-view of *La
cabeza de Goliat,* for example, could be that it is fundamentally governed by a strongly *Gemeinschaft* basis: the aversion to the dehumanizing influence of the great city (here Buenos Aires, but applicable
to any large metropolis). Similarly, in *Sarmiento* (1946) we find,

> Lo constante en un pueblo son sus sentimientos y no sus
> ideas, sus reflejos incondicionados de conducta social y no
> las adquisiciones del saber. Esto muere con cada individuo;
> pero sus gestos, como sus inflexiones prosódicas, se propagan
> en los hijos y los nietos. Eso es lo que se educa fuera de la
> escuela, lo que nosotros no hemos educado. [24]

Here again we have a direct criticism of the "saber sapiencial" that
the essayist had earlier referred to; thus it is the "natural," "non-
technical" *gestos* that really symbolize the people. At times Martínez
Estrada (unwittingly) contrasted the dual concepts of *Gemeinschaft*
and *Gesellschaft.* Referring to the view of civilization expounded by
his mentor, [25] he states,

> Para Sarmiento civilización era todo aquello que había hecho
> de Inglaterra y de los Estados Unidos naciones poderosas,
> industrialmente desarrolladas, comercial y socialmente orga-
> nizadas, económica y culturalmente eficaces; pero no se

---

be the principal formulator of these concepts, although not their originator
nor their only formulator. Concepts such as the relationship of natural to
rational will, and the dual vision of authority, witness a complexity that the
large simplification of the theories that has had to be adopted for the de-
mands of this chapter, may tend to obscure. The reader is referred to the
work itself.

[24] Ezequiel Martínez Estrada, *Sarmiento,* p. 72.

[25] It should be recalled that despite his criticism of much of Sarmiento's
diagnoses, Martínez Estrada was profoundly influenced by him, and at one
time calls himself his "fidelísimo discípulo" (*Meditaciones sarmientinas,*
p. 106).

había preguntado qué diferencias y concordancias hay entre la barbarie de los pueblos primitivos y la civilización de los pueblos decadentes. La grandeza que Sarmiento anhela es precisamente la grandeza que encubre la injusticia, la crueldad, la infamia, la codicia. Transportar esos adelantos brutos era agregarles una calamidad científicamente establecida a una calamidad libre y campesinamente engendrada... Sin un plan social de justicia, el progreso es una maldición. [26]

Thus the essayist operated a *Gemeinschaft/Gesellschaft* dichotomy in terms of "pueblos primitivos" and "civilización de pueblos decadentes," "calamidad campesinamente engendrada" and "calamidad científicamente engendrada." Similarly, in what is probably the most fundamentally *Gemeinschaft* of his essays, [27] Martínez Estrada again affirms this "community" concept of Argentina in his *Exhortaciones*:

Mi pueblo, que es el vuestro, ha sido inducido a la violación más pecaminosa y funesta de la ley, que no consiste en violarla por el delito o la transgresión, que entonces puede castigársela y hasta llegar a ser saludable, sino burlarla por el fraude... Sin una rígida norma de conducta, un pueblo civilizado se coloca o debe ser colocado debajo de los pueblos salvajes, ágrafos o primitivos... Haced comprender al pueblo, por la incontrastable potestad de la autoridad ética, que un juez es más poderoso que un presidente de la república, y que un general del ejército... tan respetable como una madre y como un sacerdote cuando lo es de verdad. Y demostrad lo que sois. Para invocar ese poder sagrado e inmenso no tenéis en la mano la espada de la justicia, ni los Evangelios, sino las tablas de la ley. [28]

This passage, from "Exhortation to the Judges" of Argentina, is replete with allusions to a "community" conception of society, which in so many instances reduces the problems of any given society to

---

[26] *Sarmiento,* p. 110.

[27] There is little or no evidence to suggest that Martínez Estrada's basic world-view was ever anything other than *Gemeinschaft* in orientation. It is, however, more evident in some essays than in others. Not unexpectedly, it is much more to the fore in the polemical and historico-sociological essays (which account for 17 out of 26 essays) than in the literary ones (9 in all), although in works like *Para una revisión de las letras argentinas* and *La poesía afrocubana de Nicolás Guillén* (1967 and 1966, respectively) it is heavily implicit where it is not self-evident.

[28] *Exhortaciones,* pp. 13-14.

the level of moral problems, and the reference to the Gospels in the last line serves to confirm the impression of the invoking of a prophetic wrath that the critic has sensed from the beginning. It is worthy of notice, also, how the essayist accords equal respect due to the mother and the genuine priest. Such conceptions, in short, could not be further from the contractual relationships, the commercial interests of the "association" view of society. From this, it may be inferred, there may arise spontaneously certain tendencies toward what may be termed a conspiratorial complex when it is felt that such "community" values are theatened by "contractual" society. Such a strand is discernible in many of the essayist's polemical essays. In *Las 40* the denunciatory tone goes hand in hand with a distinct impression that the writer feels himself on the defensive, almost under attack:

> Mercado, cuartel y templo son los tres símbolos radicales que condicionan las actividades y las empresas todas o casi todas de la ciudadanía. Yo he vivido en otra ley, caballeros, y lo que he predicado con disgusto de los pedagogos alfabetizados es la rebeldía contra el embrutecimiento por la cultura. [29]

Consonant with this attitude is the occasional demagogic tone more typical of the orator who would harangue the masses, than of an essayist before a much more restricted readership:

> Yo tengo autoridad para despreciar a esa caterva de politiqueros y escribas de la cultura. Porque he sido buen maestro y millares de hombres me recuerdan con amor y respeto; y lo digo porque impunemente se me acusa por valetudinarios del saber docente de no creer en los dioses nacionales y de extraviar a la juventud. [30]

And later he adds,

> Defiendo a mi pueblo, además, porque defiendo al ser humano de toda injusticia. [31]

---

[29] Ezequiel Martínez Estrada, *Las 40* (Buenos Aires: Ediciones Gure, 1957), p. 26.

[30] *Ibid.*, p. 53.

[31] *Ibid.*, p. 91.

Yet the implications of the *Gemeinschaft/Gesellschaft* ("community"/"contractual") dichotomy, as a method of analysing the essays of Martínez Estrada, has even deeper implications, with regard to the essayist's whole conception of civilization and barbarity, which is of primary importance to so many of his essays. Towards the end of *Radiografía de la pampa,* Martínez Estrada rejects the Sarmientian opposition of these terms as used in *Facundo;* the essayist now saw them to be part of the same reality, or rather, that both formed part of a continuum, [32] that is, that the primitivism of the rural area was carried into the city (a central idea of *La cabeza de Goliat*) where it fused with all the manifestations of modern barbarity: railways, telegraph, immigration, etc., all of which Sarmiento had advocated. [33] A clarification is called for at this juncture, however. From the foregoing it is clear that for Martínez Estrada Argentine society is essentially built upon a barbarity that has been historically perpetuated until modern times, among other reasons, because no one had exposed this "verdad profunda" (the whole cornerstone of *Radiografía de la pampa*). But the barbarity that Sarmiento conceived of, was, according to Martínez Estrada, really forms of "civilization," but this modern civilization because of its mechanized, dehumanizing action really forms a continuum with the historical barbarity of Argentine society. Hence, at the hands of Sarmiento,

> El problema quedó desfigurado más bien que simplificado. No había tal barbarie, sino formas renitentes de la civilización, tradiciones de religión, mando, pereza, inmoralidad, codicia, crueldad, influyendo activamente en sentido contrario al esfuerzo por realizar una experiencia nueva de orden, justicia, trabajo y progreso. [34]

And later in the same work (*Sarmiento*) the essayist clarifies this concept further:

> Sarmiento siguió creyendo en la antítesis civilización-barbarie, sinónimo de Europa-América, y de España-Argentina. No vio que civilización y barbarie se integraban en tipo de cultura, en un status social complejo, como la de la historia

---

[32] *Radiografía de la pampa,* p. 341.
[33] *Sarmiento,* p. 171.
[34] *Ibid.,* p. 89.

argentina (o suramericana) implica un status político, un tipo de cultura cívica de la misma complejidad: lo que el lenguaje técnico denomina "cultura bastarda". [35]

Thus Martínez Estrada really rejects modern civilization (which is virtually barbarism for him) and embraces a view of Argentina that many historians and writers have consigned to barbarism which, because of its authenticity in human terms, the essayist deems to be "civilized." This inversion of terminology — it is clearly not an inversion of values — really corresponds to the *Gemeinschaft/Gesellschaft* concept. The essayist's rejection of modern civilization (or the dehumanizing aspects of it) can now be seen as emanating from a *Gemeinschaft* view of reality, the obverse side of the situation being that he thereby rejects the contractual/association ("mechanized," "cultura kitsch") idea of society, which is a rejection of *Gesellschaft*. Thus the transformation (from usual uses of the terminology), or inversion, that has taken place is as follows:

Sarmiento favoured civilization (*Gesellschaft*) against barbarism (*Gemeinschaft*). And

Martínez Estrada favoured civilization (*Gemeinschaft*) against barbarism (*Gesellschaft*). [36]

In this broad attempt to fix the essentials of the "ideology" of Martínez Estrada, the critic is conscious of another dimension in the essayist's thought, that if less accessible to concrete description than the foregoing, is none the less real for that. We are referring to a certain mystique or mystification that the essayist at times uses to evoke the authentic nature of a given phenomenon. *Radiografía de la pampa*, in this sense, is where the author has most consistently

---

[35] *Ibid.*, p. 65.
[36] While the *Gemeinschaft/Gesellschaft* antithesis that we have used here is useful in describing some fundamental tendencies in Martínez Estrada and in his vision of Sarmiento, it is well to remember that we are not engaged in an attempt to sum up the whole personalities of both writers. If we have affirmed the importance of the "community" outlook of Martínez Estrada in practically all his works, it would be an exaggeration to say that Sarmiento's outlook was invariably "association" orientated. In fact, the basic paternalism of Sarmiento, together with his tendency to conceive of Argentina as a vast educational experiment, may well be considered as part of *Gemeinschaft* attitudes in their wider context, to which we have alluded previously.

used mystiques with greatest effect and consistency. Our previous references to the particular forces that Martínez Estrada saw as fundamental in shaping Argentine character, and in particular, *lo telúrico,* may all be conceived as an integral part of the mystique concept. Yet almost without exception the land, the stark prehistorical reality, or the later geo-political development, is essentially a negative force for Martínez Estrada; the *genius loci,* in the essayist's view, is always working against man, almost in animated revenge for the latter's refusal to come to terms with its reality upon the first impact of colonial times. Hence, within this mystique, the land is invested with a terrible, inexorable will of its own:

> Todo ese dominio de naturaleza, recintos en que la tierra defiende intactas su gea, su flora y su fauna, son confines a los que el hijo de la llanura fue arrojado y donde se extinguirá. Lo demás, la tierra plana, la pampa litoral y central es Argentina, la tierra de Europa, la tierra del blanco. Pero entre esa pampa fértil, nueva, y aquel mundo oscuro, antiguo, está el hijo del blanco y de la india, que tiene que optar y que tardará centenares de años en decidirse, dejándolo todo en suspenso hasta ese día. [37]

The mystique of the land in Martínez Estrada is invariably coupled with this deep sense of fatalism, with the conviction that the original violation of Nature has demanded a price, a reparation, down the centuries, but essentially it is a reparation that can never be made; it is the "original sin" that can have no effective absolution: "... la tierra es la verdad definitiva, la primera y la última: es la muerte." [38] The mystique of the land, in fact, is really a spiritual presence, a force that makes itself felt in diffuse ways; Argentine man may attempt to ignore it, but, says Martínez Estrada, it will be to no avail; the attempt will only serve to reinforce a consciousness of its presence. [39] José Hernández is, according to the essayist, one of the very few who has succeeded in transferring the reality of this mys-

---

[37] *Radiografía de la pampa,* p. 130.

[38] *Ibid.,* p. 16.

[39] The thesis that Argentine (and by extension, American) man uses culture as a means of effectively keeping the stark spiritual reality of the Continent at a distance, thereby making the encounter with oneself (the prerequisite for authentic life) impossible, has been well developed by a disciple of Martínez Estrada. See H. A. Murena, *El pecado original de América.*

tique of the land into literature. Evoking the ending of *Martín Fierro* as an example of the implacability of the forces of the earth, Martínez Estrada asserts:

> Tenemos en el *Martín Fierro* un cuadro más cercano a *La Araucana* que a la actualidad. Adviértase, además, que los temas, los temas como condensación de un *status* no registrado, corresponden a la etnología, la antropología y a la prehistoria más bien que a la cultura... Los hechos tienen también una técnica equivalente a la herramienta rudimentaria; sólo las reflexiones levantan al ser humano sobre el ínfimo nivel de las cosas. Cosas y hechos pertenecen a un mundo de cultura barbarizado, y los personajes se debaten como náufragos para no ser arrastrados por la corriente que todo lo destruye. [40]

There can be no doubt that there is an evocative brilliance to this piece, but it is also a good example of how the use of such intuitive effusions — necessarily the mainstay of any attempt at the communication of a mystique — presuppose a similarly attuned intuition on the part of the reader. [41] With such an affirmation, however, we have returned to the basic objection to the historicist method within the essayist's own terms of an attempt at communication: the construction of a formidable barrier to that very communication that the use of mystiques incurred. No doubt, in justifiable self-apology Martínez Estrada would have countered that such language was the only one appropriate for the expression of "verdades profundas," as he called them, that were not accessible to rational, logical description. Even so, it is consequently clear that the preference for the intuitive approach contributed to the creation of a persecution/outcast syndrome

---

[40] *Muerte y transfiguración de Martín Fierro*, II, 476-477.

[41] One of the more obvious dangers of the intuitive (or highly imaginative) evocation of a telluric reality is precisely the inherent difficulty of fixing limits, not only to the essence of the concept itself, but also to one's own imagination. Martínez Estrada himself occasionally gave the impression that he allowed free rein to his intuition where perhaps a more disciplined approach was necessary. Consider, for example, his view of *lo telúrico* in Martí:

> Todo lo que la naturaleza produce, para Martí es venerable, pero en su misma forma de acción y reacción instantáneas, no de culto o rito pagano. Las plantas más que los animales como seres absolutamente elementales, replegados en sí mismos, identificados como seres intrauterinos de la madre tierra, todavía en simbiosis con ella, pacientes, silenciosos y benéficos. (Ezequiel Martínez Estrada, *Martí revolucionario*, p. 389.)

that is characteristic of the later stages of the essayist's writings. In such a situation — that of an individual absolutely convinced of the veracity of his convictions with regard to the "real" history, the "real" reality of his country — there is an evident tendency to impute bad faith to those who will not or cannot accept the given diagnosis. From there to the engendering of a persecution complex, and the increasing withdrawal from the world, there is little distance.

With a little reflection it becomes sufficiently clear that Martínez Estrada's cultivation of the mystique of the land falls into the general historicist attitude that we have traced above. Thus, in a return to our initial affirmation of the need of a consideration of the world-view, or *Weltanschauung* of the essayist we are aware of a basically fatalistic view of man as at the mercy of supernatural forces, which, projected through history, continue to exercise their inexorable (spiritual) influence upon him, enclosing him, as it were, in his own cultural concentricity; engendered, as we have noted, as a result of man's original "violation" of nature, which, together with the whole *hijo humillado* complex inherent in American man, forms the original sin of America. Redemption, in these circumstances — and the word could not be more apt in this context — can only be partial, and not really a "baptism"; it consists of facing up to the terrible spiritual reality of America, and coming to terms with it: "Tenemos que aceptarla con valor, para que deje de perturbarnos; traerla a la conciencia, para que se esfume y podamos vivir unidos en la salud." [42] Facing up to this reality will not abolish it, but the recognition of it will mean an immense personal liberation.

Thus Martínez Estrada came to "liberate," to "redeem," from *Radiografía de la pampa* onwards, but posterity has shown that he possessed the essential trappings of "one crying in the wilderness." As we have already noted, only his work on Martí could offer sufficient consolation to a life-time spent in frequent encounters with deep disillusionment and fundamental incomprehension. Given some of the ideological elements that we have characterized in this chapter (the historicist attitudes, *Gemeinschaft/Gesellschaft* orientations, mystiques, etc.) this conclusion would not appear without a rationale, particularly since they presupposed an ideological frame of mind that ultimately restricted the reach of his work.

---

[42] *Radiografía de la pampa,* p. 342.

Nonetheless, the temptation to view such an ideology as emanating from an essential pessimism that of necessity could have no other conclusion must be resolutely resisted. Further, to characterize some of the underpinnings of Martínez Estrada's thought, as we have done, is merely (if usefully) to have pointed to elements and dimensions that incurred certain distortions that heavily influenced its social effect. Evidently questions as to the ultimate truth or fallacy of the essays — or rather, the extent to which their "accuracy" or "inaccuracy" of diagnosis of Argentine history and society affected their acceptance — must remain untouched by the patterns we have applied here, and also remain without the scope of this study.

Yet one last consideration must still claim the critic's attention: the degree to which the characteristics of Martínez Estrada's ideology — and in particular his pessimism, intuitive sensibility, as well as the distortions he incurred — developed as a result of factors that were not so much peculiar to him (which factors we have treated above) but rather as a result of factors that ultimately affect the intellectual position itself. In short, some of the essayist's attitudes proceeded from attitudes common to the intellectual as such, and not only from personal idiosyncrasies. In a description that might well have been written with Martínez Estrada in mind, Karl Mannheim asserted:

> The person who must face the daily consequences of his actions cannot but acquire pragmatic habits and a critical view within the radius of his vocational practice. The intellectual lacks some of these restraints. He meets no checks when he dwells in the long-range perspective of things, or on a level of abstraction on which one faces no consequences. Ideas which cannot misfire easily become ends in themselves and a source of solitary intoxication. The thinker whom events cannot refute is prone to forget the principal purpose of thought: to know and to forsee in order to act. Free and unimpeded ideation at times invites illusions of grandeur, for the mere ability to communicate ideas about vexatious questions seducingly resembles their mastery. Ordinarily the private conjurings of secluded individuals cause no ripples, but in a crisis an intellectual extasy may fall on fertile soil. [43]

---

[43] Karl Mannheim, *The Sociology of Culture*, p. 160.

Even if one may rightly have reservations concerning the "intellectual extasy" of Martínez Estrada, there can be little doubt that the essayist shared the great majority of the characteristics outlined by Mannheim. The sociologist most probably had in mind the rise of dictatorships in Europe of the 1930's, [44] but the concepts could equally be applied to Argentina. When the crisis came in 1945, it was the populist call to arms of Juan Domingo Perón that fell upon fertile soil, and the call to authenticity of Ezequiel Martínez Estrada, inevitably restricted, as we have shown, to a minority appeal, went effectively unheeded.

---

[44] Mannheim himself was a refugee from Hitler's Germany in 1933, and settled in England thereafter.

# CONCLUSIONS

OF PRIMARY CONCERN to the critic, in an attempt at a summation of the foregoing pages of this study, are the particular contours that the essays of Ezequiel Martínez Estrada, as a group, offer towards a wider understanding of the artist himself and that epoch of Argentinian history, society and literature in which he moved and of which was such an integral part. Commencing from these latter aspects, it is readily appreciated that the essays offer a finely focused image, above all — and as the author himself would have wished it — of an artist at work, and that work, his veritable life's work, was fundamentally one of subjecting Argentine history and literature to a relentless scrutiny; a continuous effort to discover and proclaim the authentic origins of an essentially national spiritual malaise, no matter how distasteful this process may ultimately have proved to be, and no matter the costs in personal terms.

The costs, in fact, were great. Within the role that he ascribed to himself of a latter-day prophet calling Argentina to self consciousness and thus to authenticity, Martínez Estrada conceived of no possible abdication, no possible compromise, and therein lies the essayist's essential solitude, born, ironically, of one of the most celebrated of social virtues — honesty with oneself. Accordingly, there can be little doubt that his conception of himself as a virtual stranger in his own country, if true, was motivated in equal measure by the peculiar idiosyncracies of temperament and by the actual content of his essential message as contained in the essays. For it would be a rare society indeed that would have patiently tolerated the unrelieved pessimism of one of its writers who consistently extolled its non-virtues and defects, and who maintained unflinchingly until his death that modern Argentina was grovelling in the spiritual mire of its own falseness and artificiality.

Yet intolerance, if examined, reveals a measure of interest, and if the essayist was not afforded the attention necessary for the national repentance that he considered so fundamental, his opponents could well counter that he was not effectively ignored or considered irrelevant, despite the many affirmations of the essayist to the contrary, that we have noted. For there is evidence — the affirmations of the various voices of the literary generation of 1945 in Argentina embodying the most obvious example — that Martínez Estrada, even if ultimately constituting a non-viable example for many of those equally concerned about the need for a *toma de conciencia* with their milieu, was most clearly considered as very pertinent to any discussion of modern Argentina. Clearly one hardly devotes whole issues of periodicals to irrelevant individuals, and even less so in their own life-time.

Yet Martínez Estrada was not content to be considered merely a "starting-point," and he frequently asked why he was destined not to have friends with whom to dialogue. To some extent the point is well taken in that, if the essayist did not consider himself as in full possession of revealed truth of the real condition of Argentina's spiritual ills, throughout the length of his essays there is a discernible consistency of diagnosis that reflected a coherent body of analysis, given his premises; and it was precisely in these premises — the lack of authenticity in Argentine social institutions, in turn reflective of the historical perpetuation of pseudo-social structures engendered by the colonial experience and continued throughout the nineteenth century — that the generation of 1945 saw the essential revelancy of Martínez Estrada.

That the essayist could not ultimately figure as a mentor for that generation has become clear from the gradual unfolding of certain traits of temperament that this study has had as one of its principal objectives. Lacking practically all the biographical details of Martínez Estrada's childhood, the critic encounters considerable difficulty in establishing any earlier precedent to the sentiments of melancholy and fatalism to which his first prose works — the three *Nosotros* articles of 1917 and 1918 — give expression. Fundamentally, this "telluric fatalism," this "dolor de todos," underwent little development or transition from the first essay of 1933 until the Cuban experience of 1960-1962. During those twenty-seven years the essayist waged his own private war, in the historico-sociological essays, in the literary essays and above all in the polemical essays, against the concept of Argentina as "una nueva y gloriosa nación," as the Argentine national anthem expresses it.

Yet so iconoclastic, so intimately tied were these denunciations to the temperamental peculiarities of Martínez Estrada — and not to any commonly-acknowledged ideological or philosophical orientation — that Ismael Viñas felt constrained to affirm (not without more than a hint of frustration) that the impact of the essayist's work "terrorized his generation to the point that they were impeded from dissenting." Central to Martínez Estrada's temperament was, as we noted in Chapter IV, the almost pathological need to denounce, to strive relentlessly until he revealed the very fibres of the Truth. Some critics, particularly those of the generation of 1945, saw such a need as representative of the role of a "professional denouncer" and that the essayist essentially occupied a position that was effectively "above the fray" of what he was attacking, but the whole body of the essays bear witness to a degree of commitment to what he was attacking that makes Martínez Estrada a patriot of a very special type; with particular accuracy, another contemporary and essayist, Bernardo Canal Feijóo referred to him as "un enfermo de patria."

On the other hand, if so many of the literary generation of 1945 in Argentina found that they could not share the method of denouncing and exposing the ills of their country, Martínez Estrada's message and method did not entirely fall upon deaf ears. Having noted the cultural antecedents to the formulation of the concept of *lo telúrico* in Latin America as a whole (Chapter I) this characteristic of Martínez Estrada's method for the investigation of the weight of the past on the Argentine cultural present was, as we have noted in Chapter II, not unique to him, and rather that it was adopted by many contemporaries. Those like José Clemente and Víctor Massuh who would see *lo telúrico* as a highly dubious cultural instrument for the investigation of the national reality, and would prefer to see it confined to its period of greatest vogue, the 1930's, would also be obliged to note its continuation, in a rather more refined version, in the work of one of the principal disciples of Martínez Estrada, H. A. Murena.

Due, no doubt, to the posthumous material of the essayist that has only recently become available, critics have as yet taken little notice of how the experience in Cuba — and its related publications — provide some serious qualifications to the hitherto common vision of the essential personality of Martínez Estrada. The encounter of the essayist with the whole life experience — and life philosophy — of José Martí was as fundamental an influence on the essayist as was that of Sarmiento and Quiroga, and doubtless future criticism will speculate on how Martínez Estrada might have subsequently developed had he encountered Martí to that degree earlier in life. Yet, as we have concluded in Chapter IV, part of this intense personal awakening on the part of the essayist to the reality of Martí was due to a set of historical and personal circumstances that made Martínez Estrada particularly susceptible to such an influence. The invitation to Mexico and Cuba (by the Fondo de Cultura Económica and Casa de las Américas respectively) came at a particularly low ebb in the essayist's morale with regard to his further efficacy in Argentina, and was virtually a call to bear arms in a wider, continental service. The critic may justifiably question the quality of some of the essays of this "American" period, particularly propagandistic tracts such as *El verdadero cuento del Tío Sam,* and the slightly more refined *En Cuba y al servicio de la revolución cubana,* but *Diferencias y seme-janzas entre los países de la América Latina* and *Martí revolucionario* (which we have noted as the essayist's self-confessed best work) alone should cause him to doubt that Martínez Estrada, in all justice, should continue to be known only as "the author of *Radiografía de la pampa.*"

The precise circumstances, social and emotional, that led to the virtual abandonment of a poetic career by Martínez Estrada, in favour of the essay as his principal instrument of expression (interspersed from time to time, as we affirmed in the Introduction, with dramas and short-stories) will continue to admit of various interpretations, no one of which appears definitive; even the essayist's comments on this aspect of his work, be it the personal association with Horacio Quiroga (*El hermano Quiroga*) or the Argentine military coup of 1930 (*Antología*) point to results rather than root causes. Most probably the change was motivated by an early personal recognition that he was not destined to become a really great poet and that the Establishment's applause, in the shape of the literary prizes he received (the "laureles de oro") was ultimately despised for its failure to recognize what he knew to be a personal truth. Equally importantly, if, as we have concluded above, the essays as a whole reveal an inner imperative to denounce in Martínez Estrada, then the decision to abandon poetry (virtually from 1930 onwards) may well have come from a rather pragmatic decision that prose offered greater possibilities in this sense and even despite the belated prize awarded to *Radiografía de la pampa* in 1937, effectively freed the essayist from the literary Establishment with which his poetry prizes tended to associate him.

Closely allied to these considerations are those concerned with the identification of certain phases or turning-points in the trajectory of the essays, and in general opinions have been quite speculative. As was noted at various points, there were critics who saw new phases in the essayist's work beginning with *La cabeza de Goliat* others with *Muerte y transfiguración de Martín Fierro*. Chapter IV, however, has illustrated how the most fundamental change in the essayist's production was in fact the essays of the Cuban period and particularly as a result of his work on Martí. In this regard, nonetheless, the critic should not overlook the importance of the personal, temperamental effects of the five years that Martínez Estrada was virtually confined to a sick-bed, due to a skin disease. Not unnaturally, the years 1955 (when he was cured) to 1959 (when he went to Mexico) saw the essayist rather disorientated with regard to the continued direction of his work, all within a framework of acute depression as a result of his long illness. The invitations to Mexico and Cuba, then, provided the writer with a renewed sense of purpose in life, and his work of this period, characterized, as we have considered, by an increased radicalization yet also a much more balanced tone (especially in *Diferencias y semejanzas entre los países de la América Latina*), clearly constitutes the major turning point of Martínez Estrada's career.

The wider, sociological implications of the essayist's work that have been evaluated in Chapter V are particularly revealing, more so since this particular approach may be applied to many other essayists and may contribute to the effective evaluation of a genre not always susceptible to more traditional modes of criticism. Characteristic of the essays of Martínez Estrada, and despite his vast erudition that included literature, philosophy, sociology, history and anthropology, is a clear reluctance on the part of the essayist to come to terms with the broader implications of the technological era, especially at those points where technological organization impinged upon human and general cultural values. Fundamentally, there is no doubt that the writer conceived of society and social relationships on the level of community ties, that is, with an emphasis on traditional values such as inter-dependence of people, charity, generosity; in short, a conception of social relationships that is basically rural in character. On the other hand, the association type of relationship based on commercial transactions and monetary considerations generally, was rejected by Martínez Estrada as part of the despised *kitsch* culture that was the fullest expression of another of the essayist's manias — the encroachment of scientific values on questions of culture. These affirmations, coupled with the additional evidence of the emotional experience of his work on Martí — which, as we have noted in Chapter IV, helped the author arrive at a more balanced conception of popular literature and of the masses at large, in contrast to the pre-Cuban periods — all lead the critic to the conclusion that Martínez Estrada was fundamentally reluctant to come to terms with the modernity of the twentieth century. Related themes, such as the use of mystiques (particularly that of the land) and other non-rational aspects that relied upon the basic intuitive method he employed reinforce this conclusion.

Consequently, it no longer constitutes a sufficiently accurate description of Martínez Estrada merely to see him as a perennial *inadaptado,* imbued with a congenital fatalism and carrying on a private war with his country. Chapter V has illustrated that the *Gemeinschaft* orientation together with the use of mystiques and a powerful intuitive faculty, introduced various distortions into the essayist's thinking, and a valid point of departure for subsequent studies of the author might well be that of tracing the origin and development of such distortions throughout the essays.

The scheme of study employed has been successful to the degree that it has facilitated the tracing of the dual evolution of temperamental postures and thematic preoccupations. Thus Adam's classifications (reproduced in Appendix III) have been used in conjunction with a general chronological sequence of study that has provided a more accurate sense of the stages in the development of Martínez Estrada's temperament and ideology.

# APPENDIX I

## Martínez Estrada and the Critics

*Argentine criticism*

The highly polemical nature of much of Martínez Estrada's work together with his extremes of temperament, forged for him an undeniable vital presence in Argentine literary circles for fully four decades. He was attacked and defended, praised and condemned with equal passion, but never ignored. Yet such a presence, formed in the heat of controversies and refutations — and towards the end of his life, self-imposed exile — brought forth very few, if any, objective studies of his work. This was perhaps inevitable in Argentine criticism during his lifetime, but twelve years from his death, this is still virtually the situation in Argentine and Hispanic criticism in general. While there have been several rather isolated partial studies of his works, such as the poetry, there have been no serious studies of all the essays as a *corpus,* and but one devoted to his complete works, which will be presently discussed. On the one hand this situation is not difficult to understand, since the author died in 1964, three years before the publication of his most ambitious undertaking, *Martí revolucionario* and the appearance in the later 1960's of re-printings of earlier articles in ephemeral journals, together with evidence that there is still more unedited material to be published. On the other hand, however, even a cursory reading of the body of the essays reveals that the essentials of Martínez Estrada's position towards Argentina and America, repeated again and again throughout the essays, were evident before his death, and the posthumous material has served to reinforce and clarify attitudes already expressed, not to challenge them of offer fresh material for different interpretations.

Such studies as do exist, then, reflect the polemical nature of many of Martínez Estrada's essays, since these studies themselves set out to refute particular postures of the author. Faithful to these considerations was the first of such studies, by a Marxist critic, Juan José Sebreli, who published his *Martínez Estrada: una rebelión inútil* in 1960. To a large extent his study had to be partial, since fourteen of the author's twenty-eight essays were published between 1960 and 1968. Nonetheless, as we have inferred, the essays published up until 1960 gave, for the purposes of Sebreli's objections, an accurate image of many characteristics of the author, and his study included probably the most coherent body of criticism of the author to date and also summed-up some of the principal objections against the author raised by the literary generation of 1945 in Argentina. Yet its restrictions were considerable. Purporting to examine the essential impact of Martínez Estrada (in his essays up until 1960) on Argentina, and generally through a Marxist prism, it completely ignored the conflicts within the man's personality, and the extent to which these influenced his personal ideology. Moreover, Sebreli virtually accused the essayist of being a rather bad political economist, when it was obvious from *Radiografía de la pampa* onwards that this was not at all the role that Martínez Estrada has ascribed to himself. On the other hand, Sebreli produced one very pertinent judgement when he pointed to the logical consequences of Martínez Estrada's "telluric fatalism" and his cyclical view of history, inherited in all probability from Oswald Spengler.

Three years previously, in 1957, another partial study was made of the essayist, this time in opposition to his anti-Peronist work, *¿Qué es esto?* (1956). A Peronist himself, Agustín Ferraris in his *Pido la palabra: respondiendo a Ezequiel Martínez Estrada, Mario Amadeo y Ernesto Sábato,* accused the essayist of an anti-Peronism that was a thinly disguised anti-populism. To some extent the argument was well taken in that the distinctions Martínez Estrada attempted to make, on numerous occasions, between "popular but not proletarian" literature, between "cultura popular" and "cultura de masas," reveal a certain uneasy balance that was not to be fully resolved until the essayist's encounter with José Martí, towards the end of his life. Like Sebreli's work, this type of polemical tract attempted little systematic, objective criticism nor was it to be expected, given the circumstances.

On the level of newspaper and magazine articles, Martínez Estrada was the object of a host of publications down the years, and of special interest to the critic are two issues of the leading periodicals of the literary generation of 1945, *Contorno* and *Ciudad,* both of which, in 1954 and 1955 respectively, dedicated whole issues to a discussion of the author and his continuing relevance to contemporary Argentina. Despite being united by a common desire to overcome the frivolity of the previous generation of *martinfierristas* in favour of a much greater degree of commitment with the *medio ambiente,* opinions on Martínez Estrada were not so united. Ismael Viñas, for example, saw in the author "cierto profesionalismo profético," Raquel Weinbaum found a type of pontificating in his work, while Ludovico Ivanissevich Machado affirmed that "la historia de la sociología argentina se dividirá en antes y después de Martínez Estrada." Broadly speaking, the new generation bore witness to the principal achievement of the author as that of having consistently attacked the "mentiras colectivas" of Argentina, but that it could not share the cult of pessimism which it considered fundamental to Martínez Estrada's work and personality.

Yet it was precisely on the question of the personality of the author that these studies fell somewhat short. Pessimism is capable of being accompanied by widely differing attitudes and if of fundamental importance to the study of Martínez Estrada, it cannot hope to sum up, accurately, the author's personality; more pertinently, pessimism in Martínez Estrada is not an irreducible attitude of mind, but rather symptomatic of deeper preoccupations. Further, in neither of the studies is there any attempt at a criticism of Martínez Estrada's literary views, how he saw the role of the artist in Argentine society, or more important still, how he evaluated Argentine literature, historically, given his views on Argentine history.

Despite the increased attention paid to Martínez Estrada after his death, in the form of *agasajos, homenajes* and commemorative issues of various periodicals, illuminating insights into the essential conflicts of the author's personality were not particularly common. Of a special issue of *La Gaceta,* México, XI, 124 (Dec., 1964), dedicated to the author, only José Bianco and Emir Rodríguez Monegal's recollections (both under the general heading of "Escritores y amigos recuerdan a Don Ezequiel Martínez Estrada,") provide some fresh material in the sense mentioned above. With particular insight Rodríguez Monegal wrote, "este hombre contenido y delicado, sensato y cordial, era habitante cotidiano de un infierno que sus libros apenas dejan vislumbrar." Chronologically, the next study of this type was offered by the *Suplemento de Siempre* in its "Homenaje a Ezequiel Martínez Estrada" (149, 23rd Dec., 1964), where Fernando Benítez showed considerable sensibility in his evocation of the author's tremendous difficulties throughout his life. Phrasing his words almost in the manner of Martínez Estrada himself, Benítez saw the author as among those who are "acribillados con las flechas venenosas de los que tienen como misión el engaño, la simulación y el temor a la verdad y a la justicia."

In July of 1965, *Sur* dedicated its issue to "Homenaje a Ezequiel Martínez Estrada," and typical of the quality of the periodical, constituted one of the best evaluations of the writer up until that time. Victoria Ocampo reproduced a letter from the author that shed particular light upon his little-known childhood; Adolfo de Obieta called him "lúcido avatar de los mejores exploradores del ser, no ser, y deber ser del país," and Bernardo Canal Feijóo saw him as "el último de los grandes argentinos 'poseso' de amor a la patria; esto es, preso del pathos patriótico en grado patológico. Digo el último; no volverá a darse otro así." a well-known essayist himself, Canal Feijóo had on previous occasions dissented with Martínez Estrada on basic interpretations, and in general was consistently against the telluric conception of Argentine reality that was central to the thesis of *Radiografía de la pampa*. Echoing Rodríguez Monegal's affirmation of the great personal vicisitudes of the author, Jaime Rest paid tribute to the immense personal courage and patriotism of the man. Eugenio Pucciarelli took a clear position against those (Sebreli among them) who saw Martínez Estrada's posture as ultimately sterile: "su denuncia no es inoperante: es el aldabonazo que necesitaba una generación satisfecha para despertar de su modorra y sobreponerse a la confianza ingenua en el porvenir."

The Universal Nacional del Sur (Bahía Blanca), where the author had taught in 1956, offered a "Homenaje a Ezequiel Martínez Estrada," on the 4th of November, 1965 (published in 1968). Most worthy of note was the contribution of Ricardo Mosquera who attempted to construct certain phases in the essayist's work around the convergence of world events on the domestic crisis in Argentina in 1930, thus (according to Mosquera) giving rise to *Radiografía de la pampa* in 1933; rather pertinent, too, was his observation that much of Martínez Estrada's frustrations grew from the lack of a viable, realistic concept of the function and practice of politics.

The Cuban periodical *Casa de las Américas* (whose Prize the author had gained in 1960 for his *Análisis de la cultura*) dedicated its November-December number of 1965 to an *homenaje*. In spite of the prestige of many of the contributors (Enrique Anderson Imbert, Nicolás Guillén, Manuel Pedro González among them) the studies, as a group, offered little additional critical insight into the writer's work. Of interest, however, to the interpretation of the later period of the writer's life (the Cuban Experience) were the reflections of Arnaldo Orfila Reynal, "Nada más que recuerdo," and the interviews of Emmanuel Carballo, "Tres radiografías de Martínez Estrada." Most of the views expressed were on the level of personal experiences with the writer and Camila Henríquez Ureña's, "Sobre el *Panorama de las literaturas* de Ezequiel Martínez Estrada," constituted one of the few critical analyses of his work.

Two of the most perceptive articles written on the author to date, were provided by the Argentine poet César Fernández Moreno, whose "Martínez Estrada frente a la Argentina", *Mundo Nuevo*, Paris, I (July, 1966) and "Argentina frente a Martínez Estrada," *Mundo Nuevo*, II (Aug., 1966) achieved a splendid amalgam of personal reflection and rigorous analysis. Referring to the Pampa in Martínez Estrada's work, for example, the critic states that, "La pampa es soledad, es la versión paisajística de la nada. Y donde reina la nada, el único modo de llegar a ser es el hacer," adding that for the essayist "el hacer" is of chief importance, whereas for Borges it is "el ser." With even more profundity, Fernández Moreno affirmed, with reference to the temperamental realities of Martínez Estrada, that, "Suele encontrar mediocre lo bueno, malo lo mediocre y atroz lo malo. La natural polaridad de su mente lo lleva a desmesuradas oposiciones frente a los conceptos corrientemente aceptados. Por ejemplo: la conquista de América por los españoles fue para él poco más que una mera operación de saqueo." Fernández Moreno's method has been to strike a fine balance between sympathy for the author and a certain critical detachment, with particular success.

*Foreign criticism*

As has been inferred in the introductory words to this study, criticism outside of the River Plate region and Latin America itself has been rather slow to accord to Martínez Estrada his place due in the history of Argentinian literature, and even more so with reference to the writer's continental implications. Isolated scholars such as Marcel Bataillon have paused to review a book or so, but practically none has been induced into offering more serious studies. An important and rarely-quoted exception to this virtual neglect of the writer is a long article published in 1950 by the Spanish philologist, Antonio Tovar. His insistence on the distortions of Martínez Estrada's view of history, and especially that of the Conquest (as contained in *Radiografía* ... , *La cabeza de Goliat* and *Muerte y transfiguración* ...) suggest a mild defence of *la hispanidad,* but the study also contains some balanced, well-reasoned and well-documented objections that dispel any impression of a firm ideological orientation. Basically, his most telling criticism, anticipating a later, similar judgment by César Fernández Moreno (whose critical contributions we have noted above) is that much of what Martínez Estrada saw as defects of the Spaniard and of American man generally, were in fact defects of universal man.

Given the widespread study of Hispanic literatures in the United States, the neglect of such a fundamental figure of Argentine literature is rather disconcerting. Two notable exceptions, however, are Martin S. Stabb and Peter G. Earle. In two rather penetrating articles published in 1966, Stabb provided some valuable understanding of the persistence of certain attitudes in the writer that have helped to view certain so-called changes of direction in Martínez Estrada's work as having some antecedents in his early essays and poetry; in a recent book by the same author, the essayist receives generous attention. Earle has the distinction of authoring the first comprehensive study in English of the writer, *Prophet in the Wilderness: the Works of Ezequiel Martínez Estrada* (1971), in addition to previous articles published in Argentina, one of which focuses on the short-stories and is characterized by quite solid judgements. Probably the principal achievements of *Prophet in the Wilderness* were the tracing of Martínez Estrada's place in Argentine cultural history — a history not without its antecedents of restless and rootless writers — and a rather intriguing discussion of an obsession with death and a paradise lost as constants running throughout his work. Other recent North American contributors include David J. Danielson, Joseph A. Feustle Jr., Robert G. Mead, and Alexander Coleman.

# APPENDIX II

## CHRONOLOGY OF THE ESSAYS OF EZEQUIEL MARTÍNEZ ESTRADA

1933: *Radiografía de la pampa*
1934
1935
1936
1937
1938
1939
1940: *La cabeza de Goliat*
1941
1942
1943
1944
1945
1946: *Sarmiento*
*Panorama de las literaturas*
1947: *Los invariantes históricos en el Facundo*
*Nietzsche*
1948: *Muerte y transfiguración de Martín Fierro*
1949
1950
1951: *El mundo maravilloso de Guillermo Enrique Hudson*
1952
1953
1954
1955
1956: *Cuadrante del pampero*
*¿Qué es esto?*
1957: *Las 40*
*Exhortaciones*

1957: *El hermano Quiroga*
1958: *Heraldos de la verdad*
1959
1960: *Análisis funcional de la cultura*
1961
1962: *Familia de Martí*
*Diferencias y semejanzas entre los países de América Latina*
1963: *El verdadero cuento del Tío Sam*
*En Cuba y al servicio de la Revolución Cubana*
*El nuevo mundo, la isla de Utopía y la isla de Cuba*
1964: *Realidad y fantasía en Balzac*
*Antología*
1965: *Mi experiencia cubana*
1966: *La poesía afro-cubana de Nicolás Guillén*
*Martí: el héroe y su acción revolucionaria*
1967: *Martí revolucionario*
*En torno a Kafka y otros ensayos*
*Para una revisión de las letras argentinas*
1968: *Meditaciones sarmientinas*
*Leopoldo Lugones: retrato sin retocar*
1969: *Leer y escribir*

# APPENDIX III

The organization of the essays of Ezequiel Martínez Estrada as recommended by the author in correspondence to Carlos Adam, dated 30th April, 1964. See Carlos Adam, *Bibliografía y documentos de Ezequiel Martínez Estrada* (La Plata: Universidad Nacional de la Plata, 1968), p. 197. The author gave but examples of each category, and Adam has accurately completed the table. Posthumous classifications not in Adam are mine.

## Literary

*Panorama de las literaturas* (1946)
*Nietzsche* (1947)
*El mundo maravilloso de Guillermo Enrique Hudson* (1951)
*El hermano Quiroga* (1957)
*Heraldos de la verdad: Montaigne-Balzac-Nietzsche* (1958)
*Realidad y fantasia en Balzac* (1964)
*La poesía afrocubana de Nicolás Guillén* (1966)
*En torno a Kafka y otros ensayos* (1967)
*Para una revisión de las letras argentinas* (1967)

## Historico-sociological

*Radiografía de la pampa* (1933)
*La cabeza de Goliat: Microscopía de Buenos Aires* (1940)
*Sarmiento* (1946)
*Los invariantes históricos en el Facundo* (1947)
*Muerte y transfiguración de Martín Fierro: Ensayo de interpretación de la vida argentina* (1948)
*Análisis funcional de la cultura* (1960)
*Diferencias y semejanzas entre los países de la América Latina* (1962)
*Familia de Martí* (1962)
*Martí: El héroe y su acción revolucionaria* (1966)
*Martí revolucionario* (1967)
*Meditaciones sarmientinas* (1968)
*Leopoldo Lugones: retrato sin retocar* (1968)
*Leer y escribir* (1969)

## Polemical

*Cuadrante del pampero* (1956)
*¿Qué es esto?* (1956)
*Exhortaciones* (1957)
*Las 40* (1957)
*El nuevo mundo, la isla de Utopía y la isla de Cuba* (1963)
*El verdadero cuento del Tío Sam* (1963)
*En Cuba y al servicio de la revolución cubana* (1963)
*Mi experiencia cubana* (1965) — a re-issue of *En Cuba*, with a new prologue.

## Anthology

*Antología* (1964)

# BIBLIOGRAPHY

I. THE ESSAYS OF EZEQUIEL MARTÍNEZ ESTRADA

Martínez Estrada, Ezequiel. *Radiografía de la pampa*. 6.ª ed. Buenos Aires: Losada, 1968.

———. *La cabeza de Goliat: Microscopía de Buenos Aires*. 2.ª ed. Buenos Aires: Emecé, 1947.

———. *Sarmiento*. 2.ª ed. Buenos Aires: Argos, 1956.

———. *Panorama de las literaturas*. Buenos Aires: Editorial Claridad, 1946.

———. *Los invariantes históricos en el Facundo*. Buenos Aires: Viau, 1947.

———. *Nietzsche*. Buenos Aires: Emecé, 1947.

———. *Muerte y transfiguración de Martín Fierro: Ensayo de interpretación de la vida argentina*. 2 vols. México: Fondo de Cultura Económica, 1948.

———. *El mundo maravilloso de Guillermo Enrique Hudson*. México: Fondo de Cultura Económica, 1951.

———. *Cuadrante del pampero*. Buenos Aires: Deucalión, 1956.

———. *¿Qué es esto?* 2.ª ed. Buenos Aires: Lautaro, 1956.

———. *Las 40*. Buenos Aires: Gure, 1957.

———. *Exhortaciones*. Buenos Aires: Burnichon, 1957.

———. *El hermano Quiroga*. 2.ª ed. Montevideo: Arca, 1966.

———. *Heraldos de la verdad: Montaigne-Balzac-Nietzsche*. Buenos Aires: Editorial Nova, 1958.

———. *Análisis funcional de la cultura*. La Habana: Casa de las Américas, 1960.

———. *Familia de Martí*. La Habana Editorial Nacional, 1962.

———. *Diferencias y semejanzas entre los países de la América Latina*. México: Universidad Nacional Autónoma, Escuela Nacional de Ciencias Políticas y Sociales, 1962.

———. *El verdadero cuento del Tío Sam*. La Habana: Casa de las Américas, 1963.

———. *En Cuba y al servicio de la revolución cubana*. La Habana: Unión, 1963.

———. *El nuevo mundo, la isla de Utopía y la isla de Cuba*. México: Cuadernos americanos, 1963.

———. *Antología*. México: Fondo de Cultura Económica, 1964.

———. *Realidad y fantasía en Balzac*. Bahía Blanca: Universidad Nacional del Sur, 1964.

———. *Mi experiencia cubana*. Montevideo: El Siglo Ilustrado, 1965.

———. *Martí: el héroe y su acción revolucionaria*. México: Siglo XXI, 1966.

Martínez Estrada, Ezequiel. *La poesía afrocubana de Nicolás Guillén*. Montevideo: Arca, 1966.

——. *Martí revolucionario*: Vol. I. La Habana: Casa de las Américas, 1967.

——. *En torno a Kafka y otros ensayos*. Barcelona: Seix Barral, 1967.

——. *Para una revisión de las letras argentinas*. Ed. and arr. by E. Espinoza. Buenos Aires: Losada, 1967.

——. *Meditaciones sarmientinas*. Ed. and arr. by E. Espinosa. Santiago de Chile: Editorial Universitaria, 1968.

——. *Leopoldo Lugones: retrato sin retocar*. Ed. and arr. by E. Espinoza. Buenos Aires: Emecé, 1968.

——. *Leer y escribir*. Ed. and arr. by E. Espinoza. México: Editorial Joaquín Mortiz, 1969.

II. Periodical material of Ezequiel Martínez Estrada

Martínez Estrada, Ezequiel. "Tesoros velados," *Nosotros*, Buenos Aires, 11, no. 102 (oct. de 1917), 193-199.

——. "El estímulo de vivir," *Nosotros*, Buenos Aires, 11, no. 104 (dic. de 1917), 457-566.

——. "Energías anónimas," *Nosotros*, Buenos Aires, 12, no. 106 (febrero de 1918), 225-233.

——. "Mester de juglaría," *La Vida Literaria*, Buenos Aires, I (primera quincena de julio de 1928), 2.

——. "Diálogo inverosímil: La muerte y la literatura," *La Vida Literaria*, Buenos Aires, 1, no. 6 (2.ª quincena nov. de 1928), 1.

——. "Sentido de la paradoja," *Anales del Instituto Popular de Conferencias*, Buenos Aires, v. 20 (1934), 46-61.

——. "Horacio Quiroga," *Sur*, Buenos Aires, no. 29 (febrero de 1937), 108-111.

——. "Discurso en la cremación de los restos de Horacio Quiroga," *Nosotros*, Buenos Aires, 2, no. 12 (2.ª época marzo de 1937), 324-327.

——. "Estética y filosofía de Guillermo Enrique Hudson," *Sur*, Buenos Aires, no. 81 (junio 1941), 13-24.

——. "Victoria Ocampo: '338171 T. E.'," *Sur*, Buenos Aires, no. 100 (enero de 1943), 100-107.

——. "Discurso como Presidente de la S.A.D.E.," *Boletín de la Sociedad Argentina de Escritores*, Buenos Aires, 13, v. 2, no. 24 (julio de 1944), 2 y 4.

——. "Nietzsche, filósofo dionisíaco," *La Nación*, Buenos Aires (2.ª secc. 15 de oct. de 1944), 1.

——. "Discurso," *Boletín de la Sociedad Argentina de Escritores*, Buenos Aires, 16, v. 2, no. 26 (julio de 1945), 1.

——. "La inmoralidad de *Facundo*," *Cuadernos Americanos*, México, 4, v. 23, no. 5 (set.-oct. de 1945), 207-220.

——. "Para el prólogo o para el epílogo," *Los Anales de Buenos Aires*, Buenos Aires, 1, no. 1 (enero de 1946), 11.

——. "El problema contemporáneo de la libertad," *Cuadernos Americanos*, México, 6, v. 27, no. 3 (mayo-junio de 1946), 69-76.

——. "Montaigne en la cultura," *Los Anales de Buenos Aires*, Buenos Aires, 1, no. 8 (julio de 1946), 5-10.

Martínez Estrada, Ezequiel. "Palabras pronunciadas en el sepelio de Pedro Henríquez Ureña," *Sur*, Buenos Aires, no. 141 (julio de 1946), 7-10.

———. "Sarmiento y Martí," *Cuadernos Americanos*, México, 5, v. 28, no. 4 (julio-agosto de 1946), 197-214.

———. "De *Facundo* a *Conflicto y armonías*," *Los Anales de Buenos Aires*, Buenos Aires, 2, no. 17 (julio de 1947), 3-7.

———. "Imperialismo y buena vecindad," *Cuadernos Americanos*, México (set.-oct. de 1947), 80-86.

———. "Imagen de Martín Fierro," *Cuadernos Americanos*, México, 7, v. 41, no. 5 (set.-oct. de 1948), 99-125.

———. "El 'complejo chandala'," *Cuadernos Americanos*, México, 11, v. 49, no. 1 (enero-febrero de 1950), 116-129.

———. "Norteamérica, la hacendosa," *Sur*, Buenos Aires, no. 192-194 (oct.-nov.-dic. de 1950), 156-159.

———. "Sarmiento y los Estados Unidos," *Cuadernos Americanos*, México, 11, v. 63, no. 3 (mayo-junio de 1952), 186-204.

———. "Anverso del estado," *La Nación*, Buenos Aires (2.ª secc. 15 de agosto de 1954), 1.

———. "Cultura enferma," *La Prensa*, Buenos Aires (2.ª secc. 19 feb. de 1956), 1.

———. "De las 'élites' al pueblo," *La Prensa*, Buenos Aires (2.ª secc. 4 de marzo de 1956), 1.

———. "Sucesores y albaceas del peronismo," *Marcha*, Montevideo, 17, no. 806 (23 de marzo de 1956).

———. "Nuestro periodismo y la libertad," *La Prensa*, Buenos Aires (2.ª secc. 25 de marzo de 1956), 1.

———. "'Yo escuché a distancia su voz'," *La Prensa*, Buenos Aires (2.ª secc. 10 de junio de 1956).

———. "Moreno, Rivadavia y los epígonos," *Cuadernos Americanos*, México, 15, v. 89, no. 5 (set.-oct. de 1956), 179-187.

———. "25 aniversario de la 'Radiografía de la pampa'," *La Gaceta*, México, Fondo de Cultura Económica, 5, no. 53 (enero de 1959), 1 y 4.

———. "Leopoldo Lugones (1874-1938): Retrato sin retocar," *Cuadernos Americanos*, México, 19, v. 102, no. 1 (enero-febrero de 1959), 211-223.

———. "Epílogo," *Sur*, Buenos Aires, no. 257 (marzo-abril de 1959), 38-49.

———. "Hellen Keller," *Cuadernos Americanos*, México, 18, v. 105, no. 4 (julio-agosto de 1959), 71-85.

———. "El Fondo, instituto editorial de instrucción superior y popular," *La Gaceta*, México, Fondo de Cultura Económica, 5, no. 61 (set. de 1959), 1 y 4.

———. "Lectura de la realidad argentina," *Cuadernos Americanos*, México, 18, v. 107, no. 6 (nov.-dic. de 1959), 7-34.

———. "Homenaje a Alfonso Reyes," *Cuadernos Americanos*, México, 19, v. 109, no. 2 (marzo-abril de 1960), 21-22.

———. "Un año más de 'Cuadernos Americanos'," *Cuadernos Americanos*, México, 19, v. 109, no. 2 (marzo-abril de 1960), 51-55.

———. "Los escritores frente a una actitud," *Atlántida*, Buenos Aires, 43, no. 1143 (set. de 1960), 22-28.

———. "Pedro Henríquez Ureña: Evocación iconomántica, estrictamente personal," *Cuaedrnos Americanos*, México, 19, v. 112, no. 5 (set.-oct. de 1960), 73-98.

Martínez Estrada, Ezequiel. "Almafuerte, el poeta de los humillados y ofen-
didos," *La Gaceta,* México, Fondo de Cultura Económica, 6, no. 74 (oct.
de 1960), 1-2.
———. "Cuba y el destino americano: De ida y vuelta," *Siempre,* México,
no. 495 (19 de dic. de 1962).
———. "El nuevo mundo, la isla de Utopía y la isla de Cuba," *Cuadernos
Americanos,* México, v. 127, no. 2 (marzo-abril de 1963), 89-112.
———. "Apostolado de José Martí: el noviciado," *Cuadernos Americanos,*
México, 23, v. 134, no. 3 (mayo-junio de 1964), 65-84.
———. "Nuevos 'Testimonios' de Victoria Ocampo," *Cuadernos Americanos,*
México, v. 135, no. 4 (julio-agosto de 1964), 273-278.
———. "La juventud argentina está leyendo en mis libros la vida de la na-
ción," *La Gaceta,* México, 11, no. 121 (set. de 1964), 3.
———. "Párrafos de una semblanza autobiográfica 'exhaustiva y desapasio-
nada'," *La Gaceta,* México, Fondo de Cultura Económica, 11, no. 124
(dic. de 1964), 3.
———. "Carta a Victoria Ocampo," *Sur,* Buenos Aires, no. 295 (julio-agosto
de 1965), 3-7.
———. "Dos capítulos sobre Martí: La libertad. El sindicalismo," *Sur,*
Buenos Aires, no. 295 (julio-agosto de 1965), 8-19.
———. "Cartas a Roberto Fernández Retamar y Samuel Feijóo," *Islas,* Revista de la Universidad Central de Las Villas, Santa Clara, Cuba, 7, no. 2
(julio-set. de 1965), 69-83.

III. Interviews given by Ezequiel Martínez Estrada

"Somos pasado y queremos seguir siéndolo," *Gaceta Literaria,* Buenos Aires,
1, no. 2 (marzo de 1956), 1 y 2.
"Entrevista con Martínez Estrada," *México en la Cultura,* México (7 de
febrero de 1960).
"Conversación con Ezequiel Martínez Estrada," *México en la Cultura,* México,
no. 604 (10 de oct. de 1960), 3.
"Tres radiografías del escritor profeta por nombre y obra," *La Gaceta,* Méxi-
co, Fondo de Cultura Económica, II, no. 124 (dic. de 1964), 3-4.
"En Cuba, Martínez Estrada descubrió la alegría, la juventud y la esperan-
za," *Suplemento de Siempre,* México, no. 149 (23 de dic. de 1964), 8 y 9.
"Tres radiografías de Ezequiel Martínez Estrada," *Casa de las Américas,* La
Habana, 5, no. 33 (nov.-dic. de 1965), 38-49.

IV. Criticism

a. *Partial or complete studies on Ezequiel Martínez Estrada*

Adam, Carlos. *Bibliografía y documentos de Ezequiel Martínez Estrada.* La
Plata: Universidad Nacional, 1968.
Ara, Guillermo. *Los argentinos y la literatura argentina.* Buenos Aires:
Huemul S. A., 1966.
Barreiro, José. *El espíritu de Mayo y el revisionismo histórico.* Buenos Aires:
Antonio Zamora, 1955.
Brughetti, Romualdo. *Descontento creador: afirmación de una cultura argen-
tina.* Buenos Aires: Losada, 1943.

Chávez, Fermín. *Civilización y barbarie en la historia de la cultura argentina.* Buenos Aires: Ediciones Theoria, 1965.

Clemente, José Edmundo. *El ensayo.* Buenos Aires: Ministerio de Educación y Justicia, 1961.

Cúneo, Dardo. *Aventura y letra de América Latina.* Buenos Aires: Ediciones Pleamar, 1964.

————. *El desencuentro argentino: 1930-1955.* Buenos Aires: Ediciones Pleamar, 1965.

Earle, Peter G. *Prophet in the Wilderness: the Works of Ezequiel Martínez Estrada.* Austin: University of Texas Press, 1971.

"El ensayo moderno: Martínez Estrada," *Capítulo: la historia de la literatura argentina.* Buenos Aires: Centro Editor de América Latina, no. 44 (mayo de 1968).

Feijóo, Samuel and Fernández Retamar, Roberto. "Para un epistolario cubano de Don Ezequiel Martínez Estrada," *Islas,* Santa Clara, Cuba, 7, no. 2 (julio-setiembre de 1965), 69-83.

Ferraris, Agustín. *Pido la palabra: respondiendo a Ezequiel Martínez Estrada, Mario Amadeo y Ernesto Sábato.* Buenos Aires: Capricornio, 1957.

Hernández Arregui, Juan José. *Imperialismo y cultura: la política en la inteligencia argentina.* Buenos Aires: Amerindia, 1957.

————. *¿Qué es el ser nacional?* Buenos Aires: Hachea, 1963.

Jauretche, Arturo. *Los profetas del odio.* Buenos Aires: Trafac, 1957.

Lewald, H. Ernest. *Argentina: análisis y autoanálisis.* Buenos Aires: Sudamericana, 1969.

Mastronardi, Carlos. *Formas de la realidad nacional.* Buenos Aires: Ediciones Culturales, 1961.

Mosquera, Ricardo, *et al. Homenaje a Ezequiel Martínez Estrada.* Bahía Blanca: Universidad Nacional del Sur, 1965.

Murena, Héctor A. *El pecado original de América,* 2.ª edición, Buenos Aires: Sudamericana, 1965.

Nemes, Graciela. *Comparación entre Facundo, o Civilización y barbarie, por Domingo Faustino Sarmiento, y la Radiografía de la pampa, por Ezequiel Martínez Estrada.* Unpublished M. A. thesis, University of Maryland, 1949.

Orgambide, Pedro. *Radiografía de Martínez Estrada.* Buenos Aires: Centro Editor de la América Latina, 1970.

Portantiero, Juan Carlos. *Realismo y realidad en la narrativa argentina.* Buenos Aires: Ediciones Procyón, 1961.

Ramos, Jorge Abelardo. *Crisis y resurrección de la literatura argentina.* Buenos Aires: Editorial Coyoacán, 1961.

Rodríguez Bustamante, Norberto, ed. *Los intelectuales argentinos y sociedad.* Buenos Aires: Libera, 1967.

Rodríguez Monegal, Emir. *El juicio de los parricidas.* Buenos Aires: Deucalión, 1956.

Sebreli, Juan José. *Martínez Estrada: una rebelión inútil.* Buenos Aires: Palestra, 1960.

Soto, Luis Emilio. *Crítica y estimación.* Buenos Aires: Sur, 1939.

Stabb, Martin S. *In Quest of Identity.* Chapel Hill: University of North Carolina Press, 1967.

Wilson, Shielah. *Ezequiel Martínez Estrada: a Study in the Dialectics of Determination and Indetermination.* Unpublished doctoral dissertation, University of California, Los Angeles, 1970.

b. *Signed periodical articles on Ezequiel Martínez Estrada*

Aguilera Malta, Demetrio. "Vida de privaciones y sacrificios," *Siempre,* México, no. 149 (23 de diciembre de 1964), 2.

Anderson Imbert, Enrique. "Martínez Estrada en 1926," *Sur,* Buenos Aires, no. 295 (julio-agosto de 1965), 49-54.

Anzoátegui, Ignacio B. "Los escritores frente a una actitud: Martínez Estrada y el país," *Atlántida,* Buenos Aires, 43, no. 1123 (setiembre de 1960), 24.

Ara, Guillermo. "Martínez Estrada; intuición y riesgo," *Atenea,* Concepción, Chile, Universidad de Concepción, 43, v. 161. no. 411 (enero-marzo de 1966), 115-123.

Ayala, Francisco. "Ezequiel Martínez Estrada: 'Sarmiento'," *Sur,* Buenos Aires, no. 150 (abril de 1947), 72-74.

Barletta, Leónidas. "Los escritores frente a una actitud: Martínez Estrada y el país," *Atlántida,* Buenos Aires, 43, no. 1123, (setiembre de 1960), 25.

————. "Testimonio," *Casa de las Américas,* La Habana, 5, no. 33 (noviembre-diciembre de 1965), 32-33.

Bataillon, Marcel. "Sur l'essence de l'Argentine," *Annales,* Paris, v. 3 (1948), 439-441.

Benítez, Fernando. "La cultura en México: Ezequiel Martínez Estrada," *Suplemento de Siempre,* México, no. 149 (23 de diciembre de 1964), 1.

Bermann, Gregorio. "Carta a Manuel Galich," *Casa de las Américas,* La Habana, 5, no. 33 (nov.-dic. de 1965), 36.

Bianco, José. "Escritores y amigos recuerdan a Don Ezequiel Martínez Estrada," *La Gaceta,* México, Fondo de Cultura Económica, II, no. 124 (dic. de 1964), 5-6.

Borello, Rodolfo A. "Dos aspectos esenciales de la 'Radiografía de la pampa'," *Ciudad,* Buenos Aires, no. 1 (primer trimestre de 1955), 24-30.

Borges, Jorge Luis. "'Radiografía de la pampa,' por Ezequiel Martínez Estrada," *Crítica,* Buenos Aires, 1, no. 6 (16 de set. de 1933), 5.

————. "Una efusión de Ezequiel Martínez Estrada," *Sur,* Buenos Aires, no. 242 (set.-oct. de 1956), 52-53.

————. "Los escritores frente a una actitud: Martínez Estrada y el país," *Atlántida,* Buenos Aires, 43, no. 1123 (set. de 1960), 25.

Bueno, Salvador. "Don Ezequiel, premio Casa de las Américas 1960," *Casa de las Américas,* La Habana, 5, no. 33 (nov.-dic. de 1965), 74-77.

Bullrich, Silvina. "'La cabeza de Goliat,' por Ezequiel Martínez Estrada," *Atlántida,* Buenos Aires (nov. de 1947), 172.

————. "Los escritores frente a una actitud: Martínez Estrada y el país," *Atlántida,* Buenos Aires, 43, no. 1123 (set. de 1960), 25.

Canal-Feijóo, Bernardo. "Radiografías fatídicas," *Sur,* Buenos Aires, no. 37 (oct. de 1937), 63-77.

————. "Los enfermos de patria," *Sur,* Buenos Aires, no. 295 (julio-ag. de 1965), 20-25.

Castillo, Abelardo. "Escritores y amigos recuerdan a Don Ezequiel Martínez Estrada," *La Gaceta,* México, Fondo de Cultura Económica, II, no. 124 (dic. de 1964), 6.

Ciocchini, Héctor. "Notas, sin orden, para la contribución a una imagen de Ezequiel Martínez Estrada," *Homenaje a Ezequiel Martínez Estrada.* Bahía Blanca: Universidad Nacional del Sur, 1968, 51-62.

Coleman, Alexander. "Martí y Martínez Estrada: Historia de una Simbiosis Espiritual," *Revista Iberoamericana*, vol. XLI, nos. 92-93 (July-Dec., 1975), 629-641.

Cúneo, Dardo. "Martínez Estrada, Martín Fierro y la Argentina," *Cuadernos Americanos*, México, v. 8, no. 4 (julio-ag. de 1949), 210-217.

———. "Martínez Estrada: crónica de un dolor argentino," *México en la Cultura*, México (17 de junio de 1955).

Danielson, J. David. "Death of a Master," *Hispania*, v. 48, no. 2 (mayo de 1965), 351-352.

Desnoes, Edmundo. "Ezequiel Martínez Estrada," *Casa de las Américas*, La Habana, 5, no. 33 (nov.-dic. de 1965), 33-35.

Earle, Peter G. "El perspectivismo narrativo de Martínez Estrada," *La Nación*, Buenos Aires (6 de julio de 1969).

Etchecopar, Máximo. "Sobre Ezequiel Martínez Estrada," *Esquema de la Argentina*, Buenos Aires, Club de lectores (1966), 73-77.

Feijóo, Samuel. "Para un epistolario cubano de don Ezequiel Martínez Estrada," *Islas*, Santa Clara, Cuba, Universidad Central de Las Villas, v. 7, no. 2 (julio-set. de 1965), 69-83.

Fernández Moreno, César. "Martínez Estrada frente a la Argentina," *Mundo Nuevo*, París, no. 1 (julio de 1966), 37-47.

———. "Argentina frente a Martínez Estrada," *Mundo Nuevo*, París, no. 2 (agosto de 1966), 31-42.

Fernández Retamar, Roberto. "Escritores y amigos recuerdan a don Ezequiel Martínez Estrada," *La Gaceta*, México, Fondo de Cultura Económica, 11, no. 124 (dic. de 1964), 5.

———. "In memoriam: Ezequiel Martínez Estrada," *Suplemento de Siempre*, México, no. 149 (23 de dic. de 1965), 6-7.

———. "Razón de homenaje," *Casa de las Américas*, La Habana (nov.-dic. de 1965), 5-14.

Feustle, Joseph A., Jr. "La concepción geométrica del mundo en el ensayo de Martínez Estrada," *Ínsula*, Madrid, v. 25, no. 278 (enero de 1970), 11.

Galich, Manuel. "Martínez Estrada es ya de América," *Casa de las Américas*, La Habana, 5, no. 33 (nov.-dic. de 1965), 28-29.

Gálvez, Manuel. "Los escritores frente a una actitud: Martínez Estrada y el país," *Atlántida*, Buenos Aires, 43, no. 1143 (set. de 1960), 26.

Gigli, Adelaida. "La poesía de Martínez Estrada: Oro y piedra para siempre," *Contorno*, Buenos Aires, no. 4 (dic. de 1954), 17-19.

Gil Novales, Alberto. "Ezequiel Martínez Estrada: 'Realidad y fantasía en Balzac," *Cuadernos Hispanoamericanos*, Madrid, v. 66, no. 196 (abril de 1966), 187-189.

Giner de los Ríos, Francisco. "Escritores y amigos recuerdan a don Ezequiel Martínez Estrada," *La Gaceta*, México, Fondo de Cultura Económica, 11, no. 124 (dic. de 1964), 5-6.

Giusti, Roberto. "Diagnóstico pesimista de la realidad argentina," *La Prensa*, Buenos Aires (2.ª secc. 23 de set. de 1956).

———. "La crítica y el ensayo," *Historia de la literatura argentina*. Tomo IV. Ed. Rafael Alberto Arrieta. Buenos Aires: Peuser, 1959, 486-487.

González, Manuel Pedro. "Cómo se debe amar a la patria," *Suplemento de Siempre*, México, no. 149 (23 de dic. de 1964), 2 y 3.

———. "Reflexiones en torno a Ezequiel Martínez Estrada," *Casa de las Américas*, La Habana, 5, no. 33 (nov.-dic. de 1965), 55-62.

González Lanuza, Eduardo. "Vivir y saber: Hudson a través de Martínez Estrada," *La Nación*, Buenos Aires (2.ª secc. 9 de set. de 1951), 1.

——. "A veinticinco años de 'Radiografía de la pampa'," *La Nación*, Buenos Aires (2.ª secc. 28 de dic. de 1958), 22.

Guillén, Nicolás. "Don Ezequiel...," *Casa de las Américas*, La Habana, 5, no. 33 (nov.-dic. de 1965), 25-26.

Henríquez Ureña, Camila. "Sobre el 'Panorama de las literaturas,' de Ezequiel Martínez Estrada," *Casa de las Américas*, La Habana, 5, no. 33 (nov.-dic. de 1965), 63-69.

Henríquez Ureña, Pedro. "Sobre Ezequiel Martínez Estrada," *Obra crítica*, México, Fondo de Cultura Económica (1960), 308.

Iduarte, Andrés. "Una fiel y tierna semblanza de Horacio Quiroga," *Revista Hispánica Moderna*, New York, 24, no. 1 (enero de 1958), 49-50.

Ivanissevich Machado, Ludovico. "El puritanismo en Martínez Estrada," *Ciudad*, Buenos Aires, no. 1 (primer trimestre 1955), 20-23.

Kusch, Rodolfo. "Lo superficial y lo profundo en Martínez Estrada," *Contorno*, Buenos Aires, no. 4 (dic. de 1954), 5-8.

Lancelotti, Mario A. "Ezequiel Martínez Estrada: 'Marta Riquelme'," *Sur*, Buenos Aires, no. 243 (nov.-dic. de 1956), 74-76.

——. "Martínez Estrada cuentista," *Sur*, Buenos Aires, no. 295 (julio-ag. de 1965), 55-59.

Lejarraga, Pablo. "Discurso pronunciado en el homenaje que la Cámara de Diputados le rindió a Ezequiel Martínez Estrada," *La Gaceta*, México, Fondo de Cultura Económica, 11, no. 124 (dic. de 1964), 6.

Lizarraga, Andrés. "Los escritores frente a una actitud: Martínez Estrada y el país," *Atlántida*, Buenos Aires, 43, no. 1123 (set. de 1960), 27.

López, José Ariel. "Los libros de Martínez Estrada," *Propósitos*, Buenos Aires (8 de enero de 1957).

Loveluck, Juan. "Antología de Ezequiel Martínez Estrada," *Atenea*, Concepción, Chile, v. 42, 409 (julio-set. de 1965), 284-286.

Lugones, Leopoldo. "Laureado del gay mester," *La Nación*, Buenos Aires, 1, no. 7 (secc. Magazine 18 de ag. de 1929), 2.

Maharg, James. "Reflexiones en torno a la ideología de Ezequiel Martínez Estrada," *Cuadernos Hispanoamericanos*, Madrid, no. 269 (nov. de 1972), 211-225.

——. "Los límites de la iconoclasia: la teoría literaria de Ezequiel Martínez Estrada," *Anales del XVIII Congreso Internacional de Literatura Iberoamericana* (in press).

——. "Fructiferous Exile: Martínez Estrada and the Encounter with Martí," *Estudos Ibero-Americanos*, São Paulo (in press).

Mainer, José Carlos. "Ezequiel Martínez Estrada en lo argentino," *Ínsula*, Madrid 221 (1966), 5.

Manauta, Juan José. "Los escritores frente a una actitud: Martínez Estrada y el país," *Atlántida*, Buenos Aires, 43, no. 1123 (set. de 1960), 27.

Mosquera, Ricardo. "Martínez Estrada en la lucha por una Argentina contemporánea," *Homenaje a Ezequiel Martínez Estrada*. Bahía Blanca: Universidad Nacional del Sur, 1968, 5-29.

Murena, H. A., seud. de Héctor Alberto Álvarez. "Martínez Estrada: La lección a los desposeídos," *Sur*, Buenos Aires, no. 204 (oct. de 1951), 1-18.

——. "Carta del Río de la Plata," *Asomante*, San Juan, Puerto Rico, 20, v. 20, no. 4 (oct.-dic. de 1964).

Murena, H. A., "Lo que los argentinos piensan sobre la personalidad argentina," *Diálogos*, Revista del Departamento de Filosofía, Universidad de Puerto Rico, 3, no. 6 (julio-dic. de 1966), 79-86.

Nalé Roxlo, Conrado. "Los escritores frente a una actitud: Martínez Estrada y el país," *Atlántida*, Buenos Aires, 43, no. 1123 (set. de 1960), 27.

Obieta, Adolfo de. "Ser, no ser y deber ser de la Argentina," *Sur*, Buenos Aires, no. 295 (julio-ag. de 1965), 26-33.

Ocampo, Victoria. "Los escritores frente a una actitud: Martínez Estrada y el país," *Atlántida*, Buenos Aires, 43, no. 1123 (set. de 1960), 27 y 28.

———. "Carta a Martínez Estrada," *Artes y Letras Argentinas*, Buenos Aires, Fondo Nacional de las Artes, 6, no. 24 (nov.-dic. de 1964), 2, 7 y 57.

———. "Escritores y amigos recuerdan a don Ezequiel Martínez Estrada," *La Gaceta*, México, Fondo de Cultura Económica, 11, no. 124 (dic. de 1964), 5-6.

———. "Cortina de alas," *Sur*, Buenos Aires, no. 295 (julio-ag. de 1965), 1 y 2.

Orfila Reynal, Arnaldo. "Nada más que un recuerdo," *Casa de las Américas*, La Habana, 5, no. 33 (nov.-dic. de 1965), 17-24.

Prior, Aldo. "Después de Martínez Estrada," *Sur*, Buenos Aires, no. 293 (marzo-abril de 1965), 32-43.

———. "Bibliografía de Martínez Estrada," *Sur*, Buenos Aires, no. 295 (julio-ag. de 1965), 73-78.

Pucciarelli, Eugenio. "La imagen de la Argentina en la obra de Martínez Estrada," *Sur*, Buenos Aires, no. 295 (julio-ag. de 1965), 34-48.

Real de Azúa, Carlos. "El desarraigo argentino: Mafud y el martínez-estradismo," *Marcha*, Montevideo, 21, no. 992 (31 de dic. de 1959), 1 y 6.

Rest, Jaime. "Evocación de Martínez Estrada," *Sur*, Buenos Aires, no. 295 (julio-ag. de 1965), 69-72.

———. "Trayectoria de Martínez Estrada," *Homenaje a Ezequiel Martínez Estrada*. Bahía Blanca: Universidad Nacional del Sur, 1968, 46-51.

Rodríguez Monegal, Emir. "El testimonio de Martínez Estrada," *Marcha*, Montevideo, 18, no. 871-873 (julio-ag. de 1957).

———. "Escritores y amigos recuerdan a don Ezequiel Martínez Estrada," *La Gaceta*, México, Fondo de Cultura Económica, 11, no. 124 (dic. de 1964), 5-6.

———. "Martínez Estrada en Cuba," *Mundo Nuevo*, París, no. 2 (ag. de 1966), 62-63.

Roggiano, Alfredo A. "Martínez Estrada, Ezequiel," *Diccionario de la literatura latinoamericana: Argentina*. 2.ª parte. Washington: Unión Panamericana, 1961, 332-335.

Romero, José Luis. "Martínez Estrada, un renovador de la exégesis sarmientina," *Cuadernos Americanos*, México, v. 33, no. 3 (mayo-junio de 1947), 197-204.

Sábato, Ernesto. "Los escritores frente a una actitud: Martínez Estrada y el país," *Atlántida*, Buenos Aires, 43, no. 1123 (set. de 1960), 28.

Sáenz, Dalmiro. "Los escritores frente a una actitud: Martínez Estrada y el país," *Atlántida*, Buenos Aires, 43, no. 1123 (set. de 1960), 28.

Sánchez Garrido, Amelia. "Un cuentista en su laberinto," *Homenaje a Ezequiel Martínez Estrada*. Bahía Blanca: Universidad Nacional del Sur, 1968, 29-46.

Sánchez Reulet, Aníbal. "El problema de la identidad argentina en la obra de Ezequiel Martínez Estrada." Unpublished public lecture given at the University of Illinois, Urbana, Illinois on 30th April, 1970.

Sánchez Trincado, José. "Ezequiel Martínez Estrada: 'Nietzsche'," *Revista Hispánica Moderna*, New York, Columbia University, Casa Hispánica, v. 14, no. 3-4 (1948), 300-301.

Santamaría, Haydée. "Bueno entre los buenos," *Casa de las Américas*, La Habana, 5, no. 33 (nov.-dic. de 1965), 16-17.

Schultz de Mantovani, Fryda. "Martínez Estrada en el mundo de Hudson," *Sur*, Buenos Aires, no. 207-208 (enero-febrero de 1952), 110-114.

Sebreli, Juan José. "Martínez Estrada y el fatalismo telúrico," *Gaceta Literaria*, Buenos Aires, 4, no. 20 (mayo de 1960), 19 y 30.

Solero, F. J. "Primera aproximación a Martínez Estrada," *Contorno*, Buenos Aires, no. 4 (dic. de 1954), 9 y 10.

Soto, Luis Emilio. " 'Muerte y transfiguración de Martín Fierro,' de Ezequiel Martínez Estrada," *Reseña de Artes y Letras*, Buenos Aires, 1, no. 4 (nov. de 1949), 8-10 y 12.

———. "Los escritores frente a una actitud: Martínez Estrada y el país," *Atlántida*, Buenos Aires, 43, no. 1123 (set. de 1960), 28.

Stabb, Martin S. "Martínez Estrada frente a la crítica," *Revista Iberoamericana*, Pittsburgh, v. 32, no. 61 (enero-junio de 1966), 77-84.

———. "Ezequiel Martínez Estrada: The Formative Writings," *Hispania*, v. 49, no. 1 (marzo de 1966), 54-60.

Suevo, Orlando J. "Bibliografía de Ezequiel Martínez Estrada," *Contorno*, Buenos Aires, no. 4 (dic. de 1954), 5.

Tovar, Antonio. "Introspección de la Argentina en el escritor Martínez Estrada," *Revista de Estudios Políticos*, Madrid, Instituto de Estudios Políticos, no. 49 (enero-febrero de 1950), 219-253.

Vargas, Raúl. "Ezequiel Martínez Estrada o el magisterio americano," *Islas*, Santa Clara, Cuba, Universidad de las Villas, 9, no. 3 (julio-set. de 1967), 83-87.

Vera Ocampo, Raúl. "El 'Sarmiento' de Martínez Estrada: Un ensayo de autobiografía," *Sur*, Buenos Aires, no. 295 (julio-ag. de 1965), 60-68.

Viñas, David. "La historia excluida: ubicación de Martínez Estrada," *Contorno*, Buenos Aires, no. 4 (dic. de 1954), 10-16.

Viñas, Ismael. "Reflexión sobre Martínez Estrada," *Contorno*, Buenos Aires, no. 4 (dic. de 1954), 2-4.

———. "Alrededor del 'Sarmiento'," *Ciudad*, Buenos Aires, no. 1 (primer trimestre 1955), 30-34.

Weinbaum, Raquel, seud. de David Viñas. "Los ojos de Martínez Estrada," *Contorno*, Buenos Aires, no. 4 (dic. de 1954), 1.

Wernicke, Enrique. "Los escritores frente a una actitud: Martínez Estrada y el país," *Atlántida*, Buenos Aires, 43, no. 1123 (set. de 1960), 28.

c. *Unsigned periodical articles on Ezequiel Martínez Estrada*

"En torno a un fallo literario," *La Fronda*, Buenos Aires (25 de nov. de 1932).

" 'Radiografía de la pampa,' por Ezequiel Martínez Estrada," *La Nación*, Buenos Aires (27 de ag. de 1933).

"El señor Ezequiel Martínez Estrada disertó ayer en Los Anales," *La Prensa*, Buenos Aires (8 de ag. de 1945).

" 'Sarmiento,' por Ezequiel Martínez Estrada," *La Prensa*, Buenos Aires (29 de dic. de 1946).

" 'Panorama de las literaturas,' por Ezequiel Martínez Estrada," *La Nación*, Buenos Aires (5 de enero de 1947).

" 'Nietzsche,' por Ezequiel Martínez Estrada," *La Nación*, Buenos Aires (18 de abril de 1948).

"Se entregará el gran premio de la S.A.D.E. a Ezequiel Martínez Estrada," *La Nación*, Buenos Aires (13 de nov. de 1948).

" 'Muerte y transfiguración de Martín Fierro,' por Ezequiel Martínez Estrada," *La Prensa*, Buenos Aires (2 de enero de 1949), 9.

"Hoy será evocado Federico Nietzsche," *La Nación*, Buenos Aires (22 de ag. de 1950).

" 'El mundo maravilloso de Guillermo Enrique Hudson,' por Ezequiel Martínez Estrada," *La Nación*, Buenos Aires (5 de ag. de 1951).

"El lema de una universidad nueva debe ser: 'Aquí trabajan todos, todo el día,' dice Martínez Estrada," *La Nueva Provincia*, Bahía Blanca (6 de enero de 1956).

"Acerca de la renuncia del Sr. Martínez Estrada," *La Nación*, Buenos Aires (11 de enero de 1956).

"La literatura debe escribirse para el pueblo, pero no ha de ser proletaria, sostuvo Martínez Estrada en su conferencia," *El País*, Montevideo (18 de marzo de 1956).

"Conferencias: Al pueblo argentino hay que hablarle el lenguaje de la decencia cívica," *El País*, Montevideo (20 y 21 de marzo de 1956).

"Una respuesta de Martínez Estrada," *La Nación*, Buenos Aires (3 de ag. de 1957).

"El escritor Martínez Estrada fue nombrado profesor de la Universidad del Sur," *La Prensa*, Buenos Aires (27 de marzo de 1958).

"Un homenaje a Martínez Estrada," *La Nación*, Buenos Aires (25 de ag. de 1958).

"La Sociedad de escritores celebró los 25 años de 'Radiografía de la pampa,' de Ezequiel Martínez Estrada," *La Prensa* (4 de dic. de 1958).

" 'Radiografía de la pampa': sus 25 años," *La Nación*, Buenos Aires (4 de dic. de 1958).

"Radiografía de una 'Radiografía de la pampa'," *La Nación*, Buenos Aires (11 de dic. de 1958).

" 'Muerte y transfiguración de Martín Fierro,' por Ezequiel Martínez Estrada," *La Gaceta*, México, Fondo de Cultura Económica, 5, no. 58 (junio de 1959), 4.

"Posición del escritor E. Martínez Estrada," *La Nación*, Buenos Aires (16 de julio de 1961).

"Ezequiel Martínez Estrada: Falleció en Bahía Blanca," *La Nación*, Buenos Aires (5 de nov. de 1964).

"Ezequiel Martínez Estrada: Murió en Bahía Blanca," *La Prensa*, Buenos Aires (5 de nov. de 1964).

"La Universidad del Sur evocó a Martínez Estrada," *La Nación*, Buenos Aires (16 de nov. de 1964).

"Ezequiel Martínez Estrada ha muerto en la Argentina, su país," *La Gaceta*, México, Fondo de Cultura Económica, 11, no. 123 (nov. de 1964), 1.

"Enfoque crítico sobre la obra de Martínez Estrada," *La Nación*, Buenos Aires (4 de mayo de 1965).

V. OTHER WORKS CONSULTED

Anderson Imbert, Enrique. *Historia de la literatura hispanoamericana*. 2 vols., 3.ª ed. México: Fondo de Cultura Económica, 1961.

———. "Sesquicentenario," and "Patriotismo y nacionalismo." *Argentina: análisis y autoanálisis*. Ed. H. Ernest Lewald. Buenos Aires: Sudamericana, 1969, 147-151, 151-155.

Arrieta, Rafael Alberto (dir.). *Historia de la literatura argentina*. Tomo IV. "El ensayo y la crítica." Buenos Aires: Ediciones Peuser, 1959.

Arzubide, List. *El movimiento estridentista*. 2.ª ed. México: Secretaría de Educación Pública, 1967.

Ayala, Francisco. "El nacionalismo sano y el otro." *Argentina: análisis y autoanálisis*. Ed. H. Ernest Lewald. Buenos Aires: Sudamericana, 1969, 126-144.

Borges, Jorge Luis. "Nota sobre los argentinos." *Argentina: análisis y autoanálisis*. Ed. H. Ernest Lewald. Buenos Aires: Sudamericana, 1969, 78-79.

Borges, Jorge Luis, Ocampo, Silvina, and Bioy Casares, A. *Antología poética argentina*. Buenos Aires: Sudamericana, 1941.

Bunge, Carlos. *Nuestra América: ensayo de psicología social*. Buenos Aires: Casa Vaccaro, 1918.

Cambours, Ocampo. *El problema de las generaciones literarias: esquema de las últimas promociones argentinas*. Buenos Aires: A. Peña Lollo, Editor, 1963.

Canal-Feijóo, Bernardo. *Confines de Occidente: notas para una sociología de la cultura americana*. Buenos Aires: Raigal, 1954.

———. "La superación de la antítesis." *Argentina: análisis y autoanálisis*. Ed. H. Ernest Lewald. Buenos Aires: Sudamericana, 1969, 65-75.

Carilla, Emilio. *Literatura argentina, 1800-1950: esquema generacional*. Tucumán: Universidad Nacional de Tucumán, 1954.

Caturelli, Alberto. *La filosofía en Argentina actual*. Córdoba: Universidad Nacional de Córdoba, 1962.

Cruz Costa, João. *A History of Ideas in Brazil*. Berkeley: University of California Press, 1964.

*Cuyo: Anuario de Historia del Pensamiento Argentino*. Tomo I. Cuyo: Universidad Nacional de Cuyo, 1965.

Dakin, Edwin Franden (ed.). *Today and Destiny: Vital extracts from Decline of the West*. New York: A. A. Knoff, 1940.

Dana Montaño, Salvador M. *Tres ensayos de historia de las ideas políticas*. Santa Fe: Universidad Nacional del Litoral, 1967.

Di Tella, Torcuato S. *et al. Argentina, sociedad de masas*. Buenos Aires: Eudeba, 1965.

Estrada, Juan Carlos Torchia. *La filosofía en la Argentina*. Washington: Unión Panamericana, 1961.

Farré, Luis. *Cincuenta años de filosofía en Argentina*. Buenos Aires: Peuser, 1958.

Franco, Jean. *The Modern Culture of Latin America: Society and the Artist*. London: Pall Mall, 1967.

Frank, Waldo. "El Re-descubrimiento de América: los últimos días de Europa," *Amauta*, Lima, 11, 2 (enero de 1928), 1-2.

Fuentes, Carlos. "Papel del escritor en América Latina," *Mundo Nuevo*, París, 5 (nov. de 1966), 28-30.

Galletti, Alfredo. *La realidad argentina en el siglo XX*. vol. 1. Buenos Aires: Fondo de Cultura Económica, 1961.

Ganivet, Ángel. *Idearium español y el porvenir de España*. Buenos Aires: Espasa Calpe, 1949.

García, Juan Agustín. *La ciudad indiana*. Buenos Aires: Emecé, 1954.

García Calderón, Francisco. *La creación de un continente*. París: Librería Paul Ollendorff, 1913.

———. "Ortega y Gasset y nuestro tiempo," *El Repertorio Americano*, San José, Costa Rica, 20 (1930), 147-148.

Germani, Gino. *La sociología en la América Latina: problemas y perspectivas*. Buenos Aires: Eudeba, 1964.

Halperín Donghi, Tulio. *Argentina en el callejón*. Montevideo: Arca, 1964.

Hernández Arregui, J. J. *La formación de la conciencia nacional: 1930-1960*. Buenos Aires: Hachea, 1960.

Imaz, Jorge Luis de. *Los que mandan*. Buenos Aires: Eudeba, 1964.

*Introducción a los problemas nacionales*. Buenos Aires: Centro de Estudios Nacionales, 1964. (Curso dictado en el Centro de Estudios Nacionales en el año 1964.)

Jauretche, Arturo. *Política nacional y revisionismo histórico*. Buenos Aires: A. Peña Lillo, Editor, 1959.

———. *F.O.R.J.A. y la década infame*. Buenos Aires: Coyoacán, 1962.

Jitrik, Noé. *Escritores argentinos*. Buenos Aires: Ediciones del Candil, 1967.

Jung, Carl. *Modern Man in Search of a Soul*. London: Routledge, 1962.

Keller, R. Carlos. *Spengler y la situación político-cultural de la América Ibérica*. Santiago de Chile: Imprenta Universitaria, 1927.

Keyserling, Count Hermann. *South American Meditations: On Hell and Heaven in the Soul of Man*. New York: Harper and Brothers, 1932.

Koremblit, Bernardo Ezequiel. *El ensayo en la Argentina*. Buenos Aires: Ministerio de Relaciones Exteriores y Culto (no date given).

Kush, Rodolfo. *La seducción de la barbarie: análisis herético de un continente mestizo*. Buenos Aires: Raigal, 1953.

Maffei, Francisco E. *En busca de una expresión argentina*. Bahía Blanca: Cuadernos del Sur, 1960.

Mafud, Julio. *El desarraigo argentino*. Buenos Aires: Americalee, 1959.

———. "La nueva familia." *Argentina: análisis y autoanálisis*. Ed. H. Ernest Lewald. Buenos Aires: Sudamericana, 1969, 265-269.

Mallea, Eduardo. "Sentido de la inteligencia en la expresión de nuestro tiempo." *Argentina: análisis y autoanálisis*. Ed. H. Ernest Lewald. Buenos Aires: Sudamericana, 1969, 103-121.

Mannheim, Karl. *Rational and Irrational Elements in Contemporary Society*. London: Oxford University Press, 1934.

———. *Essays on the Sociology of Culture*. New York: Oxford University Press, 1956.

———. *Systematic Sociology: An Introduction to the Study of Society*. London: Routledge and Kegan Paul, 1957.

———. *Essays on the Sociology of Knowledge*. London: Routledge and Kegan Paul, 1959.

Marichal, Juan. *La voluntad de estilo*. Barcelona: Seix Barral, 1957.

Marsal, Juan Francisco. "Las meditaciones argentinas de Ortega y Gasset," *Ciudad*, Buenos Aires, 4-5 (1956), 8-14.

Marsal, Juan Francisco. "Significado de la parasociología argentina." *Argentina: análisis y autoanálisis*. Ed. H. Ernest Lewald. Buenos Aires: Sudamericana, 1969, 235-261.

Martínez, José Luis. *El ensayo mexicano moderno*. 2 vols., 1.ª ed. México: Fondo de Cultura Económica, 1958.

Massuh, Víctor. *América como inteligencia y pasión*. México: Fondo de Cultura Económica, 1955.

Mastrángelo, Carlos. *El cuento argentino: contribución al conocimiento de su historia, teoría y práctica*. Buenos Aires: Hachette, 1963.

Matteis, Emilio de. *Análisis de la vida argentina*. Buenos Aires: Americalee, 1962.

————. *La abulia mental en Latinoamérica*. Buenos Aires: Editorial la Mandragora, 1963.

Mead, Robert G., Jr. *Breve historia del ensayo hispanoamericano*. México: Stadium, 1956.

Montserrat, Santiago. *Sentido y misión del pensamiento argentino*. Córdoba: Universidad Nacional de Córdoba, 1963.

Moreira Leite, Dante. *Caráter nacional brasileiro: Descrição das características psicológicas do brasileiro através de ideologias e estereótipos*. São Paulo: Universidade de São Paulo, 1954.

Murena, H. A. "El nombre secreto o un intento de explicación de ciertos males argentinos y americanos, pasados y presentes." *Argentina: análisis y autoanálisis*. Ed. H. Ernest Lewald. Buenos Aires: Sudamericana, 1969, 199-231.

Orgambide, Pedro and Yahni, Roberto. *Enciclopedia de la literatura argentina*. Buenos Aires: Sudamericana, 1970.

Ortega y Gasset, José. *Obras completas, IV, 1929-1933*. Madrid: Revista de Occidente, 1957.

————. *Libro de las misiones*. Madrid: Espasa Calpe, 1965.

————. *El espectador, VII & VIII*. Madrid: Espasa Calpe, 1966.

Popper, Karl R. *The Open Society and its Enemies*. Princeton: Princeton University Press, 1963.

————. *The Poverty of Historicism*. New York: Harper and Row, 1964.

Prieto, Adolfo. *Sociología del público argentino*. Buenos Aires: Ediciones Leviatán, 1956.

Rest, Jaime. *Literatura y cultura de masas*. Buenos Aires: Centro Editor de América Latina, 1967.

Rocca, Eduardo A. *Argentina: los grupos dirigentes*. Buenos Aires: Palestra, 1966.

Rodó, José Enrique. *Ariel*. 3.ª ed. México: Espasa Calpe, 1963.

Romero, Francisco. "Indicaciones sobre la marcha del pensamiento filosófico en la Argentina," *Cuadernos Americanos* (enero-febrero de 1950).

Romero, José Luis. *El desarrollo de las ideas en la sociedad argentina del siglo XX*. México: Fondo de Cultura Económica, 1965.

Russell, Bertrand. *History of Western Philosophy*. London: Allen and Unwin, 1969.

Salvador, Nelida. *Revistas argentinas de vanguardia: 1920-1930*. Buenos Aires: Universidad de Buenos Aires, 1962.

Sánchez Reulet, Aníbal. *La filosofía latinoamericana contemporánea*. Washington: Unión Panamericana, 1949.

Scalabrini Ortiz, Raúl. "La defección política." *Argentina: análisis y autoanálisis*. Ed. H. Ernest Lewald. Buenos Aires: Sudamericana, 1969, 83-99.

Shaw, K. E. "Ángel Ganivet: a Sociological Interpretation," *Revista de Estudios Hispánicos*, Alabama, v. 2, no. 2 (nov. de 1968), 165-181.

Shils, Edward. "The Intellectual between Tradition and Modernity: the Indian situation," *Comparative Studies in Society and History*, The Hague, v. 1 (Supplement I 1961), 9-120.

Siegfried, André. *Nations Have Souls*. New York: G. P. Putnam's Sons, 1952.

Soler, Ricaurte. *Estudios sobre historia de las ideas en América*. Panamá: Imprenta Nacional, 1960.

Stabb, Martin S. "Indigenism and Racism in Mexican Thought: 1857-1911," *Journal of Inter-American Studies*, Gainsville, v. 50, 4 (oct. de 1959), 405-423.

Taborda, Saúl. *Reflexiones sobre el ideal político de América*. Córdoba: La Elzeviriana, 1918.

Tönnies, Ferdinand. *Fundamental Concepts in Sociology: Gemeinschaft und Gesellschaft*. New York: American Book Co., 1940.

Torres Rioseco, A. *Nueva historia de la gran literatura iberoamericana*. 3.ª ed. Buenos Aires: Emecé, 1960.

Unamuno, Miguel de. "¿Existe una literatura proletaria?," *Amauta*, Lima, 18 (oct. de 1928), 7-8.

Van Riessen. *Nietzsche*. Philadelphia: Presbyterian and Reformed Publishing Co., 1960.

Vázquez, Juan Adolfo. *Antología filosófica argentina del siglo XX*. Buenos Aires: Eudeba, 1965.

Yunque, Álvaro. *Síntesis histórica de la literatura argentina*. Buenos Aires: Claridad, 1957.

Zea, Leopoldo. *América en la conciencia de Europa*. México: Colección "Los presentes," 1955.

———. *Dos etapas del pensamiento en Hispanoamérica*. México: El Colegio de México, 1949.

Zum Felde, Alberto. *Índice crítico de la literatura hispanoamericana, Vol. I: El ensayo y la crítica*. México: Editorial Guarania, 1954.